LIGHTBOOK

ULRIKE BRANDI

CHRISTOPH GEISSMAR-BRANDI

LIGHTBOOK

THE PRACTICE OF LIGHTING DESIGN

Birkhäuser – Publishers for Architecture

Basel · Boston · Berlin

Contents

Light drives away darkness, but creates shadows in the process, and these shadows in turn frame the pools of light. Darkness is never far away.

Homo sapiens sapiens became *homo faber*, and one of his ancestors' early works was to make light in the form of fire. Human vision, honed over millions of years without artificial light, was now subject to extended periods of use, and this fire-light made *homo faber* the most dominant species on earth – to the point where *homo faber* threatens the survival of all other life.

I believe that the history of architecture is the story of the way light enters into buildings and reveals the spatial composition and forms within.

Light is the *material* of architecture through which we can best appreciate the nature of space, surface, colours and objects. Textures are perhaps felt as much through the eyes as through the skin.

When we left the cave, we constructed our own walls and a roof. We saw for the first time our walls from the outside as well as the inside. We made openings in them and the roof to let the daylight in. Later we put glass in these openings to keep out the rain. Throughout all this time we decorated our solid walls with signs of our changing culture, and used sunlight to illuminate the glass walls.

We lived by the diurnal and seasonal rhythms of temperature and light. We moved from fire to oil lamps over a very long period, and then, in the 19th century the electric lamp arrived, and with Mr Edison, the system to light the world.

In the same century we dismantled the walls upon which we inscribed our culture and made them and the roof entirely of glass, held up by thin strips of metal.

Since then, architects have had relative freedom to design how much opacity and transparency they want in buildings. The architecture that emerges from this freedom seems rarely influenced by artificial lighting – but it should be.

I believe that lighting designers should always work with nature's own light pen as *the basis* for any lighting composition. This may sound paradoxical.

It is not through defining the lumen output required upon a surface that the lighting designer begins – that is for those who formulate regulations and for those uninspired who slavishly follow them. Instead, more and more lighting designers now allow natural light to determine the scenarios for artificial lighting. Natural light is dynamic, to be tamed, manipulated or left wild by both architect and lighting designer. This means, quite simply, that architects should now be able to work with lighting designers on the same conceptual wavelength.

Design collaboration with sensitive, skilled and professional colleagues is both a pleasure and a necessity. Lighting designers are essential to the architectural design team.

The challenge to lighting designers has never been greater – to help give us wonderful spaces both inside and outside our walls wherein we can frame our dreams and display our culture.

If we all allow the natural environment to be the instrument of design on all scales, then our designs will be more intelligent and more responsive to our senses.

Our perception of spaces and surfaces differs greatly between sunlight and moonlight, artificial light and fire or candlelight. The sky during the phase transitions between day and night provides us with some of nature's most magical moments. On a different scale, so too does the flickering candle flame, or watching the slow death of a fire.

The enduring candle is testimony to our reluctance to relinquish the fire-light, the contact with nature and the romantic atmosphere that it helps create – love and hope live in that flickering light and perfume. Light is hope and darkness fear, yet all the darkness in the world cannot extinguish a single candle.

Instinctively, I conceive internal and external spaces in natural light rather than imagine them as artificially lit environments, unless, of course, the space will always be denied the sky and sun. Subsequently, I seek the insight and skill of the lighting designer to inform the design team of the ways spaces can be connected, isolated and re-configured in artificial light.

Today, we must also recognise that we spend so much time in artificially lit spaces and in front of artificially lit screens that sensitive and intelligent lighting designers are crucial to our well-being. This is not yet fully recognised by all architects, or all clients.

My empathy lies with the lighting designer who says that the longer we keep the lights switched off the better we feel and the less energy we use.

Ian Ritchie
London, Spring of 2001

The Aim of this Book

The present book is conceived as a process-oriented handbook. Good lighting for architecture and landscape is the result of good design, of numerous little steps taken at the appropriate time, of experience, technical competence, perseverance, imagination, and of the ability to cooperate with other specialist planners and clients. In this book, we have for the first time gathered our knowledge derived from over 250 projects worldwide. We demonstrate the individual steps from the preliminary draft to the execution of the project*, and we illustrate them with examples. In self-contained individual chapters, we discuss technical questions and tools. An extensive glossary and a long bibliography on the topic of light in architecture and culture will assist with further questions. Our aim is to provide a sound and balanced reference compendium for use in the offices of architects and engineers, a resource which will contribute towards better lighting conditions.

Light in our Heads

Good lighting designers are people of experience. They have learnt to look very closely at light and its effects. The wealth of experience accumulated from this activity constitutes their most important instrument of planning. With the help of their highly trained power of imagination, lighting designers are able to judge with great precision how and where light will be effective. Moreover, they are able to describe and analyze the light which they plan for open spaces or buildings. They know the effects of the various sources of light on the very complex structure of space, surfaces, and colors. Lighting designers know how this structure – the environment of light – is perceptually altered through the choice of light. With the medium of light, designers im-

prove the quality of buildings and spaces. Their store of experience is the most important and valuable knowledge of lighting designers. They command a repertory of complementary and conflicting light, and they have learnt to describe it. Lighting designers cultivate a vocabulary of light. If a candle is lit, they see shadows, sharply contoured, moving shadows. They notice a bright light surrounding the flame and various brightly and faintly lit surfaces in the room with different reflective properties. They register the mirrored candle in the window. They perceive the wax of the candle to be translucent, while the upper region of the candle is gleaming brightly. The candlelight is warm and has a yellow-reddish color.

Described analytically or from a physical and optical viewpoint, the candle is a source of light with the characteristics of a thermal radiator. It is not directed by means of reflectors but rather radiates in all directions. It is not covered and may blind the person who looks at it directly. The candlelight falls on various reflective surfaces: a nearby tabletop, distant walls, mat, rough, shiny, or reflecting walls, and on each surface it creates a different effect. It strikes these surfaces at different angles. The light passes through the wax of the candle. If there is a glass of water or wine on the table, the light refracts in the translucent materials of the liquid.

Designers in particular are not confined to describe lighting situations in words but are also able to represent and construct them by means of drawings. It is possible to determine the direction of light as well as the angle of beam. An arrow indicates the direction of light and the opening of two arrows, the angles of beam. A diffusely radiating light source has many arrows pointing in many directions. There may be strong reflections by objects, and the reflected light will be indicated by thinner arrows. This analytical approach to phenomena of light helps in the definition and communication of lighting situations. Once attention has been directed towards light, a new and selective kind of seeing is developed: the environment now appears more as a pattern of light, while the objects recede into the background; the field of vision presents itself as a pattern of expanses of light. Since most of the light comes from above, it becomes second nature to the designers of lighting systems to turn their gaze upward and to see what light sources have created the current situation. The repertory of lighting situations already seen and stored in memory makes it possible to develop light for as yet nonexistent spaces, to design it and to talk about it. The "only" thing missing is the actual source capable of generating the desired light. Once these are found or known, the light in the head gives rise to the appropriate light in architecture.

Experiments

Aside from the imagination as the initial source of a design, there is also the experiment. One "simply" gives it a try. Within a defined framework, this can be a good way to go. Minimally, what is required is a small variable arsenal of luminaires and materials in the office and a room which can be darkened. Some lighting designers have their own manufacture for this purpose and sometimes even a large light laboratory. Some lamp manufacturers have mock-up rooms in addition to light laboratories which permit experiments on a scale of 1:1. Improvised tests are easier and quicker: how much of the light source is still visible when a spotlight is directed through frosted or opal glass? What are the limit distances of various lighting effects? What kinds of reflections are generated on metallic, on polished, or on rough surfaces?

Yet, caution is necessary: if material samples are too small, a sufficient evaluation of many properties such as reflection is not possible.

Models

Models also constitute helpful tools. For some projects, architects have working models of individual rooms or of entire buildings. These are not to be confused with the representative display models which are now frequently equipped with lavish lighting.

Fiberglass cables can be inserted into the working models in order to determine light conditions in relation to room geometries. This is not so much to test the illuminance as the directions and qualities of light. The materials and surfaces of the models must closely match those of the design at least in terms of color and surface quality. Only then can the resulting light be adequately observed. The larger the models, the more accurate are the predictions of the actual light effect in the building; the models, of course, must be true to scale. The scale varies between 1:50 and 1:20, depending on the size of the project. Very large construction projects can only be modeled in sections.

Simulations

Computer simulations offer additional means of experimenting with light in the designing process. There now exists software for the precise calculation of artificial light as well as of daylight. Yet the data entry required for the spaces to be simulated is very time consuming and thus expensive. Moreover, physically accurate computer simulations require a lot of computing time. And since the operation of the software requires further specialists, computer simulations are so far seldom financially feasible.

Sampling

In commercial construction, sampling at a later stage of construction is still the more commonly used method. Tests with sample lighting systems, of course, are only meaningful if model rooms with corresponding wall colors, floor coverings, and furniture already exist and are thus likewise expensive. Yet, such tests permit the fine tuning of the lighting concept and give clients and users the opportunity to see and examine the future space in a very realistic setting.

The Objective

In architecture, light is tremendously vivid and manifold. Intelligently positioned and well-dimensioned, light is able to generate a terrific intensity. Light can stir up emotions and help bind them to lived experience. When it gets dark, human beings undergo a change of mood. At these times good light is always in demand. The art of lighting design consists of the ability to bring out even extreme and unusual features. Beauty and harmony must make an impression, the same as inevitable conflict and the grotesque. Light must appeal to everyone, but it must also have a situational effect for individuals, couples, or groups. Good light continually redraws the fine line between harmonious variety and sharp contrast.

Ulrike Brandi
Christoph Geissmar-Brandi
Hamburg, Spring of 2001

*   This chapter reflects the European and especially the German practice.

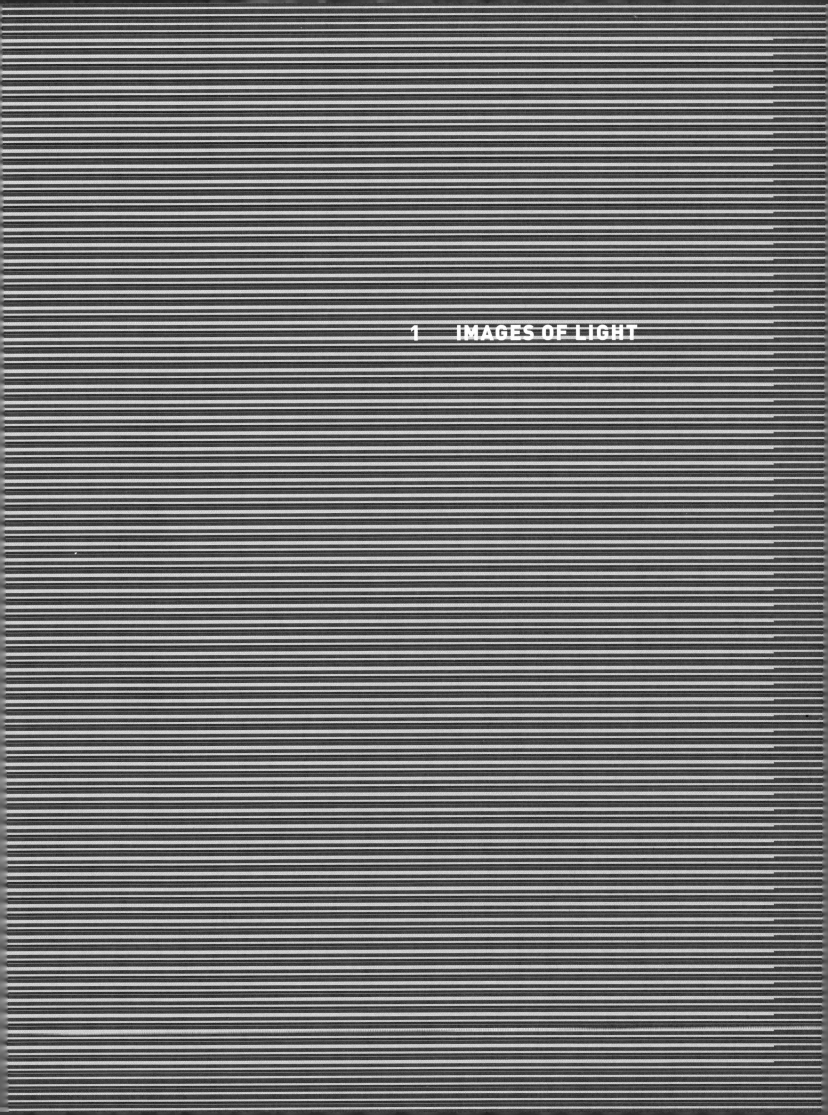

1   IMAGES OF LIGHT

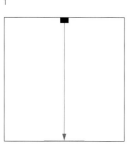

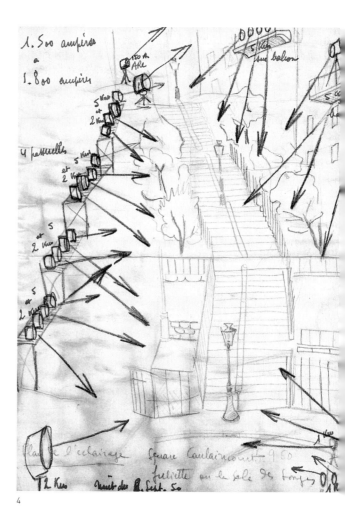

Drawings

It is a very difficult task to give a good description of light in interior spaces by means of drawings. Nevertheless, it is always an interesting experiment to try to sketch light, for clients, users, and even architects often have difficulty imagining light with subtlety of nuance. Hence, a corresponding illustration can help to visualize the design. An abstract representation of the desired light is relatively quickly achieved by means of arrows falling from the light source onto a surface. These arrows are red so as not to suggest a defined color of light, as would be the case with yellow arrows, which would suggest a warm white color. The extent of the illuminated surfaces is additionally marked in red. This very conceptual account of the effect of light is easily grasped but demands imagination of the viewer to transform the abstraction into reality or – alternatively – it demands confidence in the abilities of the lighting designer.

Light cones are frequently represented in form of colored triangular surfaces. This representation supports the false idea that one would see the color of the light and the light cone. Moreover, the light cone in the drawing looks as though as it were clearly bounded. In reality, however, with most luminaires there is a very smooth transition between the light cone and its surroundings. Some illustrations show this transition as a "penumbra", which is, for example, sketched in light yellow around a dark yellow core. This is seldom shown in the "sectional drawings".

Some lighting designers draw circles or ellipses, which in different colors are supposed to illustrate the varying illuminances as well as the light that strikes the surfaces.

Aside from these abstract geometrical manners of representation there is also the "artistic" way of illustrating moods of light. Sketches with white and colored crayons on colored or black posterboard are suitable for this purpose.

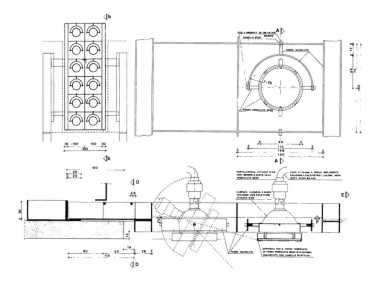

Planned lighting designs can be illustrated well by means of photographs of projects already realized. And for this purpose it is helpful to choose only those examples in which spaces rather than objects are emphasized, since otherwise the viewer's attention will be drawn to the objects depicted in the photograph rather than to the light. There is a real danger that the client will infer from the illustrated mood of light immediately to the planned light. This is hardly possible if the illustration depicts a different room. Thus it may be useful to exaggerate or distance the photographs by means of colorization (with a computer program such as *Photoshop* or, more simply, *Paintshop Pro*) and other graphical techniques. Transparent positives which look atmospherically delicate and unreal if superimposed onto a colored background also belong to this type of technique. Photographs of models are further aides in describing a planned lighting situation or light setting.

1   The luminaire in space: a red arrow indicates
    the direction of light, while the red line symbolizes the
    illuminated surface.

2   The representation of a light cone distinguishes
    narrow-beam and wide-beam luminaires, but falsely
    suggests that the cone is visible.

3   Theater and film professionals plan the effect of each
    individual spotlight, ...

4   ... sketching the positions and the directions of light.

5   In this space, luminaires illuminate large recessed
    panes of glass. In their staggered arrangement, they are
    represented in various levels of brightness.

6   When the light of a narrow-beaming spotlight strikes
    a surface, ...

7   ... it creates bright elliptical areas. The various colors of
    the surrounding lines distinguish various illuminances.
    The floor plan illustrates the idea of creating a transition
    of light from the floor to the wall. There, both ellipses
    are cut; in the actual room, they will be bent by 90° from
    the horizontal to the vertical plane.

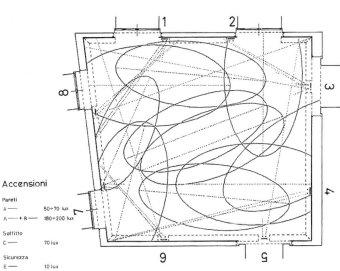

8 When modifying scanned photographs, designers should ensure that the seemingly realistic design can actually be executed.

9 The abstract representation of the directions of light in a sectional view gives a technical impression. Photographs showing details of illuminated surfaces describe the atmospheric component of a design.

Graphs

16

By means of light calculation programs, which luminaire manufacturers normally used to hand out free of charge, the distribution of light in rooms can be demonstrated very quickly in various ways, and simple rendering programs with false colors in the software also allow for graphical accents. The software is easy to use, but it cannot do anything more than calculate and represent the illuminances for each room. These representations of light are used more as evidence of correct planning or in internal discussions of alternatives than as material for presentations. Most programs first of all allow for the representation of the lamp positions. Once the reference plane and the mean reflectance factors have been entered, the programs calculate the corresponding illuminance values. In the numerical output, these values appear as a number field (matrix).

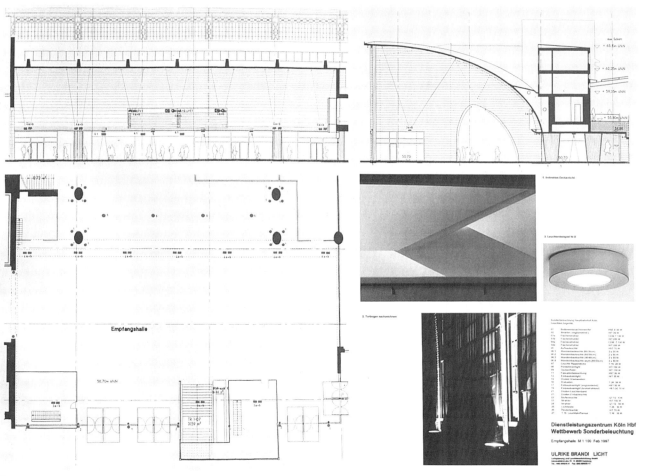

10 Every designer will find his own individual style of presentation. Here, the photograph is superimposed as a
transparency onto a sheet with a gradient color scheme.

11 Many individual strands of fiberglass are lead into this
working model, directing light onto objects within.
When the light is switched on, the intended alternation
of transparent and non-transparent walls is revealed.

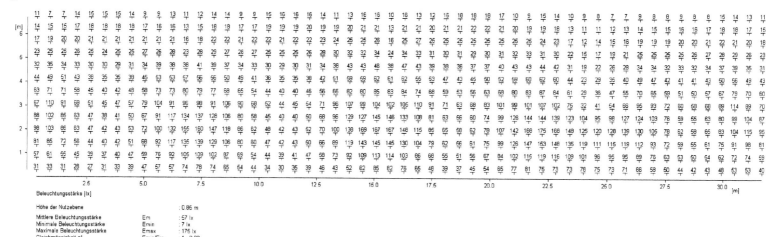

Beleuchtungsstärke [lx]

Höhe der Nutzebene		: 0.85 m
Mittlere Beleuchtungsstärke	Em	: 57 lx
Minimale Beleuchtungsstärke	Emin	: 7 lx
Maximale Beleuchtungsstärke	Emax	: 175 lx
Gleichmässigkeit g1	Emin/Em	: 1 : 8.68
Gleichmässigkeit g2	Emin/Emax	: 1 : 26.71

Graph of the Numeric Output

The numerical output indicates the precise illuminance value at the respective point of calculation.

Graph of the Illuminance Output

Translated into a two-dimensional graph, these values yield the illuminance curves. On the indicated reference plane, they show the brightness variation in definable gradations. If desired, they are also represented in color. The gradations result from the bandwidth of the illuminances in the lighting proposal. For interior spaces, a standard would be, for example, the representation of illuminances between 20 and 1000 lux.

Graph of the Grayscale Output

And finally, a three-dimensional grid diagram – a "mountain range of illumination" – may be derived from the data obtained. The bright zones then appear as proportionately high "mountains", while it gets darker in the "valleys". Here too, there is a danger of a false interpretation. If, however, uniformity of the planned installation is an important criterion, this can be verified very well by means of the grid. Some programs permit the two-dimensional representation in false colors of the brightness values on ceilings, floors and walls of simple interior spaces. This representation may help in detecting dark corners or abrupt transitions. The programs of the various manufacturers are mutually incompatible. The program DIALUX of the German Institute for Applied Lighting Technology (Deutsches Institut für angewandte Lichttechnik) in Lüdenscheid could create a new and uniform standard in Germany. More and more manufacturers and designers, however, use the multilingual RELUX of the firm Relux Informatik AG in Basel.

Simulations

Occasionally splendid, frequently "cold" and "lifeless" computer-generated light representations can be conjured up by means of visualization software as long as the planning schedule permits it, for processing times are sometimes considerable. Depending on the process (raytracing, radiosity, or a combination), even PCs equipped with multiple processors sometimes require days to perform complex lighting situations!

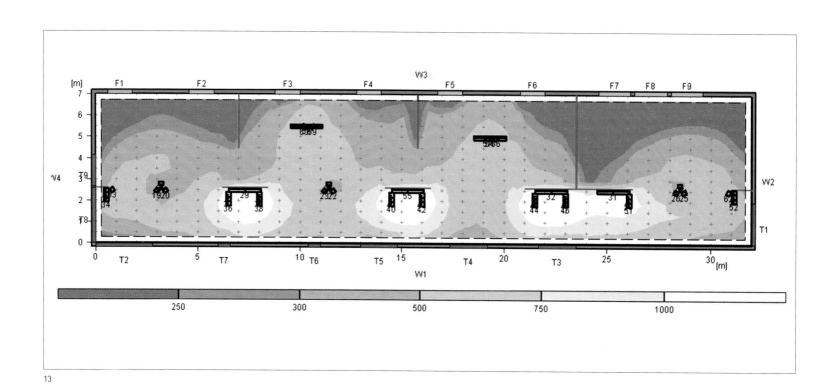

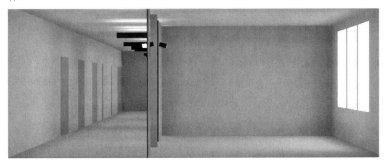
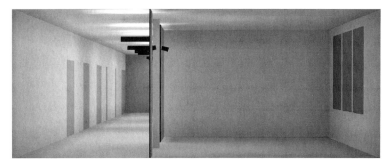

The "photorealistic" representations thus generated, however, are less suitable for the representation of an idea than for depicting a virtual reality. In the mere depiction, reproduction, or mirroring of this virtual reality, the artistic conception can easily be lost. Nevertheless, the possibilities are continually becoming a little more manifold and faster as well.

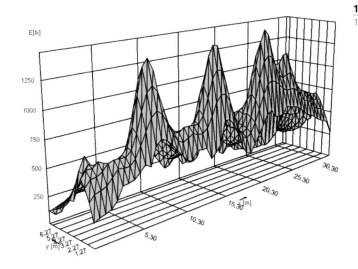

12 This representation is less intuitive, but more detailed. The graduations can usually also be captured in grayscale, although this falsifies the visual impression of reality.

13 Grayscale or false colors clearly illustrate the distribution of the levels of illuminance.

14 These visualizations show a section of the room in Fig. 12 during the day and at night.

15 The "mountain range" of the gridded chart especially illustrates the transitions between high and low illuminances.

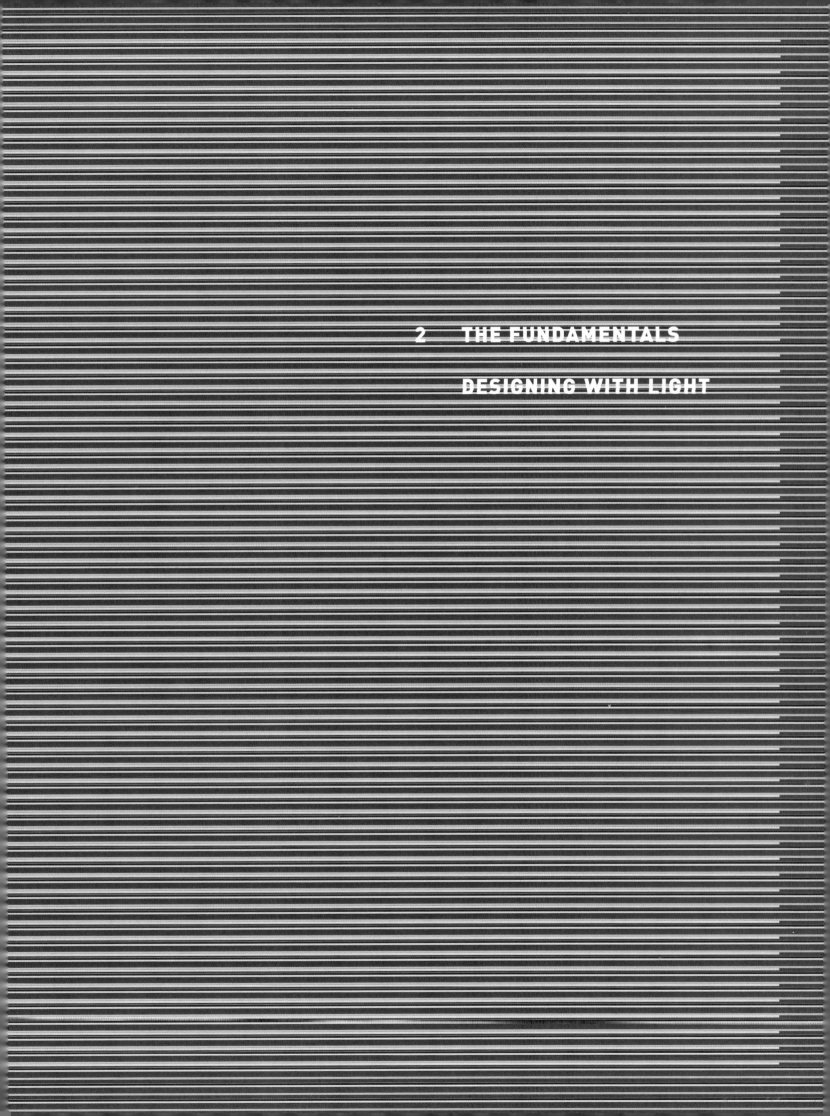

2   THE FUNDAMENTALS

DESIGNING WITH LIGHT

1 Originally, the movement of the sun was supposed
to be reproduced on the glass ceiling of the *Galerie de
l'Evolution* in Paris through a round opening in the roof.

22

Paris 23.7.-23.6.
Tageszeit Monat/
Höchster Stand am Tag

Juni

16.00 Juni
64.8733
184.8494

Mai

15.30 Mai
61.9236
184.5092

April

15.00 April
53.7920
183.7345

Februar

14.30 März
42.2320
183.0003

Januar

14.00 Februar
31.3733
182.5285

Dezember

13.30 Januar
21.8503
182.2343

November

13.00 Dezember
18.0158
182.1743

12.30 November
21.1232
182.3174

Oktober

12.00 Oktober
30.0822
182.6236

11.30 September
41.4539

11.00 August
52.9859

September

10.30 Juli
61.5951

August

Juli

Daylight

The common view reduces "lighting design" to "artificial lighting design". There are historical reasons for this. Up until the first half of the twentieth century, the architect as universalist was responsible for lighting. With his façades, roofs and floor plans, he planned the daylight conditions in his buildings, subsequently adding artificial lighting. At first, the means of artificial lighting employed were various types of incandescent bulbs. Already beginning around 1925, however, the nowadays ubiquitous fluorescent lamps made their first appearance.

With the progress in lamp technology and the wide selection of available lamp types, lighting design became the purview of specialized engineers, whose task it was to devise technically sophisticated and economical lighting solutions. Thus, the planning of artificial lighting fell to electrical engineers, while the daylight conditions continued to be determined by the architects. In twentieth century architecture, new materials such as concrete, steel and glass gave rise to new forms and uses of buildings. Natural light has always played an important role in the design of buildings. In the last hundred years, however, architecture has taken a real turn towards light as a determining element of designs. And it makes no difference in this regard whether architects chose "closed" structural designs or had buildings erected with the transparency of steel and glass.

The buildings always display a reverence for natural light such that in the twentieth century one could also speak of a new architecture of light. In the meantime, daylight planning too has become a very specialized field. For about the last 20 years, the use of daylight has been gaining further prominence on the side of engineering. For the purpose of energy conservation, engineers are looking for ways of utilizing as much daylight as possible for illumination while reducing the negative effect of increased daylight incidence in buildings, that is, the accompanying heat irradiation. This new coupling of daylight planning with air-conditioning technology has a promising future in which, even architecturally speaking, many issues still need to be resolved.

Characteristics of Sunlight

In addition to the ecological and economic advantages of daylight in interior spaces, there are the artistic advantages and the positive effects on the physical and psychological well-being of people. There are no substitutes for the qualities of daylight. Hence, the question regarding the daylight conditions in a given space (indoors and outdoors) should be considered at the beginning of any artificial lighting design. An initial answer is derived from the orientation of the building, from its location

(degrees of latitude and longitude) and from the environment of the building (a possible blocking of light through surrounding buildings). Needs vary according to the building's geographical location: In the north, where sun, light and heat are scarce, an extensive utilization of light is desirable. The nearer one draws to the equator the more light there is and the more closed off the buildings become.

As a simple first consideration, it is helpful to establish the extreme insolation at noontime and to take all seasons into account. The times of sunrise and sunset also need to be considered.

In addition to the positions of the sun, various weather situations must be taken into account: glaring sun, mucky weather, fog, the redness of the sky at sunset, brilliant fall weather, thunderstorms, rain and snow. It is desirable that daylight enters the building in such manifold ways that it continually affects the atmosphere inside the building.

Sometimes it will be necessary to block the rays of the sun, while in other cases daylight will have to be supplemented with artificial light. It is precisely this variation which affects the well-being of people in a room. For years, experts sought to determine and guarantee by means of standards the ergonomically "correct" light. Especially in office spaces, the result

Sunrise and Sunset in Central European Time

Date	January	February	March	April	May	June
1st	8:27 am / 4:25 pm *	8:00 am / 5:12 pm	7:07 am / 6:12 pm	6:58 am / 7:55 pm	5:55 am / 8:45 pm	5:11 am / 9:29 pm
15th	8:20 am / 4:43 pm	7:36 am / 5:38 pm	6:36 am / 6:27 pm	6:27 am / 8:18 pm	5:31 am / 9:07 pm	5:05 am / 9:40 pm

	July	August	September	October	November	December
1st	5:10 am / 9:41 pm	5:46 am / 9:09 pm	6:35 am / 8:08 pm	7:22 am / 7:00 pm	7:15 am / 4:56 pm	8:04 am / 4:17 pm
15th	5:23 am / 9:32 pm	6:08 am / 8:44 pm	6:57 am / 7:37 pm	7:46 am / 6:29 pm	7:39 am / 4:33 pm	8:20 am / 4:14 pm

*Sunrise / Sunset

2 Deep reveals painted in bright colors reflect light from outside into interior spaces.

3 On a much smaller scale this also occurs with window bars.

4 The dome of the Pantheon in Rome allows the various types of daylight to enter into the building.

5 The light appears as a narrow cone in the hazy air, models the ceiling panels ...

6 ... and migrates as a contoured circle across the walls.

7 Water surfaces create moving light reflections on the ceilings in neighboring houses.

8 The light shelf protects the area of the room near the window against excessive sunlight and directs this light against the ceiling in the inner recesses of the room.

9 Heliostats are reflectors which follow the sun while transmitting its light in a uniform direction, in this case an inner courtyard.

10 Light is filtered by thin straw mats. Direct sunlight creates sharp shadows.

11 In the interior of the Hongkong-Shanghai Bank, the movable mirrors direct sunlight onto the public square below the building.

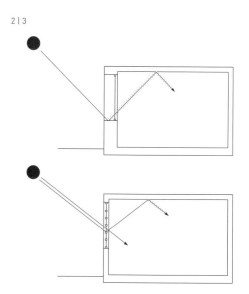

was a monotone uniformity of illuminance and a reduction of contrast and reflection. With a little exaggeration, one could say that this approach regarded every window as a nuisance rather than a positive quality. While the standards continue to exist, they are now no longer defined as the sole objective of lighting design. Rather, the aim is now to imitate qualities of daylight in artificial light. Even in terms of quantity, daylight is far superior to artificial light: outdoors, the prevailing illuminance on sunny days measures between 10,000 and 100,000 lux. By contrast, the German DIN standard prescribes 500 lux for office lighting. A further feature affecting the human organism is the spectral composition of light, which, as we know from admiring the steel blue sky during the day and the red sky at sunrise and sunset, can change dramatically. There are traditional, sometimes simple yet effective, means of controlling and directing daylight. Besides, there are the technical and often very sophisticated systems developed over the last 20 years.

Traditional and Simple Daylight Systems

The Pantheon in Rome is a famous example of a clever use of daylight through a simple opening positioned in the right place. Simple shutters which, with the appropriate slats, block just the right amount of light are effective means of directing light, as are wide eaves, pergolas and trees. Some of these devices are adjustable (shutters) and can be used

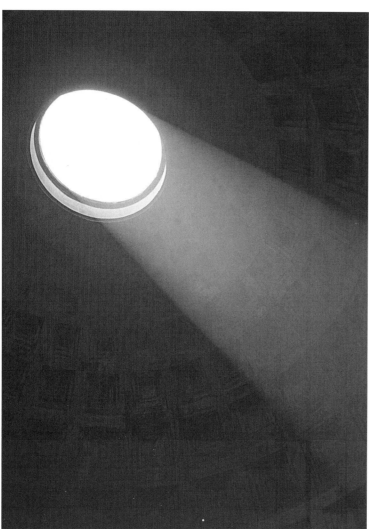

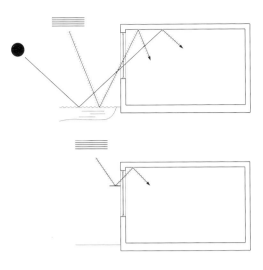

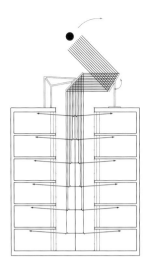

in accordance with the time of day, some change with the seasons (plant-covered pergolas), allowing only a small amount of light to pass through in the summer and a large amount in winter. Deep white-washed window reveals direct daylight far into the room. Even the bars on old windows direct some light against the ceiling of a room, making such windows, in spite of their comparatively smaller glass surface area, hardly inferior to windows with large glass surfaces, as far as the utilization of daylight is concerned. A body of water along-side a building is also an ingenious way of reflecting daylight into the interior.

The "lightshelf" too reflects daylight against the ceiling of a room. It is mounted onto the façade outside in the upper third portion of the win-dow and simultaneously protects the area close to the window against exposure to direct sunlight.

Fundamentally, one can distinguish systems and principles of directing daylight according to whether they are used in the area of the façades/windows or the roofs/skylights of buildings. While some systems use direct sunlight or the diffuse light of the sky, others shade and shield against glare.

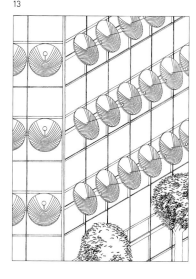

Movable and Fixed Systems

Protective Glass Against Solar Radiation

In the 1970s, coated glass began to be used for filtering out thermal radiation in the infrared part of the sunlight spectrum. Nowadays, there are many different varieties of protective glass:

· strongly shielding varieties of glass which appear like mirrors from the outside can have an unpleasant blinding effect on the surroundings; especially during bad weather, the interior is quite dark.
· less strongly shielding varieties which are more like clear glass but are also less effective. These types of glass are frequently used in skylights and glass-covered atriums.
· glass coated with durable stove-enamels. Partial covering of glass is possible. Fine grids on glass-covered atriums are hardly noticeable from below and scarcely reduce the translucence of the glass.

Heliostats

Heliostats are mirrors for "pursuing" the sun and channeling its rays in a uniform direction. Thus, the light of the sun can be transmitted, e.g. from the roof of a building through an inner courtyard into the lower stories. Conventional heliostats must be guided in two directions, since in travelling from east to west, the sun also rises and sets. The mechanism of heliostats requires maintenance and their effect depends on the size of the mirror capturing the light. The heliostat depicted is an asymmetric parabolic reflector that is partitioned into segments and embedded in a dual pane of glass. Over the course of a day, it must only turn about its own axis; thus, its mechanism is simpler than that of conventional heliostats.

Slats and Blinds

In principle, horizontal slats and blinds offer very precise control. Sunlight may be blocked completely or directed against the ceiling in order to utilize it in the inner reaches of the room. There are a variety of coatings avail-

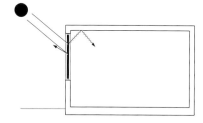
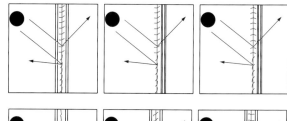
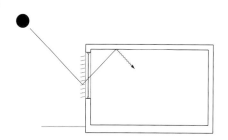
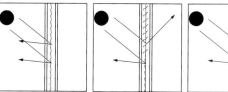

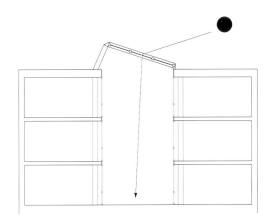

able. Exterior blinds, however, are susceptible to wind, while interior blinds do not protect well against thermal radiation. Blinds may be installed inside a dual pane window, where they do not get dirty. Slats on the façade – made of anodized aluminum or glass – may be of larger size with various profiles. The curvature of the reflective surface spreads out the light.

Light-Directing Glass

Several systems utilize the interstice of dual panes of glass in order to accommodate minimized optical objects and profiles. Light-directing glass is filled with acrylic profiles which throw light onto the ceiling of a room by means of a total reflection within the acrylic substance. An additional prismatic profiling of the inner window pane helps better distribute the light entering the room at an angle.

Mirror Profiles in Dual Panes of Glass

The mirror profiles of the "Köster sheets" are likewise contained within dual panes of glass. The variously shaped parabolic mirror surfaces are

arranged in such a way that they allow the horizontal sunlight in winter to pass through, while blocking the steep radiation in the hot summer season. The profiles are rigid and are designed differently for the various directions and types of installation. They are used in the façade and roof areas.

Prism Sheets in Dual Panes of Glass

Prism sheets also make use of the total reflection in acrylic glass: while direct sunlight is reflected back to the outside or directed against the ceiling of the room, diffuse light of the sky can pass through the material. Prism sheets are used in windows (even hooked-out with mirror) and in skylights. Up to three layers with various prism geometries and partial mirror vaporization of the prism flanks may be combined, in order to ensure sun protection, glare protection and redirection for the various positions of the sun. Prism slats have a simpler construction. Like Venetian blinds, they are adjustable and are mounted either horizontally or vertically. In combination with light-conducting mirror blinds, prism

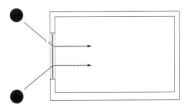
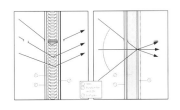
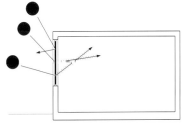
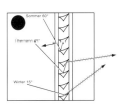

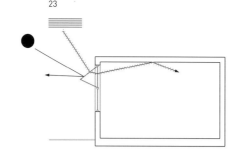
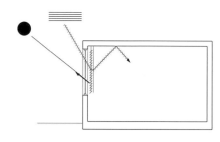
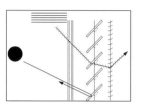

23 Hooked-out prism panels collect a larger amount of zenith light than prism panels vertically integrated into the window.

24 Prism panels in combination with interior blinds.

25 Laser cut panels react differently to the sun in summer and in winter.

26 Minute spaces as slits in acrylic glass create horizontal reflective surfaces, which reflect light coming in vertically, while allowing light coming in horizontally angles to pass through.

slats permit the utilization of daylight especially in the inner reaches of rooms.

Laser Cut Panels (LCP)
Laser Cut Panels are used as a fixed system within dual panes of glass in skylights or as swivel elements on the front of a façade. They redirect sunlight at the surface of small incisions created by means of lasers in a sheet of acrylic glass. Although they hardly obstruct the view, they must be installed above windows, since blinding effects can occur on their inside.

Holographic-Optical Elements (HOE)
Holographic-optical elements consist of holographic film inserted into multi-layer glass so as to redirect sunlight. The disagreeable separation into the spectral colors occurring in the refraction of light is largely concealed by the slightly scattering quality of the glass. HOE are only effective for limited angular ranges. Hence, a variety of different HOE exposed side-by-side or one above the other are used. Installed in the upper window area in the façade or in the skylight, the elements redirect direct sunlight. In façades facing north, they also direct diffuse light of the sky into rooms as hook-out elements. Their specially designed optics offer sun protection. HOE can bundle sunlight on photo-voltaic surfaces arranged behind them and thereby increase their efficiency by up to 50%.

Mirror Screens and Anidolic Systems
Flat mirror screens inserted into dual panes of glass serve to block direct sunlight in the utilization of the diffuse light of the sky. They open towards the north and reflect the sun entering from the east, south, and west. These screens are found in skylights. Anidolic or non-imaging systems work on a similar principle, although spatially they are constructed differently: they form a wide "chimney of light" which is oriented northwards. The desired light is concentrated, and as a consequence, the required size of the opening is reduced by a third as compared with traditional skylights.

Many of these new systems for the direction of light, sun protection and glare protection may be combined. The redirection of direct sunlight into rooms may lead to surprisingly brilliant effects; of course, only when the

27 Holographic-optical elements redirect light in skylights ...

28 ... or in front of façades. Here they are combined with photo-voltaics.

29 Charming colorful images are visible from below, which hardly affect the transparency.

30 Spatially shaped mirror screens protect interior spaces against direct sunlight. They were used in museums.

31 Anidolic systems reflect light from the north into interior spaces.

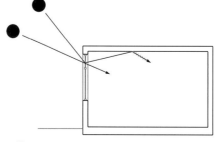
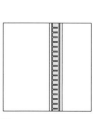

25   26

sun is shining. Thermal loads must always be considered in this context. The amount of daylight gained depends on the size and the orientation of the collecting surfaces (the zenith is two thirds brighter than the horizon). Many systems have unwanted side effects such as the separation of white sunlight into its spectral colors. Some redirecting systems impede the view to the outside. For this reason, today, mostly the overhead areas of façades are used for redirecting systems. Some systems form their own distinctive patterns: the streaks of prisms, the squares of individual sheets, the dovetails formed when such sheets are combined are details which do not suit all architectures. Vaulted metal ceiling elements which may be required can spoil the view in interior spaces.

The manufacture of prism sheets, LCP and HOE is technically very sophisticated and hence costly. In some cases, the manufacture of the systems consumes large amounts of energy. This expense must be set off against the energy conserved later, in order to evaluate the total costs of the system. It is difficult to compare the various systems directly, since for a certain task one system will be more practical and effective, while for another building another system will be more suitable. Lighting de-

signers must rely on their experience and their feel for the material. Currently, comparative calculations with computers are possible, but only in a limited and improvised way, since current software has difficulty in dealing with the dynamic situations which must also be considered.

The daylight systems presented here follow promising approaches which require further development. Frequently, simple arrangements are sufficient to create a well thought-out system of daylight direction in interior spaces. A precondition for sound daylight planning is an early involvement of the lighting designer in the design process.

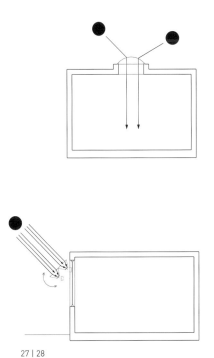

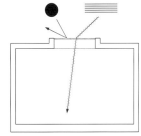

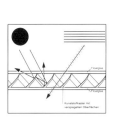

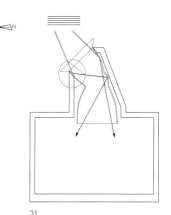

32 The various seasons are brought about by the changing incline of the earth's axis with respect to its orbit.

33 The length of the days and the highest position of the sun varies in the course of the seasons. Designers pay special attention to the solstice in summer and in winter and to the equinox.

34 The incline of the earth's axis affects the length of the shadow of every object on earth.

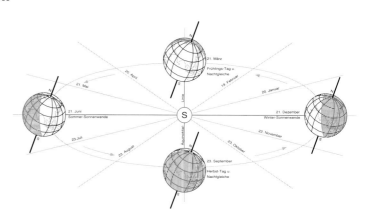

Determining Daylight Conditions

Direct Insolation and the Daylight Factor

Daylight in interior spaces changes with the time of day and with the season. Hence, the extreme values are particularly important for making general statements about lighting conditions. For planning purposes, the lighting designer needs to know the degree of latitude of the locale, which determines the angles and duration of solar radiation, the orientation of the building and information regarding adjacent structures which might cast shadows on the building. In addition there are tables listing the probabilities of sunshine in a region.

Direct insolation illustrates how the various positions of the sun arise during the different seasons. The reference point is the city of Hamburg. The earth's axis is tilted towards the plane of the earth's orbit around the sun by 23.5°. Hamburg is located at 53.5° north. The highest position which the sun ever achieves in this city (that is, at 12 noon on June 21) is

$$90° + 23.5° - 53.5° = 60°.$$

The lowest position at 12 noon on December 21 is

$$90° - 23.5° - 53.5° = 13°$$

and at the equinox in spring or in fall on March 21 and on September 23, the sun at 12 noon is

$$90° - 53.5° = 36.5°$$

above the horizon.

The various angles are explained when one looks at the illustration more closely and considers the earth's surface as the tangent of the sphere. The sun's rays enter the house in Hamburg parallel at an angle γ. This angle forms a right-angled triangle (the right angle is β) with the latitude of Hamburg (53.5°) and the incline of the earth's axis towards the earth's orbit around the sun (= direction of the sun's rays at an angle of 23.5° (α)). The following applies:

$\alpha + \beta + \gamma = 180°$ and:
$\alpha = 53.5° + 23.5° = 77°$;
$\beta = 90°$;
$\gamma = 180° - 77° - 90° = 13°.$

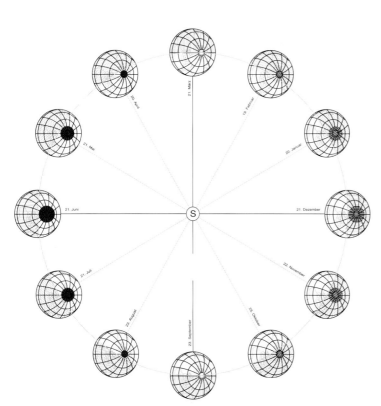

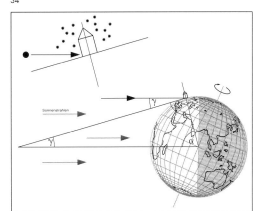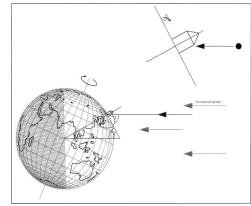

This calculation yields the insolation of a building in the northern hemisphere in winter. The next illustration shows the situation in summer. The corresponding formula is:

$\alpha + \beta + \gamma = 180°$;
$\alpha = 53.5° - 23.5° = 30°$;
$\beta = 90°$;
$\gamma = 180° - 30° - 90° = 60°$

This value – the angle between the sun and the horizontal plane – is called the altitude of the sun. Every additional degree of latitude in the northerly direction equals a reduction of the altitude of the sun by one degree, while every degree of latitude in the southerly direction equals an additional degree in the altitude of the sun: the sun's position is higher in the south than in the north. With the help of sun position diagrams, which in each case refer to a certain degree of latitude, the insolation of a building can be drawn into the floor plan and the sectional view. The graph refers to a particular time of day and season. The elongated floor plan of the *Franckesche Stiftungen* in Halle allows for the simultaneous representation of the direct insolation at various times of day and during various seasons.

Daylight Simulations

Models

Models offer another way of gaining insight into the daylight conditions within a building. Required is a light source emitting parallel rays of light in order to simulate the sun. The parabolic mirrors which produce this type of radiation usually have a diameter between 60 and 100 cm. The model must not exceed this size, if it is to be completely insolated. Now the artificial sun can be adjusted in such a way that every desired location and every desired time can be simulated; even entire days can be run through in quick motion. The simulation rooms have an evenly illuminated ceiling so as to take the light of the sky into account. Some universities, luminaire manufacturers, and lighting designers operate daylight simulators.

Altitude of the Sun:

At 12 Noon	Degree of Latitude	21.6.	21.3./23.9.	21.12.
Murmansk				No Sun
Hamburg	53.5° N	60.0°	36.5°	13.0°
London	51.5	62.0	38.5	15.0
Paris	49.0	64.0	40.5	17
Munich	48.0° N	65.5°	42.0°	18.5°
Milan	45.5	68.0	44.5	21.0
New York City, Rome	41.5	72.0	48.5	25.0
Beijing	40.0	73.5	50.0	26.5
Tokyo	36.0	77.5	54.0	30.5
Los Angeles	33.5	80.0	56.5	33.0
The Tropic of Cancer	23.5° N	90.0°	66.5°	43.0°
Hongkong	22	93.5	68.0	44.5
Dakar	15	98.5	75.0	51.5
The Equator	0°	113.5°	90.0°	66.5°
Brisbane	27.5 S	86.0	62.5	39.0
Cape Town	33.5 S	80.0	56.5	33.0

35 The sun position graph depicts, for all locations at 51.5°
northern latitude, the course of the sun from east to west
together with its various elevations throughout the day
and throughout the seasons.

36 The measured values are entered in a shadow construction with the help of the section and the floor plan of a
building.

37 A model in the daylight simulator (ERCO) indicates
the shadows formed in the space. The effect of the diffuse
light of the sky can be seen as well.

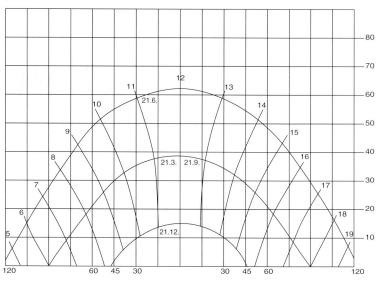

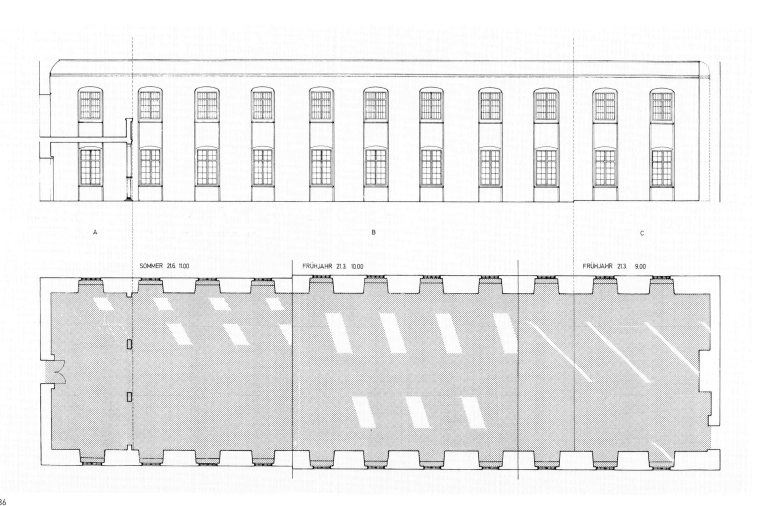

SOMMER 21.6. 11.00   FRÜHJAHR 21.3. 10.00   FRÜHJAHR 21.3. 9.00

A   B   C

Computer Simulations

A number of programs allow daylight simulation in various degrees of quality. First, this involves the preparation of a three-dimensional model room with the respective window openings and skylights. Second, a location and sky values in accordance with the CIE standard sky (sunny, overcast, etc.) must be attributed to the model. Afterwards, the incidence of light is calculated. Unfortunately, the programs on the market today do not yet permit dynamic calculations. Further, they only provide a very limited simulation of systems for the direction of daylight, shadowing and glare protection. For this reason, the use of the computer programs remains limited.

The Basic Rules of Daylight Planning

Irrespective of how the building is simulated, the planning process is determined by the following rules:

Checklist
- The more horizontal a daylight opening is, the more effectively will it bring light into the room, since the zenith light of the sky is three times brighter than the light of the horizon.
- The more square a room is, the higher is its room utilization factor and the higher will be the mean daylight factor with the same daylight opening.
- As a rule, a number of smaller daylight openings are more favorable (especially with regard to uniformity) than one large opening.

The following exemplary calculations demonstrate the influence of various parameters such as room proportions, size and position of the daylight opening or window, and the reflectance factors in the room. The sample room is located in Basle (47.5 degrees north). The calculation was done for a medium overcast sky, and the measuring plane for the illuminance is 0.20 m above the floor.

In addition to carrying out the comparisons just mentioned, it is advisable to compare examples from the five tables before planning daylight openings. This should be followed by some project-specific experiments.

Please note that in the following illustrations, the software for the calculations does not represent the rooms true to scale. The numerical specifications on the floor plans provide the actual measurements. The line of sight into the rooms changes, i. e. the view is not always from south towards north. The first table shows the effect of the position and the distribution of the windows on the daylight factor and the illuminances in the room relative to an exterior illuminance of 10000 lx. The room measures 6 x 10 m² with a ceiling height of 3.50 m. The window surface area is 4 m² for rooms I – VI. The level of reflection of the walls was changed between Fig. I and Fig. II. In Fig. III and Fig. IV, the windows are at different vertical positions. In Fig. V, four windows are located in one wall, while in Fig. VI, each wall has one window.

I

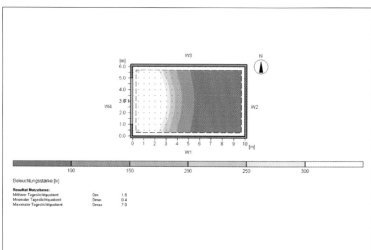

III

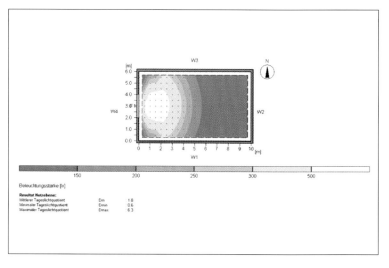

V

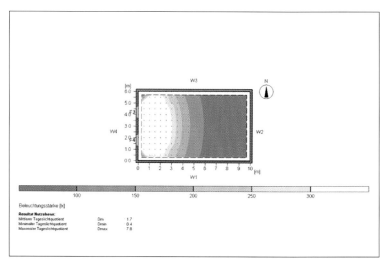

II

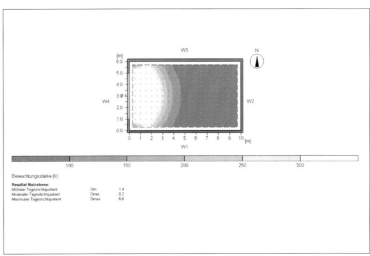

W3

N

[m]
6.0
5.0
4.0
W4   3.0 (FH
2.0
1.0
0.0
0 1 2 3 4 5 6 7 8 9 10 [m]
W1

W2

Beleuchtungsstärke [lx]

100   150   200   250   300

Resultat Nutzebene:
Mittlerer Tageslichtquotient   Dm   1.4
Minimaler Tageslichtquotient   Dmin   0.2
Maximaler Tageslichtquotient   Dmax   6.6

IV

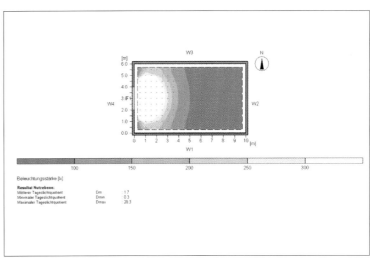

W3

N

[m]
6.0
5.0
4.0
W4   3.0 (FH
2.0
1.0
0.0
0 1 2 3 4 5 6 7 8 9 10 [m]
W1

W2

Beleuchtungsstärke [lx]

100   150   200   250   300

Resultat Nutzebene:
Mittlerer Tageslichtquotient   Dm   1.7
Minimaler Tageslichtquotient   Dmin   0.3
Maximaler Tageslichtquotient   Dmax   20.3

VI

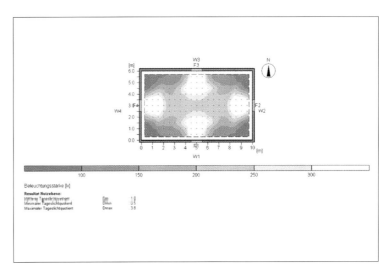

W3
F3

N

[m]
6.0
5.0
4.0
W4   3.0 (F4
2.0
1.0
0.0
0 1 2 3 4 5 6 7 8 9 10 [m]
W1

F2
W2

Beleuchtungsstärke [lx]

100   150   200   250   300

Resultat Nutzebene:
Mittlerer Tageslichtquotient   Dm   1.8
Minimaler Tageslichtquotient   Dmin   0.6
Maximaler Tageslichtquotient   Dmax   3.6

aThe following table shows the influence of room proportions on the daylight factor and the illuminances in the room. All rooms have the same surface area and a ceiling height of 3.50 m. In Fig. I–VI, the total window or skylight surface area is constant at 4 m².

In Fig. I and Fig. II, the room is square (7.75 x 7.75 m²), in Fig. III and Fig. IV it is rectangular (6 x 10 m²) and in Fig. V and VI, it forms a long rectangle (3 x 20 m²).

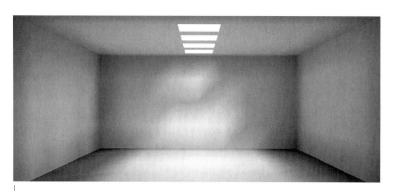

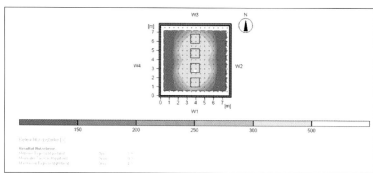

I

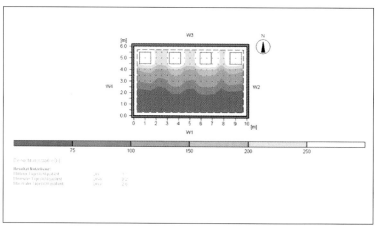

III

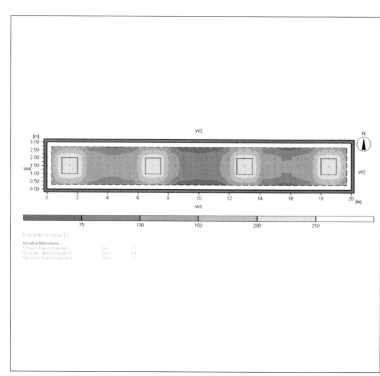

V

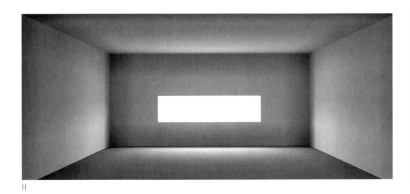

II

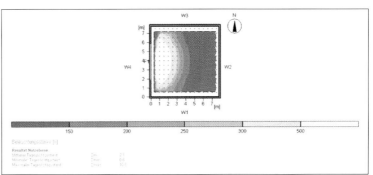

IV

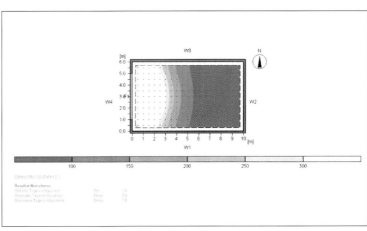

VI

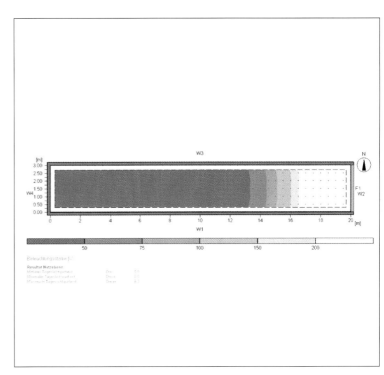

The next table shows the influence of the reflectance factor of the walls on the daylight conditions in the room.
In Fig. I and II, the walls reflect at 70 %, in Fig. III and IV at 20 %, and in Fig. V and VI at 0 %.

I

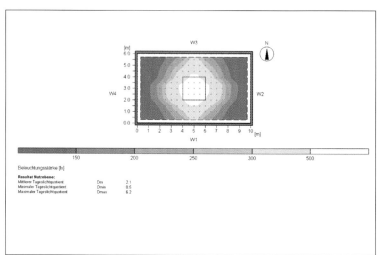

III

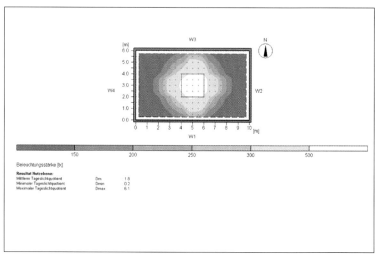

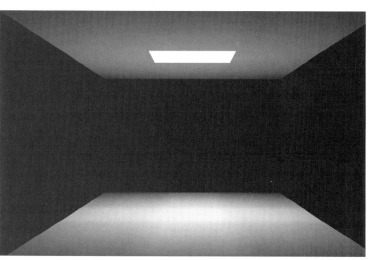

V

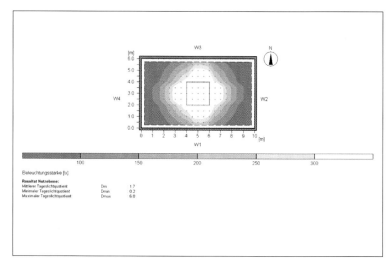

II

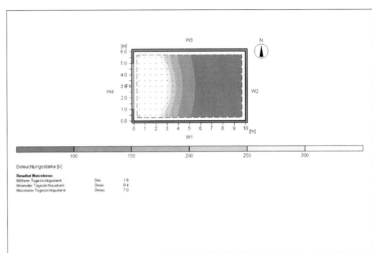

IV

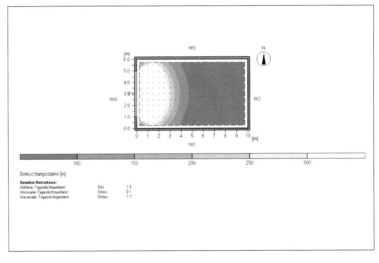

VI

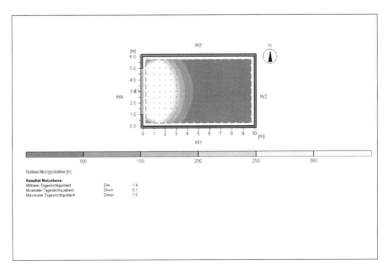

The final table shows the influence of the height of the
ceiling on daylight conditions: at a constant surface area
of 6 x 10 m², the height of the room is 2.50 m in Fig. I, 3.50 m
in Fig. II, and 5 m in Fig. III.

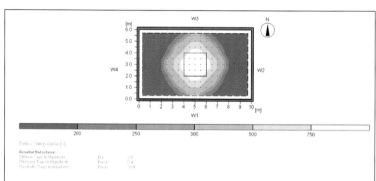

I

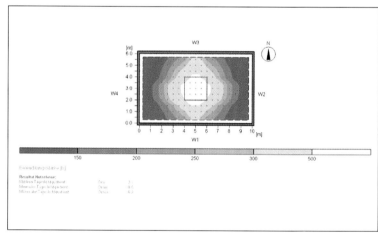

II

III

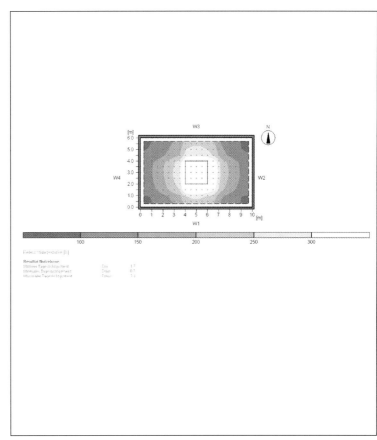

1 Rough surfaces in the landscape reflect light diffusely, while the sun is reflected in the water. The reflection moves with the observer across the surface of the water.

2 On this old photograph, the light of the window subtly retraces the faces and the pleats of the dress.

3 On a reflective surface (and on other smooth surfaces), the angle of reflection corresponds to the angle of incidence.

4 The snow appears in various shades of white: here, the smooth surface appears darker than the plowed uneven field, which reflects light more diffusely.

5 Rough surfaces reflect light unevenly.

6 Direct sunlight produces harsh shadows. Diffuse soft light of the sky brightens the shadows.

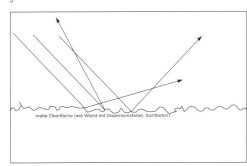

Artificial Light

Light as "Material"

The Spreading of Light

The sun, the fixed stars, candles and lamps are all sources of light or luminous bodies. There are natural and artificial sources of light. On the other hand, there are the illuminated bodies such as the planets, the moons, or a wall which cast light back into our eyes as a reflection. The abilities of the eyes are tied to the surrounding light. Light only becomes visible where it strikes surfaces and "creates" them in such a marvelous way. In the process, shadows are created which look like "holes" in the light. They are part of the ordinary perception of everyone: however, we are not always conscious of the shadows, nor are they always noticeable. Yet, they bear witness to the manifest relation between light and space. Three gradations of shadows may be distinguished; shade, half-shade and cast shadow. Shadows are formed on the imaging body itself through the light that falls on it, producing brightness, semi-darkness, and complete darkness. The zones of transition from brightness to darkness lie in half-shade. The dark shadow is the image of a body on the ground or on other surfaces onto which a shadow falls.

The various shadows are produced by light; they inform the eye, whose power depends on the presence of light, well about the visible characteristics of what is seen. The first element touched upon is the surface: how light is absorbed, reproduced and reflected. We see whether the body is translucent, whether it refracts, filters, or absorbs light. Indeed, this observation, however, quickly illustrates the many varieties of light.

Diffuse light portrays a surface differently than direct sunlight, and artificial light creates different shadows than the residual light at the onset of night, as the light of the sky creates differently shaped shadows than those visible through artificial light. The shape of the shadow depends on the proximity of the source of the light that produces it.

Materials have various degrees of translucency (transmittance). There are transparent materials such as clear glass, water, air, translucent materials such as opal glass, and non-transparent materials such as wood and metal. The boundaries between these types are blurred. As a thin layer, wood can be translucent, as a very thick layer, water can be non-transparent. Light passing through gold leaf looks green, while light passing through thin silver foil looks blue.

Reflection

Most of the time, it is indirect light that enters our eyes. In the form of candlelight, direct light may be pleasant; as a bare electrical lamp, however, it may blind and thus be a nuisance: the blinding headlights of oncoming traffic at night are a familiar and unpleasant experience.

Flat glass mirrors or high-gloss reflecting materials can produce reflections that are just as powerfull as direct light. Luminaire manufacturers exploit the effect of a directed reflection in their darklight downlights. The reflectors are adjusted to the corresponding lamps in such a way that they give off their light over the darklight mirror reflector at a precisely defined angle. The luminaire has no glare and, from a distance, seems completely inconspicuous.

7 Shiny and creased materials show both: even and uneven reflectance.

8 Small experiments can prevent unintended side effects. On the shiny surface, three light sources are visible. If the surface were dull, it would appear evenly illuminated.

High-gloss surfaces which are not flat but irregular or textured, such as latten, corrugated sheet metal, even the surfaces of fabrics or stucco lustro, often reflect in surprising ways. If they are to be illuminated, only experiments with sufficiently large material samples viewed from various angles can guard against undesired reflections. A lighting designer with a good command of the laws of optics can make explicit use of surfaces and their reflections to achieve charming effects. Diffusely reflecting materials scatter the light falling on them from all points in all directions. White surfaces can reflect just as well as mat aluminum, and both materials only reflect diffuse light.

Reflectance Factors:

Color	Reflectance Factor %
White	70–85
Light gray	45–65
Medium gray	25–40
Dark gray	10–20
Black	< 5
Yellow	65–75
Yellowish brown	30–50
Dark brown	10–25
Light green	30–55
Dark green	10–25
Pink	45–60
Light red	25–35
Dark red	10–20
Light blue	30–55
Dark blue	10–25

Material	Reflectance Factor %
Lacquer, brilliant white	87–88
Aluminum, high-gloss anodized	75–87
Aluminum, mat anodized	75–84
Sound absorbing ceiling, white, perforated	60–80
Marble, white	60–70
Mortar, light	35–50
Concrete, light	30–40
Concrete, dark	15–25
Sandstone, light	30–40
Sandstone, dark	15–25
Granite	15–25
Brick, light	20–30
Brick, dark	10–15
Wood, light	30–50
Wood, dark	10–25

Ground Surface	Reflectance Factor %
Meadow, lawn	approx. 5
Snow, fresh	approx. 70
Snow, old	approx. 50
Fields	approx. 25
Concrete	approx. 50
Gravel	approx. 20
Grit	approx. 10

 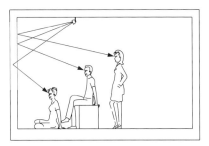

9   The point of reflection migrates with the observer.

10 A refraction of light occurs at the boundary between air and the denser medium of water.

11 If a ray of light passes twice through the boundary between two media of different densities, it will be refracted twice.

12 If the ray of light strikes such a boundary at a very shallow angle, a total reflection will occur. This phenomenon is exploited in fiber optic light guide technology.

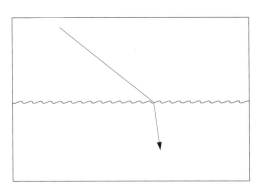 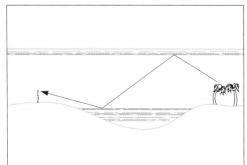 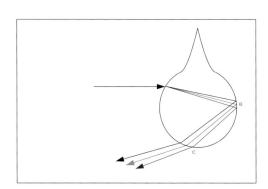

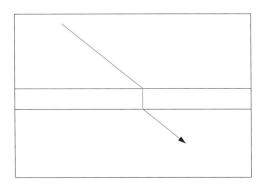 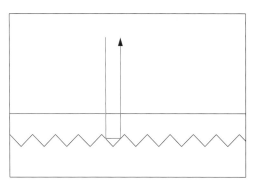 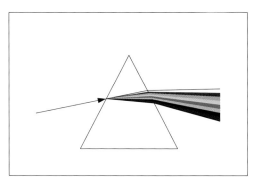

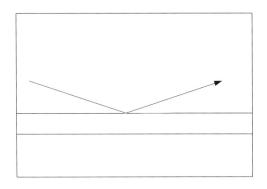 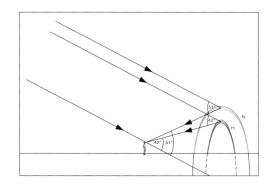

10 | 11 | 12   13 | 14   15 | 16 | 17

13 The shimmering heat that can be observed in temperate regions above asphalt roads arises in a similar way as a mirage.

14 The phenomenon of a total reflection is utilized in prism panels and in the reflectors attached to roadside guiding posts.

15 A raindrop dismantles sunlight into its spectral colors ...

16 ... similar to a prism.

17 The resulting rainbow can only be seen from certain angles.

18 The reason why crystal sparkles so intensely is that with its high refractive index, it spreads out the spectral colors in a very broad way.

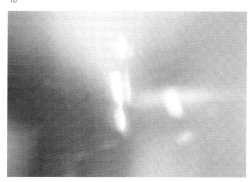

It is of importance for the practice of lighting design to bear in mind that the reflectance factors of walls, ceilings and floors have a very great effect on the brightness of the room and on the illuminances achieved in the final result.

The more mat a surface, the better it can be illuminated over large areas. A shiny golden wall, the oils of a painting, or glass are treacherous materials. With a directed illumination, they develop a reflective light in one spot (which moves with the viewer), while otherwise remaining relatively dark.

Also, the frequent attempt to emphasize glass roofs by shining light on them must fail due to the fact that the light is reflected and yet the glass surface does not visually appear as a bright surface. The glass only looks bright as a surface if it is covered in dust.

Light refracts as a ray of light passes from a dense into a less dense medium or the other way round. As long as the ray of light touches the denser medium (e.g. water) at a right angle, it passes through unrefracted. As soon as it strikes the medium at an angle smaller than 90°, the angle of the ray continuing in the denser medium, e.g. water, decreases relative to the perpendicular.

If, thereupon, the ray of light reenters the less dense medium, e.g. when it passes from glass back into air, the ray of light is again refracted away from the perpendicular such that it continues, slightly offset, in the original direction.

A total reflection occurs when the angle of incidence from the denser to the less dense medium is so small, i.e. so large relative to the perpendicular, that the light is reflected at the boundary. This occurs, for example, in the technology of light-conducting fibers.

In practice, reflection also means that the frequently cited transparency of glass façades is only effective when viewed from certain angles. Under certain illumination and viewing conditions, glass can have a mirroring and harshly rebuffing effect. A total reflection can also occur between two quite sharply divided air layers of different temperature, a dual reflection known as a "mirage".

A retroreflection occurs when the entering light is not, as in a mirror, reflected at the same angle in another direction but when it is reflected into the direction from which it came. Reflectors have prism structures on the back; special road markers, frequently employed at road construction sites, have glass globules in their colored layer, road studs have larger glass spheres which reflect the light from the headlights back into the direction of the automobile.

Rays with a perpendicular incidence can also be totally reflected. To achieve this, the back of a glass pane or of acrylic glass is moulded as a prism structure.

The refraction of light signifies the breaking down of white light into its spectral components. Rays of longer wavelength (orange – red) are refracted less than rays of shorter wavelength (violet – blue). This is how the rainbow arises in the refraction of rays of light in numerous small drops of water. It is visible only from a certain relative angle between the sun, the rain drops, and the observer.

In the guidance of daylight, the refractory effect can be a nuisance. It arises in the redirection or refraction of light on prism sheets, prism foils and holograms. Only by means of the combination of prisms is it possible – if one ignores the edge areas – to restore the white light through the superposition of the colored light. Depending on their specific properties, different materials refract light to various degrees in the transition to air. Glass refracts light in the transition from air more strongly than water, diamond more strongly than glass. The various wavelengths are also refracted to different degrees, which explains the glitter of quartz crystals and diamonds.

Refractive Indices from Air to:

Ice	1.3
Water	1.33
Crown glass	1.51–1.62
Quartz	1.54
Flint glass	1.61–1.75
Diamond	2.5

19 Frosted glass scatters light and is thus suitable as a projection surface.

20 Clear embedded particles appear as holes in the material.

21 Perforated sheet metal is often used to cover the lamp in a luminaire. In the same way, it may be used to scatter the incident daylight in interior spaces.

Transmission

Materials allow light to pass through in various ways. Glass transmits light especially well. As frosted glass, opal glass, etched, sand-blasted, bead-blasted glass, or textured glass, however, glass can also scatter light. This occurs either at the surface (frosted glass: surface scattering) or in the material itself (opal glass: volume scattering). In the Ecology Gallery of the Museum of Natural History in London, the various qualities of glass in light can be distinctly observed. The glass with a low iron content does not have a green cast. The arched glass walls, matted through a coating, are suitable as a screen for changing colored light projections and thus appear either closed or transparent. In the floor of the bridge, partial areas of the glass in the shape of ginkgo leaves have been left transparent. Here the glass appears as though it were punched out. From the position of the viewer, some leaves appear dark (dark background on the ground floor), some very bright (reflections of the light from above), and some indifferent (mixture of both phenomena). Colored glass in filters, sunglasses and solar protection glass filter out certain wavelengths of the light (and of the invisible part of the spectrum of solar rays) but darken the space correspondingly. This filtering effect can also be achieved by coatings (frequently by means of vapor-deposition) which is typical for solar protection glass and cold-light reflectors.

Surfaces

Perforated plates and rib mesh are defined in their transmittance factor by the proportion between the material and the opening, making them transparent in varying degrees. In order to avoid unwanted projections of perforated plate or rib mesh patterns, however, additional mat foils or glass must generally be installed behind them. Rib mesh has a preferred direction. It is important to conduct tests before using these materials. If they are finely grained, technical fabrics (wire, plastic, or textile) used in photography or in stage lighting have the same effect as soft-focus lenses, similar to frosted glass or foil. Spatial fabrics or mesh react differently to all angles of light incidence.

Luminous Surfaces – Phosphorescence and Fluorescence

Materials similar to those used in the coatings of fluorescent lamps can also be applied to other surfaces. These are usually inorganic crystal phosphors. In fluorescent lamps, the excitation takes place by means of ultraviolet radiation, and the emission of the light quantum takes place in the visible part of the spectrum. Phosphorescing colors, as on watch faces, are likewise excited by visible light. In the case of fluorescence, the material glows within 10^8 seconds; in the case of phosphorescence, this takes longer, and there is an afterglow. Ian Ritchie made use of this effect in his installation for the exhibition *Lichtfest* in Ingolstadt. The phosphorescing material was applied to the walls of a tunnel of glass. The visitors used flashlights to paint their "graffiti" which disappeared after half a minute.

Electroluminescence

Electroluminescence achieves only a low luminous efficacy of about 6 Lm/W. It is used on information boards and as emergency lighting on airplanes (lighting strip on the floor). In the process of electroluminescence, illuminants are excited by an electrical alternating field.

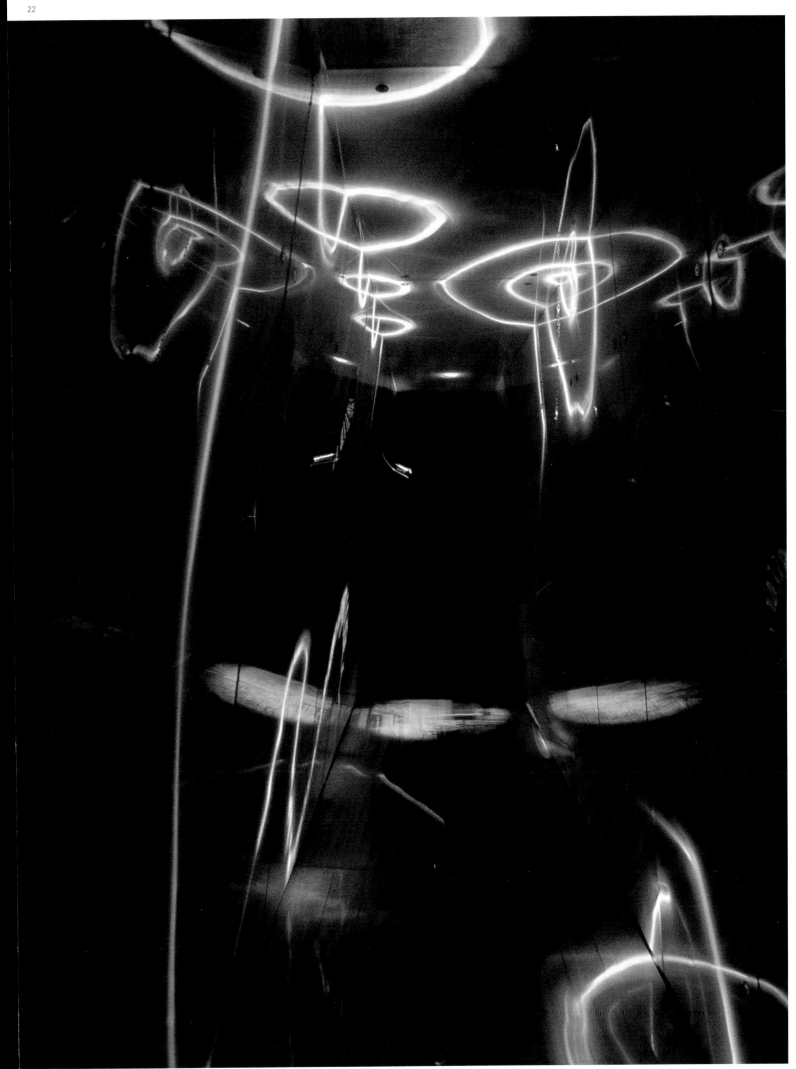

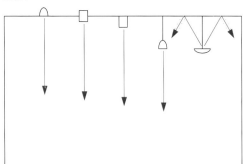

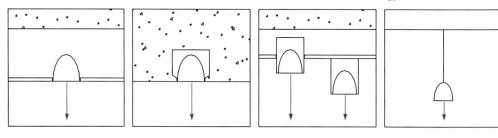

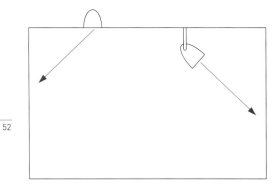

Luminaires and Lamps

Luminaires may be categorized under many different aspects, the distinction between "indoor luminaires" and "outdoor luminaires" being the most obvious. But one speaks also of "technical luminaires" in contrast with "residential luminaires" or "decorative luminaires". This is an unfortunate choice of terminology, since, of course, every luminaire has technical components. The distinction with respect to the generated luminous effect and luminous quality – direct, indirect as well as direct-indirect light, would seem to agree with the approach of the designer. These categories, however, are often too abstract and theoretical, since there exist many mixed forms. A concrete and practical first distinction concerns the manner and place of installation, that is, the specification, whether the luminaire in question is a wall, floor, or ceiling luminaire and whether it is recessed or surface-mounted.

Ceiling Luminaires

All luminaires which emit their light in a downward direction and have a round or square shape belong to the large family of downlights. These range from freely suspended industrial floodlights of the highest protection classification for the illumination of large shops to the miniaturized reflector with a halogen incandescent lamp for installation in plasterboard ceilings.

The reason for the popularity of the classical recessed downlight is that it discreetly disappears into the ceiling. If the downlight has a large antiglare angle and therfore, the eye is hardly blinded by the high luminances of the lamp or reflector, one can scarcely discern where the light in the room is coming from. The object character of a luminaire in space is eliminated.

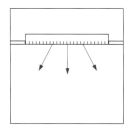
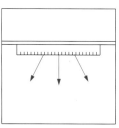
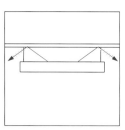
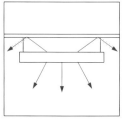

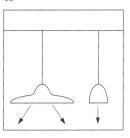

23 Ceiling luminaires are distinguished according to type of mounting, type of lamp and accessories: recessed downlights, semi-recessed downlights, surface-mounted downlights, pendant downlights, indirectly radiating pendant luminaires.

24 On the ceiling, these built-in luminaires have the appearance of downlights. Yet they radiate asymmetrically, illuminating a wall like spotlights.

25 The conditions for recessed or built-in luminaires vary: installation in a suspended ceiling is less complicated than in a concrete ceiling.

26 Luminaires hanging by a chord are among the original forms of this luminaire family. The principle is simple, which is perhaps just the reason for its great popularity.

Downlights fitted with halogen incandescent lamps have the smallest openings. If equipped with fluorescent lamps, downlights have a diameter from 20 cm up to 40 cm, especially if several compact fluorescent lamps are being used. In the usual, rotationally symmetrical reflectors, point sources of light achieve a higher efficiency than large-surface lamps. As directionally neutral elements, round downlights can be planned in an infinite variety of arrangements. Accessories such as diffuser panels which illuminate ceilings and make the light source visible, filters which protect against UV radiation, slats and grids which hide the lamp from view are complemented by decorative accessories such as rings and glass covers. Fixed or adjustable built-in wall washers may outwardly be shaped like built-in downlights. Downlight-wall washers are preferred for the extremely uniform illumination of large wall surfaces. The asymmetric angle of beam and the wattage are dimensioned in such a way that the luminaire, positioned at a sufficient distance from the wall, eliminates glare and illuminates the wall in the best possible way. Wall washers were initially developed for museums in order to achieve an even illumination of the display areas.

Linear Fluorescent Luminaires

The term linear fluorescent luminaire points to the elongated shape of the fluorescent lamp which can measure up to 1.80 m in length. Whether as a lighting strip or as a row of individual lights, the universal linear fluorescent luminaire illuminates industrial workshops, train stations, offices, and foyers in a variety of forms.

In office spaces, reflectors block the glare from the light of linear fluorescent luminaires. For an optimal glare reduction, the geometry of these luminaires requires their alignment with the line of vision, especially in

the workplace. Nowadays there are grids which block glare well in all four directions. The high gloss mirror screens used in the 1980s had the unpleasant effect of conspicuously reflecting every movement in the room and thus creating an atmosphere of restlessness. Moreover, dust and finger prints are visible on these sensitive surfaces. Today, the high gloss mirror screens are being replaced by mat screens. Direct light from linear fluorescent luminaires provides the most economical office lighting, although the subjective well-being of employees frequently suffers under this light. Ceiling height or room proportions permitting, suspended linear fluorescent luminaires can create a direct-indirect light. This is a pleasant combination, since the diffuse and uniform indirect light and the shadow-forming direct light complement each other.

Linear fluorescent luminaires with two radiating light components ("secondary lights") and their square variants were developed in the early 1990s. Their lamps are partially shaded from below and emit indirect light into the room via a relatively large, mat silver or white reflector, while giving off only defined portions of light in a downward direction. Due to the bright reflective surfaces, the room has a much more pleasant appearance than in the direct light of the mirror screen luminaires. Since pendant luminaires fall into the line of vision, it is important that they have a pleasing form and be small in size. Linear fluorescent luminaires with a more simple design are found in all types of spaces: bare lamps in warehouses and discount stores, white reflectors and perhaps slats in supermarkets, mat or translucent covers in train stations, in underpasses and tunnels as well as in explosion and corrosion-proofed versions in industrial plants.

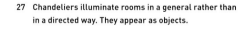

27 Chandeliers illuminate rooms in a general rather than in a directed way. They appear as objects.

28 Pendant luminaires with reflectors, on the other hand, produce islands of light.

29 This pendant luminaire emits light both directly and indirectly, making it suitable for office spaces.

30 Linear fluorescent luminaires are available in recessed and surface-mounted versions ...

31 ... and as pendant luminaires.

32 This linear fluorescent luminaire is well suited for offices, radiating direct and indirect light into the room.

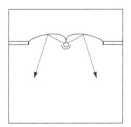

LOCATION	TYPE OF INSTALLATION	TYPE OF LIGHT	LAMP	LIGHTING ACCESSORIES
CEILING LUMINAIRES	RECESSED	DOWNLIGHT	QT	LOUVRE / LAMELLAE
			TC	BULKHEAD
			HIT	GLASS
		LINEAR RECTANGLE	TC	LOUVRE / LAMELLAE BULKHEAD
			T	LOUVRE/LAMELLAE BULKHEAD
		SECONDARY	TC	SHIELDING
			T	OF THE
			HIT	LAMP
	SEMI-RECESSED	DOWNLIGHT	QT	WITHOUT/WITH AURA
			TC	WITHOUT/WITH AURA
			HIT	WITHOUT WITH AURA
		LINEAR RECTANGLE	TC	LOUVRE / LAMELLAE BULKHEAD
			T	LOUVRE / LAMELLAE BULKHEAD
		SECONDARY	TC	SHIELDING
			T	OF THE
			HIT	LAMP
	SURFACE-Ł MOUNTED	DOWNLIGHT	QT T HIT	
		LINEAR RECTANGLE	TC	LOUVRE / LAMELLAE BULKHEAD
			T	LOUVRE / LAMELLAE BULKHEAD
		SECONDARY	TC	SHIELDING
			T	OF THE
			HIT	LAMP
	PENDANT	DOWNLIGHT	QT T HIT	
		WITH SHADE OR HOUSING	QT	
			T	TRANSLUCENT
			HIT	
		LINEAR ONLY D*	TC	
			T	
		LINEAR. D/ID*		
		LINEAR ONLY ID*		

* D = directly radiating
 ID = indirectly radiating
 D/ID = directly/indirectly radiating

LOCATION	TYPE OF INSTALLATION	TYPE OF LIGHT	LAMP
FLOOR LUMINAIRES	RECESSED	DIRECT SYMMETRICAL	QT
			TC*
			HIT
		DIRECT ASYMMETRICAL	QT
			TC*
			HIT
		DIFFUSELY RADIATING	TC /T
			LED
		SIGNAL LIGHT	LED
			FIBER-GLASS TECHNO-LOGY
	SEMI-RECESSED	DIFFUSELY RADIATING	TC
			LED
		SIGNAL LIGHT	LED
		SHADED, ONLY RADIATING ONTO FLOOR	QT
			TC
			HIT
	SURFACE-MOUNTED	FLOOR FLOODLIGHT	TC
			HIT
		DIFFUSELY RADIATING	TC
			LED
		SIGNAL LIGHT	LED

* within Limits

LOCATION	TYPE OF INSTALLATION	TYPE OF LIGHT	LAMP
POLE LUMINAIRES	FIXED H= 2–25 METERS	ROTATIONALLY SYMMETRIC TOP	TC
			HIT
		DIRECTABLE SPOTLIGHT	TO
			HIT
		DIFFUSELY RADIATING	TC
			T

Left column table:

LOCATION	TYPE OF INSTALLATION	TYPE OF LIGHT	LAMP	LIGHTING ACCESSORIES
	RECESSED	CEILING FLOODLIGHTS	QT / TC / T / HIT	
		FLOOR FLOODLIGHTS NIGHT LIGHT	QT / TC / HIT	
WALL LUMINAIRES		DIFFUSED LIGHT	QT / TC	HIT / FROSTED PANE
	SURFACE-MOUNTED	CEILING FLOODLIGHTS	QT / TC / T / HIT	
		FLOOR FLOODLIGHTS NIGHT LIGHT	QT / TC / HIT	
		DIFFUSED LIGHT	QT / TC	HIT / FROSTED PANE*
		D/ID RADIATING AGAINST CEILING AND FLOOR SCREENED	QT / TC / HIT	ALSO COMBINATIONS
		RADIATING ONLY AGAINST THE WALL	QT	* without or with Aura

LOCATION	TYPE OF INSTALLATION	TYPE OF LIGHT	LAMP	LIGHTING ACCESSORIES
	FIXED	RADIATING ON TO GROUND	A / QT / TC	
BOLLARD LUMINAIRES		DIFFUSELY RADIATING	A / TC / QT	
		SIGNAL LIGHT	LED	

Right column table:

LOCATION	TYPE OF INSTALLATION	TYPE OF LIGHT	LAMP	LIGHTING ACCESSORIES
	FIXED OR SWIVELLING	DIRECTLY RADIATING	QT / TC	
		INDIRECTLY RADIATING	QT / TC / HIT	
STANDARD LUMINAIRES		DIRECTLY-INDIRECTLY RADIATING	QT / TC / HIT	OR IN COMBINATION
		DIFFUSELY RADIATING	QT / TC	
	FIXED	DIRECTLY RADIATING	A / QT / TC / T	
TABLE LUMINAIRES		DIRECTLY-INDIRECTLY RADIATING	TC / QT	
		DIFFUSELY RADIATING	A / TC / QT	
	SWIVELLING MOVABLE	DIRECTLY RADIATING	A / QT / TC	

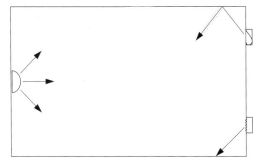

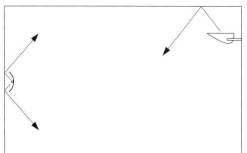

Pendant Luminaires

As a variant of suspended downlights and suspended linear fluorescent luminaires, the pendant luminaire exists, as the primordial form of an electric light with the historical enamel reflector in industrial workshops and with a variety of lampshades in residential spaces. These luminaires, which mainly radiate in a downward direction, are well suited for dining tables or, mounted in series, for bars and look best when fitted with all-purpose lamps or halogen incandescent lamps. In these areas, the warm and dimmable light of these luminaires has many advantages over the light of fluorescent lamps.

Wall Luminaires

The classical wall-mounted luminaire is a further development of the sconce. A lampshade around the light source distributes the light softly over the wall and into the room. A lower mounting height in comparison with ceiling lamps creates a warmer, more intimate atmosphere. At times, ceiling areas crowded with installations may force a designer to fall back on wall luminaires.

Some wall-mounted luminaires for general lighting shine on the floor in front of them, while others illuminate the ceiling, which in turn reflects soft light towards the ground. Some wall luminaires combine both light effects, either from one light source or even from two lamps of different types. Wall luminaires which direct their light only against the wall and are screened off even towards the front can be used to bring old masonry or brickwork to life. A nice example of the screened wall luminaire is found in the cafeteria of the Spiegel Verlag publishing house in Hamburg designed by Verner Panton. The orange-colored plastic wall elements reflect a warm light. Motorists passing by in the evening are greeted with a powerful spectacle.

Specially designed ceiling washers are a suitable means for using wall-mounted luminaires to illuminate ceilings. Fitted with fluorescent lamps, they form a mural frieze or act as swiveling surface radiators. With point sources of light, e.g. halogen incandescent lamps, there is the danger that the illuminated area is sharply outlined. In order to avoid an unintended effect of restlessness at the ceiling, the designer will conduct a lighting test or use frosted or partially frosted glass. The first built-in wall luminaires were night lights, the kind which one also finds built into steps in theaters and cinemas and which then also became popular outdoors with angled slats or frosted covers. The luminaires were small eith a low wattage. Nowadays, there exist many variants of this type of luminaire.

Built-in Floor Luminaires

For a long time, light emanating from the ground or light close to the ground was a domain of outdoor lighting and was especially used in the illumination of objects and parks. Today, built-in floor luminaires, which often produce a narrow-beaming light, are quite common indoors as well as outdoors. The luminaires are installed either in casings flush with the surface of the ground or inserted directly into the corresponding recesses. The use of built-in floor luminaires is not completely without problems. Often, users feel blinded by these lights. Integrated ring slats can reduce the glare but cannot prevent it completely in close proximity to the source. With clear glass covers there is the danger of skidding; frosted and hence skid-proof materials would make the light too diffuse. Finally, the surface of this type of lamp often heats up to more than 120°C. Users often do not expect such temperatures. Hence, it is advisable to install built-in floor luminaires off the footpaths. Luminaires which try to solve these temperature problems by means of a dual glass cover and a deeply recessed light source require a relatively large installation depth. The planning of built-in floor luminaires in interior spaces demands a very good knowledge of installation procedures and requirements in order to prevent possible problems. A type of luminaire which has been in use in outdoor spaces for a long time emits its light sideways on the ground through flat lenses (in one, two, or four directions). This results in a dramatic, often very atmospheric sided light.

The safety concerns of pedestrians on public paths cannot be satisfied by means of lights on the ground: vertical illuminances at eye level are much better suited for recognizing people at night.

The built-in floor luminaire as well as built-in luminaires with a slight dome, which are found more often outdoors than indoors, are available in a diffusely radiating version (see above) and as a point light with a signal rather than an illuminating function.

In both cases, end-emitting and side-emitting glass fiber lights as well as light-emitting diodes have proven successful and offer lighting designers great new design options. The higher purchase costs compared to traditional lamps are offset by the durability of the new technology and in the case of LED by the fact that they are as maintenance-free as possible.

The light distribution of the built-in floor luminaires corresponds to that of underwater luminaires, which, however, mostly must be operated in or under water for thermal reasons.

36 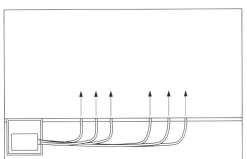 37 38

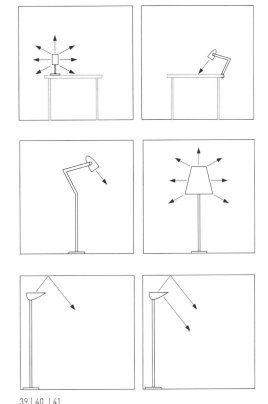

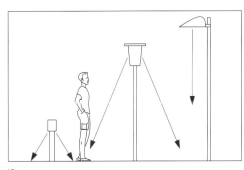

Floor Standard Luminaires

The classical floor standard luminaire in living quarters features a translucent shade made of paper, plastic, or fabric and thus has a pronounced object character. It emits primarily non-directed light on all sides and creates a cozy island of light. The swiveling and directable standard luminaire is well suited as a reading luminaire.

Ever since standard luminaires as ceiling washers fitted with halogen incandescent lamps have been increasingly used to illuminate living quarters, standard luminaires have also started to complement the range of available office luminaires. Users and designers wish to keep the ceiling free of pendulum luminaires and at the same time produce the pleasant character of indirect light, perhaps in combination with direct work space illumination. The flexible light allocated to the work space, however, comes at the price of an additional floor installation. Standard luminaires for offices are equipped with fluorescent lamps (often with two levels of brightness) or metal halide lamps. The lighting technology of standard luminaires is qualitatively so varied that they should definitely be tested in the intended space: uneven illuminances on the ceiling, sharp edges of shadows on the wall or ceiling, and too little light for the work space are often points of criticism. Via an integrated reflector or a second lamp, some of these luminaires offer a direct component for the work space.

Desk Luminaires

Two basic types of desk luminaires should be mentioned: First, the rigid, miniaturized standard luminaire with a translucent shade, as it is found in hotels and living spaces, where it creates a warm and cozy atmosphere; second, the swiveling and directable desk luminaire, which has already become a design classic in various versions. The direction and distance of the light can be individually adjusted. Incandescent lamps, halogen incandescent lamps, and compact fluorescent lamps require luminaire heads of various sizes and produce various amounts of heat.

33 Because wall luminaires can be mounted at arbitrary heights, they are convenient means for creating varying light atmospheres.

34 A wall that reflects light lends a different atmosphere to a room than a bright ceiling.

35 Here, the wall and the lamp amalgamate in an organic way, transforming the room into a lantern.

36 Built-in floor luminaires are used to illuminate façades or objects. They can also throw sided light onto the floor.

37 End-emitting fiberglass technology is used to create many small points of light in the floor at a relatively low installation cost.

38 Sided lights on the ground are rich in contrast and have a dramatic effect.

39 Table luminaires follow two principles: the principle of the translucent lantern and of the directable spotlight.

40 Standard luminaires provide various types of light: with reflectors, they create a directed light; with a translucent shade, they produce a diffuse light.

41 As ceiling washers, standard luminaires can be used for purely indirect illumination. Some additionally provide a portion of direct light.

42 Outdoor luminaires: the mounting height varies from bollard luminaires to top-mounted and side-mounted pole luminaires.

39 | 40 | 41   42

Bollards and Pole Luminaires

These two types of luminaires are typical examples of outdoor lighting. They illuminate streets, squares, parks and other outdoor areas. The atmosphere they produce is largely determined by their mounting height: a taller luminaire will have a more anonymous effect (athletic field, intersection), while a lower luminaire creates a more homely and cozy atmosphere (pedestrian zones, parks). The color of the light is just as important: While mercury vapor lamps with their cool light effect were used until the end of the 1980s, today, metal halide lamps or the new high-pressure sodium vapor lamps predominate. Luminaires with good antiglare systems and directed light are replacing luminaires radiating diffuse and undirected light.

The Choice of Luminaires and Lamps

When implementing a lighting concept, it is important to examine the various design options in terms of their economic efficiency. Designing something beautiful is relatively easy with liberal spending and a large budget. It is a far greater feat, however, to create something special by modest means. Along with the economic aspect, there is the ecological aspect to consider – the obligation to conserve natural resources. The best option, of course, is not necessarily the most economical one, but the option which strikes the right balance between the aesthetic expression, the utility value and the economic efficiency of a lighting system.

In the generation of light, as much of the electrical energy as possible should be converted to light rather than heat. The corresponding value is known as the luminous efficiency. For a luminous flux of 1380 lumen, an incandescent lamp requires a power of 100 W. A high pressure sodium

43 Induction lamp, not yet very widespread, with an extremely long life. Suitable for hard-to-reach places such as tunnels.

44 LED, lamps with a very compact construction, very low power requirement and a long life, also dimmable. A pioneer in lighting technology.

45 Metal halide lamp. Good color rendering and a variety of colors of light, for exterior or interior use. With suitable lenses, this lamp produces extremely narrow bundles of rays of high intensity.

46 High-pressure sodium discharge lamp, with a very warm (yellow) color of light and a long life, hence often used in street lighting.

Power Consumption and Luminous Flux of Lamps

Lamp	Power p (W)	Luminous Flux φ (lm)
Low voltage halogen lamp	20	320
	50	930
	75	1300
	100	2200
High voltage halogen incandescent lamp	40	460–490
	60	780–820
	100	1430–1500
	150	2400–2500
	250	4000–4200
	300	5000
	500	9500
Incandescent lamp	25	190–200
	40	380–400
	60	730
	100	1380
	150	2220
Mercury vapor lamp	50	2000
	80	4000
	125	6500
	250	14,000
Metal halide lamp	70	5500–6300
	75	4900–5500
	150	11,250–13,500
	250	20,000
	400	32,000–43000
High pressure sodium vapor lamp	50	3500
	53	2300
	70	5600–7000
	97	4800
	100	9500
	150	14000
	250	25,000
Fluorescent lamp	8	450
	13	930
	18	1300–1350
	24	1740
	28	2580
	35	3250
	36	3200–3350
	54	4350
	58	5200
Compact fluorescent lamp	5	250
	9	580–600
	18	1150–1200
	26	1750–1800
	36	2800–2900
	55	4800
Induction lamp	150	12,000
Sulfur lamp*	1425	135,000

* not manufactured at the present time

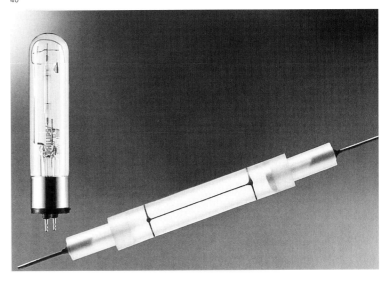

vapor lamp, by contrast, produces 9500 lumen from 100 W. The incandescent lamp produces approx. 5% light and 95% heat, the high pressure sodium vapor lamp, fluorescent and other discharge lamps, on the other hand, produce approx. 20% light and 80% heat.

The choice of the type of lamp also determines some of the parameters of the luminaires itself and of its operation. The type of lamp determines the size of the luminaire. This is an issue which must not be underestimated in practice: architects and clients are familiar with the tiny units of the low voltage halogen incandescent lamps: they frequently confront the lighting designer with the expectation of employing similar, almost invisible units in public and commercial spaces as well. Arguments for lamps requiring a larger version of the luminaire are economic efficiency and longer service life, the economic advantage of which can be demonstrated mathematically. Even for identical lamps, manufacturers produce luminaires of various sizes, since the larger luminaire:

· dissipates heat more effectively (therefore the lamp actually attains its potential life),
· has more precise and effective optics,
· can be employed in a more universal way (permitting the use of several lamps, offering options for accessories).

Therefore is why in many cases it is not advisable to follow the principle of using the smallest luminaire possible.

The operation of lamps may vary from case to case. The essential questions the user must address are:

· Should the luminaires be dimmable?
· Should they emit nearly the full luminous flux immediately upon being switched on? (This is not the case, for example, with halogen metal vapor lamps)
· Should they re-ignite immediately following a power failure? (This would be required of emergency escape route lighting, and halogen metal vapor lamps are only capable of this when equipped with special auxiliary devices)

Luminaires with a high operational efficiency are not necessarily the best: a bare incandescent bulb has a higher efficiency than one installed in a reflector. Nevertheless, the reflector luminaire is more economical, since it directs the light to the place where it is needed rather than "wasting" it without direction in space. Within the category of "lamp with reflector", however, there are great differences in efficiencies. These depend on the size and arrangement of the lamps as well as on the quality and the surface precision of the reflector.

Louvered luminaires and also indirect luminaires "swallow" a lot of light due to the way they are constructed, yet they were designed to improve vision by avoiding glare or excessive contrast.

Operational Efficiencies of Luminaires

· The required power supplies should consume as little energy as possible. Fluorescent lamps are operated with conventional ballast units, low-loss ballast units, or electronic ballast units. The latter have the lowest amount of loss.
· With the additional use of control units to reduce the operating times of the lamps (the lamps are switched on only on demand), further energy savings can be realized.

Type of Luminaire	Operational Efficiency [1]LB
Exposed Luminaires	
for Fluorescent Lamps, Reflector Luminaires	approx. 0.9
Open	approx. 0.7
With screen, white-diffuse	approx. 0.6
With mirror reflector	approx. 0.7
With mirror screen	approx. 0.6
With plastic cover, clear or clear-prismatic	approx. 0.6
With plastic cover, white-diffuse	approx. 0.5
Bulkhead Luminaires	
Clear or clear-prismatic	approx. 0.7
White-diffuse	approx. 0.6
Pendant luminaires, radiating upward and downward, with screen, white-diffuse	approx. 0.7
With mirror screen and indirect light component	approx. 0.8

Dimming

The dimming of fluorescent lamps and incandescent lamps saves energy. A 100 W halogen incandescent lamp dimmed down to the luminous flux of a 50 W lamp will still use more energy than the 50 W lamp, but it will use less energy than the 100 W lamp operated at 100% capacity. In the case of incandescent lamps, dimming has an effect on the life of the lamp. Merely dimming to 95% almost doubles the life of the lamp.

47　Incandescent lamp, the most commonly used lamp by far. Inexpensive to manufacture, with a beautiful light but a short life and poor luminous efficacy.

48　Mercury vapor lamp with a very cool, neutral-white color of light, especially suitable for exterior use. The lamp emits a diffuse light and is now only seldom used.

49　Low-voltage tungsten halogen lamp: a very small lamp with an integrated reflector for interior use in the creation of lighting effects. Costly to install and some have a high power consumption.

50　Fluorescent lamp: a universal lighting product. Long life, relatively low power consumption, but often regarded as "unsightly".

51　Compact fluorescent lamp: a further development of the fluorescent lamp with similar properties, but smaller construction.

52　PAR-reflector lamp: lamp with integrated reflector, producing a very nice spotlight.

53　High-voltage tungsten halogen lamp, for unproblematic and particularly bright light.

54　Metal halide lamp with short arc. Especially suitable for decorative lighting effects and accent lighting.

Maintenance

Maintenance is an important cost factor consisting of the frequency of maintenance work, the expenditure of time for maintenance work, and the costs of replacement parts. In the case of large lighting installations, it makes sense to set up a maintenance schedule.

Calculation of Economic Efficiency

All of the factors mentioned above can be stated in monetary terms. Thus, it is possible to demonstrate the effect of a renovation of a lighting installation and to measure the savings.

47

48

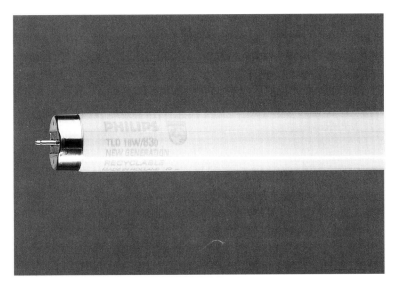

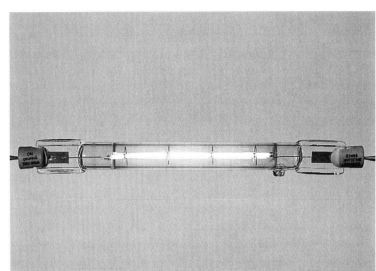

3 PROCESSES AND PROCEDURES

DESIGN
IMPLEMENTATION
SUPERVISION

Tenders and Contracts

Frequently, an architect proposes a team of specialist engineers and will then be asked by the client to obtain tenders from the individual planners, including the lighting designer. The lighting designer then receives supporting documents from the architect to carry out his/her calculations:

· Plans, frequently competition drafts or preliminary designs. The key factor in making a tender is the information regarding room size and usage. To estimate the cost of the lighting system, the lighting designer requires, in addition to the floor plans, sectional views or information regarding the height of the rooms. For old buildings, the lighting designer will sometimes receive plans that do not yet contain the new design but which show the parts of the building to be renovated.

· Perhaps supplementary texts explaining the artistic and functional approach of the architect. These help the lighting designer decide whether to assume a low, medium, or high budget, or whether the work can be carried out within the limits of a fixed budget. The lighting designer's fee depends on the budget's size.
· Perhaps cost records stating either the total electrical budget or simply the luminaire budget. Even if cost records already exist, the lighting designer should verify these records for tendering purposes.

In order to estimate the prospective budget, the surface areas of the various types of room must first be determined. The surface areas are multiplied by a value for the specific costs ($cost/m^2$). The specific costs are based on figures drawn from the past experience of the individual light-

Organizational Structures Among Participants in the Planning of a Construction Project

Project Manager [sometimes]	Client		User
	Public [specialist client]		[not necessarily same as client]
	Private firms [hired architects]		
	Individuals [not specialist client]		
monitors costs, schedule, coordinates	commissions		sets up program, requirements
	Architect		**Specialist Engineers/Other Specialists**
	Project architect	suggests [usually]	Landscape architect	Structural engineer
	Construction manager		Ground expert	Acoustics specialist
			Interior architect	Façade architect
			Designer	Engineer for energy – efficient construction
			Exhibit planner	Color consultant
			Mechanical engineer	
			Engineer for air conditioning/heating	
			Electrical engineer	
			Lighting designer	
			Artist	

ing designer. Hence, it is advisable for lighting design firms to maintain statistical records of completed projects in order to obtain average specific costs. Through this additional work, the lighting designer develops a feeling over time for the costs of various types of installation. While it is possible to make surprisingly precise estimates, every client should know that at the time of tendering, the tenderer can only speculate as to the client's precise wishes.

If a budget is fixed, the lighting designer should point out at the time of tendering that he considers the budgeted amount to be too low, for designers must adequately calculate their costs. It does not make sense to offer services at prices which neither reflect one's own costs nor meet the client's.

The specific costs entered in this table are values drawn from the past experience of our firm. They turned out to be lower in the years from 1995 to 1997 than in previous years, presumably because investors were more cautious. As clients, governmental construction offices must later present their budget documents for construction (Haushaltsunterlage Bau or HU-Bau) to the respective Ministries of Finance (Oberfinanzdirektion or OFD). The Ministries of Finance sometimes have limits of specific costs which they derive from previous comparable projects, while other Ministries of Finance work with costs per enclosed space (cost/m³).

In 1994, the Governmental Construction Administrative Authority (Staatliche Hochbauverwaltung) of the state of Baden-Württemberg published the following standard values for equipment costs under item number 44,5 Lighting Equipment (Beleuchtungsanlagen):

An estimate might look as follows:
Project: Office Building xy

Room	Length x Width	m²	DM/m²	Total
Entrance hall	28 x 35	980	160	156,800
Exterior	estimated	2000	30	60,000
Façade	Length 2 x 180 and 2 x 80	520	estimated	80,000
			estimated	300,000
Grand Total				**DM 74,700**

Project: School Building xv

Room	Length x Width	m²	DM/m²	Total
Gymnasium	MUFS	2400	100	240,000
	SUFS	1200	80	96,000
	Technical	400	60	24,000
Classroom Building	MUFS	10700	100	1,070,000
	SUFS	7600	80	608,000
	Technical	1500	60	90,000
Entrance	MUFS everything	1200	100	120,000
MUFS	Main Useable Floor Space			
SUFS	Secondary Useable Floor Space			
Technical	Technical Equipment Floor Space			
Grand Total				**Approx. DM 2,228,000**

Lighting according to DIN 5035 or Lighting Guidelines Lighting 92
Fixed lighting systems including lamps, installation, all
necessary installation materials and accessories,
bright room, max. ceiling height 3 m, nominal illuminance 100 lx with:

	DM/m² Net Building Floor Space Specific Costs	DM/m² Net Building Floor Space Upper/Lower Limit of Costs
Bare linear fluorescent luminaires up to IP 50	12	10/15
Extra charge for: electronic ballast, up to 80%		
Version up to IP 54, approx. 35%		
Bulkhead and louvered luminaires	16	12/20
Extra charge for: electronic ballast, up to 75%		
Version up to IP 54, approx. 40%		
Mirror screen luminaires, bulkhead luminaires for computer monitor workplaces in versions of higher quality, luminaires with compact fluorescent lamps	28	20/35
Extra charge for electronic ballast 25–80%		

It is difficult to determine specific costs based on past experience for outdoor areas, since the perceptible quality of light can vary much more drastically outdoors than in enclosed artificial light spaces. Sometimes it is necessary to make a "quick" preliminary design for the bid, a substitute, so to speak, for the design proper. In this way, the designer arrives at roughly the cost per luminaire and can multiply this amount by the number of units required. It is the same with the illumination of façades, with light objects or creative "plays of light". For parking lots, pedestrian and traffic areas, however, specific costs can again be derived from past experience.

Usually, the budget determined by the lighting designer includes the costs of the luminaires and their accessories (such as filters, antiglare flaps, lighting tracks, poles), for the lamps and for the installation of the luminaires. The question of whether the control systems will be planned by the lighting designer or by the electrical engineer must be decided in a concrete case; but it is important to state the interface of the areas of responsibility in the tender explicitly so as to avoid misunderstandings. The electrical wires needed to feed the luminaires, the switches and the switch boxes are accounted for in the budget of the electrical engineer. Guidelines for the wiring system (various circuits, light settings), however, are drawn up by the lighting designer. For public clients, the budget includes sales tax, while private clients state the net budget without sales tax. The fee is calculated from the net costs of the construction. In order to avoid misunderstandings, it is advisable to state both amounts.

In Germany, the fee according to a budget is regulated by the HOAI (Honorarordnung für Architekten und Ingenieure, Teil IX, § 74 "Technische Ausrüstung" – Regulations Regarding Fees for Architects and Engineers, Part IX, § 74 "Technical Equipment"). The fee level usually lies between the middle of Level II and the top of Level III, since lighting designers are not consulted for projects at a lower level. Governmental construction offices usually accept only the lowest rate of a level, that is, the bottom of Level III.

The HOAI provides for the classification of the level of difficulty on the basis of the procedure of charging: (point-to-point charging: Fee Level III, efficiency method: Fee Level II). From the perspective of professional, artistically demanding lighting systems design, this is completely absurd; the method of charging does not determine the level of difficulty of a design but merely concerns the desired precision of a calculation. The service of a lighting designer lies above all in achieving a good design with the inclusion of all aspects of a building and the subsequent realization of his plan.

The tender should contain the following points:

Object of the tender

Name of the project, precise enumeration of all individual areas or rooms (especially if only sections of a building are to be planned by the lighting designer).

Services

Individual stages according to the HOAI (planning for approval usually does not apply to lighting design in interior spaces) and (if applicable) "special services" are remunerated separately at an hourly rate or at a flat rate. In the area of "special services" there is room for maneuver in lighting, since the HOAI does not spell out lighting design sufficiently in the area of its basic services to which the fee table exclusively applies. Design services (see below), for example, are "special services" according to the HOAI.

Fees

List of fees for the individual stages in accordance with the HOAI and following the anticipated budget (construction costs, luminaires and their accessories). This may need to be calculated in an exemplary fashion, even when the reference quantity (= the estimated costs or costs of construction already carried out) is still liable to change. Light simulations and design services necessary for the design of special luminaires fall under the category of "special services", which, according the HOAI, must be remunerated separately. This may be done either at a flat rate or at an hourly rate. The lighting designer should point out expressly that simulations or design are not included among the basic services according to the fee table of the HOAI, for the design of lamps is very expensive and cannot be provided within the HOAI fee. For this reason it is useful to list as a standard of cost the hourly rates of the individual staff members of the firm (owner, project manager, project team members, draftsmen). Remuneration is also calculated at an hourly rate, if changes for which the lighting designer is not responsible require a repetition of planning. The question of how wise it is to insist upon this requirement must be decided from case to case. The situation is especially difficult if the changes were not caused by the client but by other planners involved in the project.

Incidental expenses

The mode of charging for incidental expenses can be based on itemized records (= submission of receipts), on flat rates for individual incidental expenses (e.g. travel from the firm of the lighting designer to the project site), or the handling of incidental expenses can be arranged as a percentage of the total fee (approx. 5%). A combination of charges is also common. Incidental expenses represent a substantial cost factor; invoicing is very time-consuming and the costs are frequently not taken seriously, even though they may sometimes amount to 10% of the total fee. Hence, the designer should ensure that the percentage share for incidental expenses of the total fee does not turn out to be too low.

Other

Agreements about copyrights, for example.

The individual service stages are described in the HOAI for general "Technical Equipment":

The Service Stages of the HOAI for "Technical Equipment"

Services	Valuation of the Basic Services as a Percentage (= Percentage of Total Service) of Fees
1. Preliminary inquiries Investigation of the preconditions the technical undertaking	3
2. Pre-Design (preparation of project and planning) Working out the essential components of the planning	11
3. Design Development (system and integration planning) Working out the final planning	15
4. Planning for approval Working out the documents for the building proposal	6
5. Construction documents Working out and presenting realizable planning solutions	18 (14)
6. Preparations for the tender process Quantity survey and specifications for tendering	6
7. Participation in awarding procedure Examination of tenders and participation in awarding procedure	5
8. Contract administration (construction supervision) Supervision of the execution of the project	33
9. Take-over procedures, commissioning and post-occupancy evaluations Supervising the elimination of deficiencies and documenting the overall result	3

Unless the drawing up of plans for slots and openings is stipulated in the contract, service phase 5 is to be assessed at 14 percent of the fees of § 74.

Services	Valuation of the Basic Services as a Percentage (= Percentage of Total Service) of Fees
1 HU-Bau – Pre-Design**	
2 Design Development– in part	11
3 Special services such proof of economic viability and	10
calculation of operating expenses	
4 Planning for approval	
5 AFU-Bau – Completion of the design development ***	6
6 Construction documents: Working through the results of the previous services stages	5
Working drawings + slot plans	
Verification of the working drawings and slot plans	
7 Preparing the contract awards	18
8 Resubmission for tender	6
9 Construction supervision	5
	33
Total	**94**

* RBBau = Richtlinien für die Durchführung von Bauaufgaben des Bundes

** HU-Bau = Haushaltsunterlage Bau = Budget Document Regarding Construction

*** AFU-Bau = Ausführungsunterlage Bau = Implementation Document Regarding Construction

Lighting Design Services in Accordance with RBBau *

Public clients often use a performance schedule which refers to the HOAI and is derived from it but which better reflects the business practice of the governmental construction offices. In these models, the service stages of the preliminary inquiries is always excluded, since the governmental construction offices see themselves as expert clients who conduct their own basic investigation.

Types of Tendering and Commissioning

The preparation of a tender is a first consideration of a project, which already contributes to its later design. The lighting designer should dedicate sufficient time to this and consider very carefully whether he/she is really willing and able to take on the project and whether it is to his/her advantage. On the one hand, projects may be too large for a given design firm; on the other, many projects cannot be handled by a design firm in an economically viable way: the construction costs and the associated fees are so low that it is hardly possible to finance extra staff.

The billing scheme according to the HOAI completely ignores the fact that lighting cannot be designed in a routine fashion, but rather that good lighting design requires an intensive engagement with the overall design of the planned architecture including many small and time-consuming details. In addition, there is the fact that the lighting designer must consult with many project participants, which is also very time-consuming. Hence, every project must be calculated very carefully.

A lighting design firm can also be active in consulting. Consulting tenders are calculated differently. They are based on the estimated time spent on the service provided, which is usually established in terms of days and in rare cases on an hourly basis. An advantage consists in the fact that (with the appropriate contract) the liability for faults is more limited in consulting than in designing; a disadvantage is that the influence on concrete developments can indeed be very limited. For this reason, the result, which lies in the hands of the designers and not of the consultants, can diverge substantially from the intended design. When a lighting designer is called in as a consultant in projects that are already underway, it is usually to remedy planning hitches or mistakes. Besides, design firms may have to implement the new proposals while sacrificing their own design. The consulting firm should not draw up binding plans, but should deliver sketches and consulting statements, from which the information can be integrated into the corresponding existing plans by the architects and electrical engineers.

Commissioning can take several forms:

· Verbal commissioning is legally valid in Germany and counts as a concluded contract, yet in France, for example, this is not the case. To be legally covered, it is advisable to confirm a verbal commission by means of a letter addressed to the client.

· A written commission is preferable, for example, by means of a letter from the client, commissioned architect or specialist planner, on the basis of a tender or a telephone conversation. The letter should state the scope of services, the fee, and the provisions regarding incidental expenses.

· A contract is concluded: this is either the client's standard contract (governmental construction offices – see above) or a contract proposal by the lighting designer. Formulating a contract oneself or having one drawn up by a specialist lawyer is quite an expense. Hence, it is not necessarily a disadvantage to have the client present the contract. If there is a proposal, it is negotiable. If one commands a strong starting position and aims for long term cooperation, it can be favorable to present one's own contract proposal.

· In some cases, the client will not want to conclude a separate contract with the lighting designer but will prefer subcontracting, for example, through the electrical engineer. In this case, the chargeable costs will be high, according to the HOAI, but the fee low according to the progression in the fee table. A total budget of DM 1,000,000 corresponds to a fee of DM 167,520 on top of Level II and thus divided is DM 83,760. Chargeable costs of DM 500,000 each, by contrast, results in the much higher fee of DM 92,660. Since lighting designers are already very limited in their calculations, the loss is substantial and often not economically justifiable (see above).

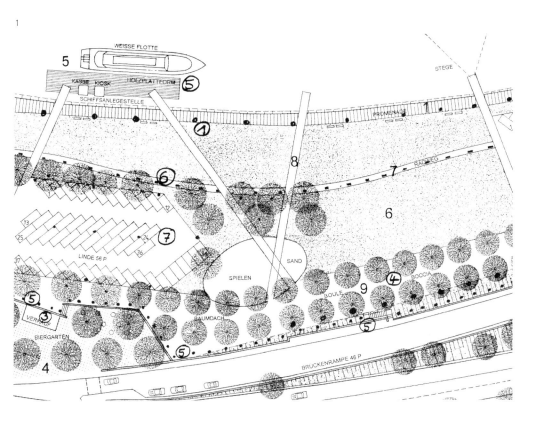

1   For a tender of exterior facilities, it is helpful to sketch a rough hypothetical design with diverse sections and to calculate the respective costs, on the basis of which the fee is then determined.

The Lighting Designer Communicates with Participants in the Planning Process and with Suppliers

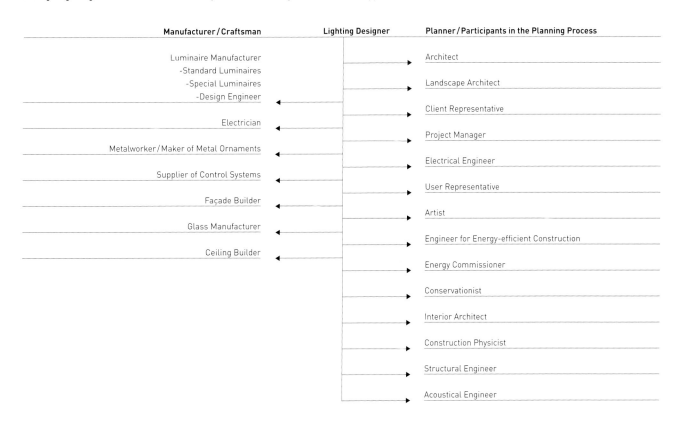

Manufacturer / Craftsman	Lighting Designer	Planner / Participants in the Planning Process
Luminaire Manufacturer		Architect
-Standard Luminaires		
-Special Luminaires		Landscape Architect
-Design Engineer		
		Client Representative
Electrician		
		Project Manager
Metalworker / Maker of Metal Ornaments		
		Electrical Engineer
Supplier of Control Systems		
		User Representative
Façade Builder		
		Artist
Glass Manufacturer		
		Engineer for Energy-efficient Construction
Ceiling Builder		
		Energy Commissioner
		Conservationist
		Interior Architect
		Construction Physicist
		Structural Engineer
		Acoustical Engineer

2 A site inspection (of existing buildings) and a review of the existing planning documents are part of the preliminary inquiries.

3 An examination of the space produces a preliminary plan.

4 Drawings or other plans show up weaknesses in the design.

The Starting Point

Preliminary Inquiries

Determining the basic conditions of planning usually begins in discussion with the architect, who explains the building and points out relevant details. If the object of planning is an existing building, inspecting the rooms to be redesigned may be part of the initial informative consultation. The lighting designer receives the preliminary drafts from the architects and landscape architects as well as all necessary information such as annotations to competitions, user requirements, or findings regarding the existing historical substance of the building. In a first meeting, the lighting designer puts the most important points down in writing.

Pre-Design

A lighting design begins with a thorough study of the building's interior and exterior spaces, and the explanation of the architect's intentions. The level of development of an architect's idea of light varies greatly. Some architects have a very precise idea of the light situation in a building; all that is missing is the knowledge required to realize it: what luminaires to choose and how to arrange them. Others have given only basic consideration to lighting and wish to make this more concrete in dialogue with the lighting designer. Other architects are completely open to suggestions from the lighting designer. All three starting points are fine; provided that there existstet mutual trust and interest, a good lighting concept can be developed on each of the three premises. The architect's explanation often takes place in the form of an imaginary inspection of the building. Such an inspection "in the mind's eye" and the imagination of the lines of vision will later be helpful in the design. Since the artificial light design also begins with a consideration of daylight, information regarding the location of the building, the orientation of the windows, the daily periods of main usage and the surrounding buildings and vegetation is important. Fundamentally, it must be clear what design idea the architect is pursuing, how the building will be used and what special conditions

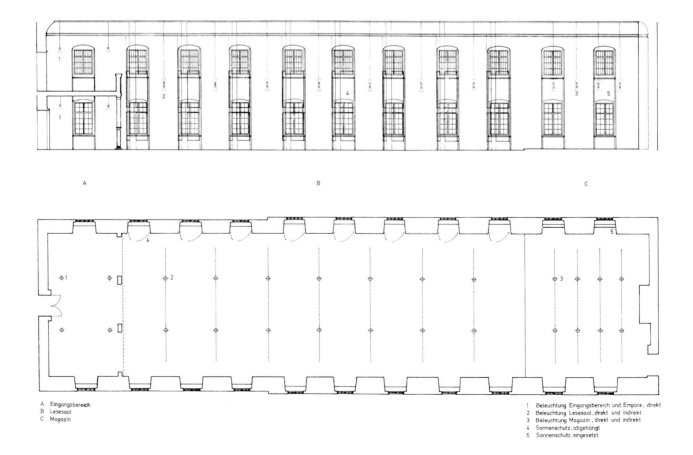

A Eingangsbereich
B Lesesaal
C Magazin

1 Beleuchtung Eingangsbereich und Empore, direkt
2 Beleuchtung Lesesaal, direkt und indirekt
3 Beleuchtung Magazin, direkt und indirekt
4 Sonnenschutz, abgehängt
5 Sonnenschutz, eingesetzt

and specific limitations already exist.

The pre-design for the chapel of the *Frankesche Stiftungen* in Halle was done in 1990, shortly after the opening of Germany's internal border. At that time it was not known how the special situation and hence the jurisdictions would develop over the long term. The local architects who, over the years, had saved the building from dilapidation in a makeshift manner presented the state of the construction site.

The *Frankesche Stiftungen* was founded in 1695 as an educational institution, and the buildings at times accommodated 2000 pupils from all parts of Europe. Access was to be restored to the natural history collection and to the library. The former chapel was designated to house the library. It had lost one of its two high galleries through bombing. On this side, bookshelves were to be installed as an open stack. The reading area was also to be usable as a venue for evening concerts or readings. On clear days, wonderful sunlight enters the hall. Two long, two-story window frontages face precisely to the south and north. The windows reveals are positioned in two rows one on top of the other and enclosed in

of a depth of 1.70 m. From east to west, following the longitudinal axis of the room, brilliant, warm sunlight appears on the southern side and is reflected by the paint peeling off from the reveals of the windows. On the northern side, soft, brighter light falls into the room, forming a counterbalance to the richly varied play of light and shadow on the southern side. It is rare to find such harmony, and it is probably also due to the height of the ceiling, the proportions of the room and such details as the deep reveals and the small hollow moulding between the walls and ceiling. A historical photo showed one of the old chandeliers in the hall and prompted the idea of the architects and conservationists to recall the old chandeliers through modern ones.

Upon closer inspection, however, it was revealed that:

· Daylight is the most important light for this room.
· The room does not require chandeliers.

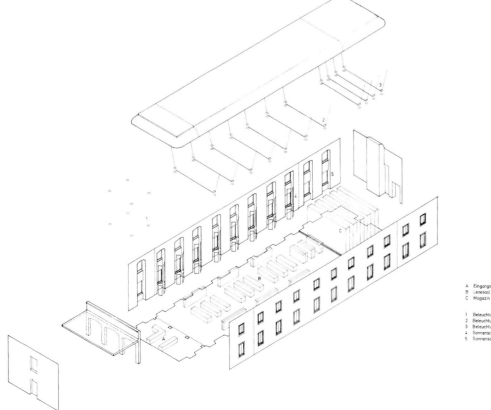

A Eingangsbereich
B Lesesaal
C Magazin

1 Beleuchtung Eingangsbereich und Empore, direkt
2 Beleuchtung Lesesaal, direkt und indirekt
3 Beleuchtung Magazin, direkt und indirekt
4 Sonnenschutz, abgehängt
5 Sonnenschutz, eingesetzt

The Role of Daylight

The reading room shouldt not be exposed to sunlight without protection, for this would cause irritating glare in the reading areas, and some books are very sensitive to light. The quality of changing daylight, however, should not simply be shut out. A simple daylight investigation drawn up by hand answers the question of which area receives direct sunlight and how the extent of sun protection can be minimized. The deep window frames help to prevent much insolation.

Any exterior form of sun protection had to be excluded already for reasons of historical preservation. The inner unwinding of the façade is so beautifully profiled by the reveals that, rather than being smoothed away, these reveals should be accentuated. Hence, curved panels made from a simple wire mesh would provide sun protection. Semi-transparent, they are to form recesses into which one can step to take a break from reading and gain a view of the outside. The size of the panels was just large enough to prevent the entry of solar radiation without hiding the entire window. According to the plan, these panels were to be offset towards the bottom of the window and stayed between floor and ceiling.

The Requirements on Artificial Light

Artificial lighting also was developed on the basis of the intended use of the room rather than for formal reasons. The reading room would receive uniform light throughout and no isolated "islands of light". Two pairs of luminaires serve this purpose, one in each pair radiating upwards, the other downwards. The indirect light produced by the economically efficient metal halide lamp illuminates the ceiling, accentuates the height of the ceiling, and reveals the surrounding hollow moulding. The pendant downlights radiating downwards are fitted with incandescent halogen luminaires and when dimmed can create a warm and festive concert atmosphere. The historical room is touched by the suspension of luminaires only in a few places, and the wiring is run through the attic. With these considerations, the pre-design has arrived at the threshold to the stage of design development. It subsequently puts the quantities and technical aspects of this preliminary plan into concrete terms.

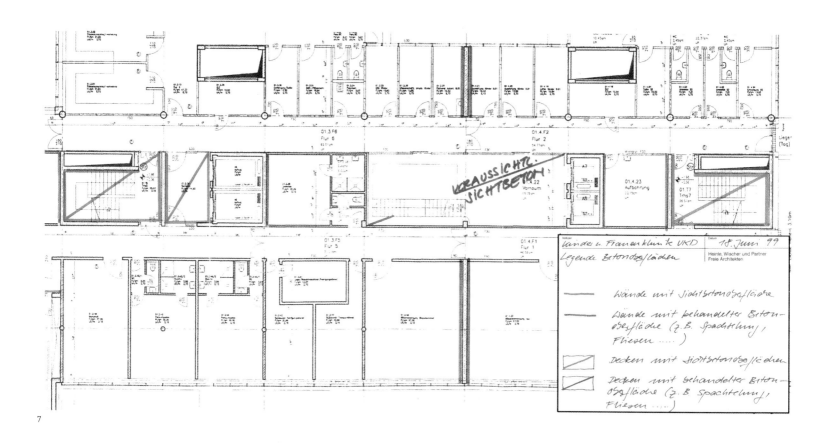

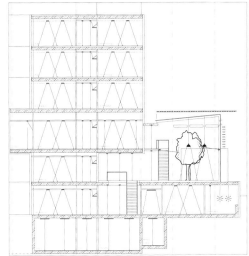

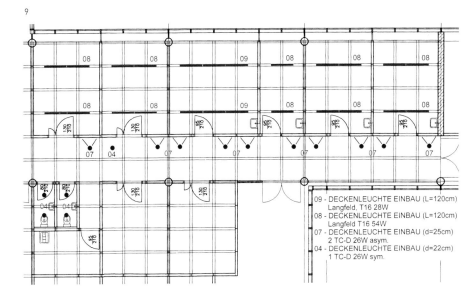

09 - DECKENLEUCHTE EINBAU (L=120cm)
Langfeld, T16 28W
08 - DECKENLEUCHTE EINBAU (L=120cm)
Langfeld T16 54W
07 - DECKENLEUCHTE EINBAU (d=25cm)
2 TC-D 26W asym.
04 - DECKENLEUCHTE EINBAU (d=22cm)
1 TC-D 26W sym.

The Situation of Design

Design Development

Design development continues to work out the ideas of the pre-design. Every step towards a concrete application requires a verification of its feasibility. The ambitious and grand ideas developed earlier are now to be transformed as "simply" as possible into a concrete lighting plan. The balancing act performed by the lighting designer between the "far-out idea" and the "realistic design" is an important expression of his skills. In this regard, architects and lighting designers (and other specialists) inspire or restrain each other.

In the design phase, designers awaken the expectations of the client. These expectations could possibly take on their own life, which later leads to (often unjustified) disappointments. Designers are well advised to make very realistic proposals and to seek further dialogue with the client in order to gain additional improvements. For an example of a design plan which is much more complex than the *Frankesche Stiftungen* (see preliminary concept) existed special, known user requests. It is the lighting plan for the *University Clinic* in Dresden, a public construction project.

In terms of the service stages, the HU-Bau (= Haushaltsunterlage Bau/Budget Document Regarding Construction) corresponds to the first two thirds of the design stages described in the HOAI (= Honorarordnung für Architekten und Ingenieure/Regulations Regarding Fees for Architects and Engineers), whereas the final third is reserved for a possible revision. As a procedure, the HU-Bau pursues a clear goal: the verifiable reporting of costs. For this purpose, the lighting designer draws up a design that already puts together quantities, chosen types and prices. The respective authorities (the governmental construction office and the Ministry of Finance) do not verify the artistic design, but they do verify whether the technical and economic requirements of investment and the operation of the lighting installation are fulfilled.

In this example, the basis for the lighting design was the revision of the architects' competition design. In their commentary, the architects name the urban situation as the overriding reason for structuring the building into a main thoroughfare and wards, with garden courtyards in between. A further guiding principle was the desire to create an architectural environment that will make a hospital stay as pleasant and friendly as possible for the patients, many of whom are children. These two themes of "structuring and orientation" and "pleasant atmosphere" would to find their concrete counterpart in the lighting design.

The main points in the discussions with the architects were:

· The diverse character of light in the various areas, the transition from direct to indirect light or illuminated ceilings. The architects' drawings were useful here.
· The type of construction involving prefabricated elements. Various sketches were drawn concerning the integration of the ceiling luminaires into the ceiling elements in the examination room area. With an axial measurement of 1.20 m x 1.20 m, various luminaire positions and various lamps were possible. The exterior effect and the geometry of the luminaire arrangements were also discussed.
· The lighting of the patients' rooms. How is it possible to produce a homey and cozy light atmosphere given the stringent requirements on hygiene and practicality in a hospital? Fortunately, there was a trend against sterility and coolness, even on the side of the client and user.
· As a grand and spacious common area, the glass hall received much attention in the discussions.

These talks were followed by a process of coordination with the mechanical engineers. With the design plan, the engineers received the information regarding the power requirements of the luminaires (lamp and power supply) and the approximate positioning (wall, ceiling) for each room. This tells the electrical engineers the required wiring paths, the

5 A model of the *Pediatric and Gynecological Clinic of the University Hospital* in Dresden.

6 The eastern side of the building consists of the connecting corridor and the glass foyer.

7 The listing of the various wall and ceiling materials aided the lighting planners in their design.

8 The sectional view shows the direction of the light: mainly direct light, indirect light in the hallways.

9 After careful consideration, this ceiling mirror – with lamps inserted into the ties between the ceiling panels – seemed to be the one best suited for the various room situations.

10 These plans (detail) of the ground floor with the foyer
and the lecture hall, a wing with patients' rooms, and the
laboratory and examination rooms are part of the HU-Bau
or "Budget Document Regarding Construction". Every
luminaire is specified in the legend and appears again
under the same number in the luminaire catalogue.

length of the wires, and the installation expenses involved. The space required by the various installations in the bare suspended ceiling should also be discussed in a timely manner. At this point, electric circuits and options are planned in principle but not in detail. The light planning documentation generated for the *Pediatric and Gynecological Clinic* of the *University Hospital* in Dresden is composed of the following parts:

1st Part of the Documentation: Explanatory Text

Light for the *Pediatric and Gynecological Clinic* of the *University Hospital* in Dresden

Dresden, December 7, 1998:

The Pediatric and Gynecological Clinic consists of two blocks, which are connected by a cross tract. The lighting design aims at providing a pleasant atmosphere for patients as well as for employees and students, which will help people recover, work and orient themselves in the building. The artificial light complements and enhances the use of daylight. In the evening and at night, it is the sole source of light.

The clear structuring of the building is reflected in the arrangement and repertory of luminaires. The artificial light brings out the cheerful materials and surfaces in a fresh and natural way and enhances the effect of the room proportions.

For efficient operation and maintenance of the luminaires, most of them were equipped with fluorescent lamps and compact fluorescent lamps. A relatively small number of luminaire types provides lighting throughout the building.

*A few downlights in the ceiling and under the gallery illuminate the **entrance hall**. In this area, different switch settings are desirable during the day and in the evening. The high airspace of the hall appears bright and cheerful in the indirect light of ceiling washers. These indirect floods as well as the downlights are equipped with discharge lamps on account of the ceiling height; an illuminance of 200 lx is sufficient.*

*Only in the **common area** for children do pendant luminaires appear as objects with lower mounting heights. These are equipped with compact fluorescent luminaires. In special areas such as the cafeteria and the kiosk, halogen lamps are planned.*

*Linear fluorescent luminaires provide for general illumination in the **auditorium**. A second system of downlights with halogen incandescent*

lamps provides dimmable light for slide shows. Together, these result in an illuminance of 750 lx.

*A long **hallway** connects the two complexes of the clinic like a backbone. This hallway has a higher architectonic significance and will feature a large plasterboard ceiling. Soft light emanating from wall bracket luminaires fitted with compact fluorescent lamps illuminates the ceiling while shining direct light onto the floor. All connecting hallways within the wards will receive downlights as well as wall washers. The latter, however, will resemble the downlights in terms of their light opening. Most of the luminaires are arranged laterally towards the walls so as not to blind the patients as they are being wheeled through the hallway in their beds. A two-stage switch allows for illuminances of 200 lx by day and 100 lx by night.*

***Offices, examination rooms and laboratories** receive their light from recessed lamps integrated into the ceiling grid. A variety of wattages in these luminaires permit a fine adjustment to the size of the rooms to avoid excessively high illuminances (the nominal illuminance is 500 lx) and provide a good energy balance in the building.*

*The **patients' rooms** receive indirect illumination via luminaires integrated into the electricity distribution tracks. These luminaires will be supplemented with downlights according to the size of the room. Luminaires for reading spaces allow patients to regulate light according to their individual preferences, while night lighting at the exits provides safety.*

The prescribed illuminances of 100–300 lx for examination lighting are met by means of luminaires exclusively equipped with compact fluorescent lamps.

2nd Part of the Documentation: Design Plans

In the original, the plans are drawn at a scale of 1:100, without dimensioning (shown here only in excerpts and reduced in size).

3rd Part of the Documentation: Index of Luminaires

The luminaire index registers all the luminaires with luminaire numbers. The luminaires are specified with regard to type of installation and type of lamp. For larger projects, it is advisable to keep records according to floors, since this facilitates rough verification calculations.

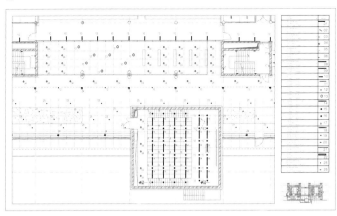

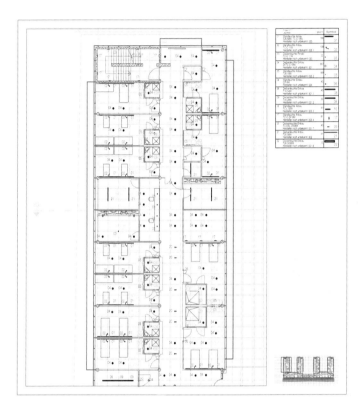

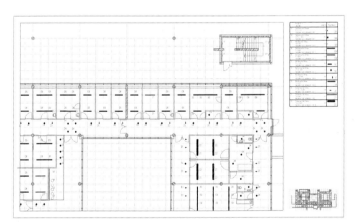

Luminaire Index
University Hospital Dresden, Pediatric and Gynecological Clinic

Luminaire	1	2	3	4	5	6	7	8
Name	2nd	1st	1st	2nd	3rd	4th	5th	6th
	Base-ment	Base-ment	Floor	Floor	Floor	Floor	Floor	Floor
Total								
1 Wall luminaire, surface-mounted								
T26 58 W, TC-D 18 W 513		20	26	122	168	177		
2 Wall luminaire, surface-mounted								
TC-D 11 W 272		10	14	45	108	95		
3 Ceiling luminaire, pendant								
TC-D 11 W 104		8	26	16	17	22	15	
4 Ceiling luminaire, recessed								
2XTC-D 18 W 1753		239	290	279	248	367	330	
5 Wall luminaire, surface-mounted								
26 18 W 894		110	129	108	176	189	182	
6 Wall luminaire, recessed								
QT 9 W 138		5	18	30	40	45		
8 Ceiling luminaire, recessed								
T16 54 W 695		152	236	60	129	40	78	
9 Ceiling luminaire, recessed								
T16 28 W 451		190	76	30	77	30	48	
10 Wall luminaire, surface-mounted								
L 55 W 229		44	47	35	31	41	31	
11 Ceiling luminaire, pendant								
T16 54 W 52		52						
12 Spotlight								
HIT 35 W 28			28					
13 Ceiling luminaire, pendant								
TC-TEL 32 W 8		8						
14 Ceiling luminaire, recessed, asymmetrical								
T16 54 W 60		30	30					
15 Ceiling luminaire, recessed								
QT32 250 W 24		12	12					
16 Ceiling luminaire, recessed								
QT 18 150 W 84		36	24	24				
17 Wall luminaire, surface-mounted								
TC-D 2X18 W 548	24	88	82	88	89	81	84	12
18 Wall luminaire, surface-mounted								
T16 54 W 34		8	26					
19 Ceiling luminaire, recessed								
QR-CBC 51 50 W 29		29						
20 Ceiling luminaire, recessed								
TC-DEL 2X26 W 458		148	105	73	47	40	45	
21 Ceiling luminaire, surface-mounted								
T26 58 W 567	230	101	40	44	54	41	44	13
22 Ceiling luminaire, recessed								
T26 3X36 W 333		85		224	4	12	8	
23 Spotlight								
HIT 150 W 25		25						
24 Ceiling luminaire, recessed								
HIT 70 W 71		71						
25 Wall luminaire, recessed								
TC-D 10 W 42		42						

UB-Licht 07.12.98

Cost Estimate

University Hospital Dresden, Children's and Gynecological Clinic

1st Floor

Luminaire Name Total	Quantity	Price / per Unit / DM	Total / DM
1 Wall luminaire, surface-mounted			
T26 58 W, TC-D 18 W 513	20	1,716	34,320
Manufacturer not yet known			
2 Wall luminaire, surface-mounted			
TC-D 11 W 272	10	230	2,300
Manufacturer not yet known			
3 Ceiling luminaire, pendant			
TC-D 11 W 104	26	330	8,580
Manufacturer not yet known			
4 Ceiling luminaire, recessed			
2XTC-D 18 W 1753	290	400	116,000
Manufacturer not yet known			
5 Wall luminaire, surface-mounted			
26 18 W 894	129	120	15,480
Manufacturer not yet known			
6 Wall luminaire, recessed			
QT 9 W 138	5	180	900
Manufacturer not yet known			
8 Ceiling luminaire, recessed			
T16 54 W 695	236	300	70,800
Manufacturer not yet known			
9 Ceiling luminaire, recessed			
T16 28 W 451	76	250	19,000
Manufacturer not yet known			
10 Wall luminaire, surface-mounted			
L 55 W 229	47	300	14,100
Manufacturer not yet known			
11 Ceiling luminaire, pendant			
T16 54 W 52	52	400	20,800
Manufacturer not yet known			
12 Spotlight			
HIT 35 W 28	28	450	12,600
Manufacturer not yet known			
13 Ceiling luminaire, pendant			
TC-TEL 32 W 8	8	500	4,000
Manufacturer not yet known			
14 Ceiling luminaire, recessed, asymmetrical			
T16 54 W 60	30	500	15,000
Manufacturer not yet known			
15 Ceiling luminaire, recessed			
QT32 250 W 24	12	284.60	3,415
Manufacturer not yet known			
16 Ceiling luminaire, recessed			
QT 18 150 W 84	24	350	8,400
Manufacturer not yet known			
17 Wall luminaire, surface-mounted			
TC-D 2X18 W 548	82	130	10,660
Manufacturer not yet known			
18 Wall luminaire, surface-mounted			
T16 54 W 34	26	600	15,600
Manufacturer not yet known			
19 Ceiling luminaire, recessed			
QR-CBC 51 50 W 29	29	179	5,191
Manufacturer not yet known			
20 Ceiling luminaire, recessed			
TC-DEL 2X26 W 458	105	400	42,000
Manufacturer not yet known			
21 Ceiling luminaire, surface-mounted			
T26 58 W 567	40	100	4000
Manufacturer not yet known			
22 Ceiling luminaire, recessed			
T26 3X36 W 333			
Manufacturer not yet known			
23 Spotlight			
HIT 150 W 25	25	431	10,775
Manufacturer not yet known			
24 Ceiling luminaire, recessed			
HIT 70 W 71	71	370	26,270
Manufacturer not yet known			
25 Wall luminaire, recessed			
TC-D 10 W 42	42	110	4,620
Total Price / DM			**464,811**

UB-Licht 07.12.98

4th Part of the Documentation: Costs

Cost records include all luminaires with their prices in order to determine the corresponding total budget. DIN 276, which is still often applied, groups luminaires into the following four categories: general lighting, special lighting, emergency lighting and other lighting. This is no longer a very practical system. In Germany, the current system of rebates leads to the following approximate determination of costs: the rebate that manufacturers offer merchants corresponds approximately to the costs of luminaires, assembly and profit of the tenderer. Thus, including the list price in the calculation gives realistic results. For very high quantities, the rebates are higher as well. In some cases, one should consult the manufacturer in advance about the prices for certain luminaires. The retail price for the client must be distinguished from the intermediate price for the merchant and the electrician; in this case (see above), the price for the lamps and their assembly must be added. The reference to net or gross costs in the tender help avoid misunderstandings. Since the rebate systems (in Germany) are currently changing, the simple calculation just presented (see above) will probably have to be replaced by the second method (see below) in the long term. The line, "manufacturer not yet known", signifies that, during the phase of the design development, the precise brand of the relevant luminaire was not yet determined. For the purpose of determining prices, however, a certain type of luminaire, which is offered by one or more manufacturers is often listed here. At this stage, it is only important to know that a luminaire using a certain lighting technology with the required quality and at a certain price is on the market. This "stand-in luminaire" is the example pictured in a luminaire catalogue. In such a catalogue, all the participants in a construction project will find a photo and measurements, giving them a concrete idea of a particular luminaire (the illustrated luminaire catalogue is not a necessary component of design development but rather a pragmatic tool of communication). Whether the "stand-in luminaire" or another will eventually be chosen is only decided at the stage of preparing the construction documents, and sometimes only following the tender. The lighting designer and the architect jointly present these documents to the client. Following a possible revision, the client will receive them for examination. In the case of a private client, this may be done very informally. The public client, of course, must strictly abide by formal requirements. Usually after three to four months, the planner will receive the audit report from the Ministry of Finance (Oberfinanzdirektion or OFD). The lighting designer may only receive the "lighting" excerpt as part of the general electrical documentation.

11 Excerpt from an illustrated lamp catalogue. The architects, engineers and the client may gain a first impression
of the formal properties of the lamps and study technical aspects in more detail. This facilitates the task of
convincing them to trust one's choice.

The subsequent revision of the HU-Bau, the final third of the design development stage in accordance with the HOAI, consists of the integration of the auditor's comments into the design. In practice this can be quite a difficult task.

Unfortunately, there are audit reports in which a wholesale demand is made to reduce costs by up to one half. Auditors justify this with cost comparisons, sometimes with projects at a much lower standard than the building currently being planned.

A project will benefit greatly if the designer examines the proposals carefully and provides a thorough response to the reduction of costs. A solution can often be found by consulting with the client, taking the concerns of the designer and the cost auditor into account. Even if this phase of construction often seems laborious and sometimes hopeless, a good cooperation between architects, who are likewise concerned to ensure quality, and lighting designers will often lead to a positive end result. This is valid for the own quality requirements:

The more sound and solid the design development, the simpler and more uncomplicated is the preparation of the construction documents. Solid design development, after all, will contribute to an efficient execution of the project and represents one of the few ways of influencing costs by the design firm. Many other aspects like the willingness to communicate, straightforwardness in contrast to frequent requests for modifications are in hands of the other participants in the project.

For the *Pediatric and Gynecological Clinic of the University Hospital Dresden*, the audit report made moderate demands, which could be integrated into the existing plan without too much difficulty.

Audit Report
Governmental Construction Office ...
Statement on Budget Document of ...
Electrical Engineering Section

A) General

Conformity to DIN 276
Assignment Costs – Cost Divisions

B) Explanatory Report on Cost Division 44,5

Detailed Statements on Lamps
Statements Regarding the Adherence to Regulations
Assignment of Lighting Calculations to the Various Room Locations
Comments on Mean Illuminances (which must be neither too high nor too low)
Call for Further Lighting Calculations

C) Drawings

Assignment Luminaires – Costs

D) Calculation of Costs

Exclusion of Luminaire Types for Reasons of Costs
Exclusion of Quantities of Luminaires for Reasons of Costs

E) Other

Scheduling of Meeting for the Revision of Budget Document (HU-Bau)

Checklist

The following checklist may help in the internal planning process of a lighting design firm:

Preliminary Design
· Minutes of meetings
· First sketches as preliminary design

Design Development
· Completion of the sketches prepared in the preliminary design in terms of floor plan and sectional view
· Preparation of project-specific checklist and internal schedule
· Listing of important unresolved issues: for example, the reflectance factors of the desired colors on walls, ceilings and floors
· Preparing a presentation plan for the architect
· Items to be marked in the plans: illuminated surfaces, illuminances, positions of luminaires, rough idea of luminaires (type of lamp, beam spread wide/narrow etc.)
· Establishing the number of luminaires; calculation of the illuminances in model rooms
· Design of emergency lighting
· Coordination of the designs with architects, electrical engineers, building technology engineers etc.
· Checking whether special luminaires are necessary, if so: design of special luminaires, suggestion of possible manufacturers (three)
· Preliminary presentation to the client (possibly)
· Presentation to the client, with complete documentation and tentative list of luminaires
· Cost estimate
· Drawings for all areas, possibly as an example
· Explanation of text
· Entry of desired modifications

Planning Tools for the Office

The preparation of drawings using (personal) computers, called CAD (computer aided design) or CAAD (computer aided architectural design) has become standard for professional design firms. In spite of the high complexity of the software and the untrained imagination, especially of older designers who began their careers without computers, there are, after a difficult learning phase, two advantages in particular in comparison with traditional techniques: the speed of drawing and the design options are increased substantially – provided, of course, that one has mastered the programs with practice and understanding. In addition, the management of the gathered data and hence the preparation of tender specifications is simplified. The data moreover can be transferred to facility management applications for later use.

Almost all solutions in this area (with the exception of *Bentley System's Microstation*) run on *Windows NT*, while a few run on *UNIX* or more recently on *LINUX* server operating systems (although *LINUX* solutions are at present still problematic, they will hopefully soon be viable). Although there are many software applications for architects and engineers on the market, their capabilities do not usually match the services of lighting designers. Hence, the software must be customized. There are some approaches on the basis of the popular *Autocad* by *Autodesk,* a software application which has become standard in spite of certain shortcomings. *Autocad* is actually the only open CAD system that, with an acceptable amount of effort, allows customized solutions.

A start was made around 10 years ago on mainframe computers, and later on *UNIX* and *DOS,* by the developers of *Adeline* (further developed and distributed by the Fraunhofer Institut in Stuttgart), a hefty program package that took years to master. Although they took a long time to obtain, the resulting "simulated environment for daylight and artificial light calculations" was extraordinarily good for those days. Yet the program was unusable in practical planning applications.

The lighting component of *Elaplan* (formerly *AEG*, now *Aston*), which is also an older product, presents itself as part of a large modular system on electrotechnology. It is designed to calculate the correct illuminances in interior spaces using many different processes. The same thing is achieved by the *Autocad* application *Rocad* for building technology (Distribution: *Mensch und Maschine)* with a simple, integrated light calculation program (*Minicophos* by Zumtobel) and an interface to the freeware by *DIALUX* (an older attempt by several large manufacturers to establish a software standard for light calculation programs).

Sie View (manufacturing and distribution: formerly *Siemens*, now *Siteco)* was the first software that made physically correct renderings in *Autocad* possible using the application program *Radiance*. The required processing times are now substantially reduced through the combination of *Autocad* and *Lightscape* (a light rendering program purchased by *Autodesk*). The company *ERCO* offers parts of its product program in the required 3DS format.

A completely different route is taken by *L.E.O.S.* (Light, Energy Optimization and Service (Licht, Energie-Optimierung und Service); Rights: *HEWContract*; Concept: *Ulrike Brandi Licht*; Distribution: *Relux Informatik AG)*. This process-oriented software developed by our firm works via the CAD user interface and with reference to actual buildings. It covers the entire process (spanning many years) from the preliminary design to the operation and final disposal of lighting systems (facility management) using *Autocad* and an extensive database, and leaves nothing to be desired as expert software. Every luminaire on the market can be represented in all the characteristics relevant for planning. Daylight calculations can be combined with artificial light calculations. Renderings (with the addition of the light calculation program *RELUX*) are possible as well. The system also offers electronic measurement (mobile data collection) with the automated preparation of drawings of buildings. The preparation and exchange of professional drawings is the basis of *L.E.O.S.*

Two current developments affect the work of a lighting design firm: the variety of popular CAD systems (*AutoCAD* with *R 2000* or *Architectural Desktop* and numerous applications, *Nemetschek*, *Microstation*, *Speedikon*, *RIB*, *Archicad*, *Apple Computer* systems such as *Minicad)* as well as the mechanical services management systems such as *pit-cup* and many customized developments, although they still lead to compatibility problems.

Lighting designers using CAD are affected by this issue, for they must cope with many firms and their diverse systems and individual preference settings. It is not just a matter of being able to read someone else's data but also of being able to "export" the data produced on one's own system in such a way that the cooperating firms can use them in turn. Practically speaking, this works as long as knowledgeable people are in charge. Yet much information present on the individual systems in the firms is still lost in the process. A lot of the data is simply not transferred by the interfaces. In essence, these interfaces are still conceived as "analog", geared towards the preparation of drawings. Attempts at creating platforms for new interfaces (e.g. ifc = industrial foundation classes) have so far remained without tangible results. They are supposed to facilitate the universality and supplementation of all relevant data in all types of work. Such a solution would bridge the old gap between numerical databases and graphical interfaces. To the present, it is not easy to combine these two distinct systems. It is one thing to analyze data entered or stored in databases according to formulae, but quite another to generate the vector data of graphical interfaces and make them visible. In addition, there is the rapid development of the possibilities of three-dimensional planning. The usual drawing levels like floor plan, elevation, section or wall elevation developments will perhaps soon no longer be means to the design; a new generation of computer-skilled designers will probably be able to set up many drawing elements more efficiently on the computer within the next 10 years. This requires practice and understanding, as the mind of a designer is now being strained once more with the establishment of CAD and computer. First, the familiar repre-

12 The present-day conference room of the Hapag Lloyd is located in the former booking hall for passages to America. Natural light creates an abundance of brightness.

13 The historical photograph of the foyer appears just as bright and friendly. Small lamps below the glass ceiling illuminate the space in the evening.

14 The natural light simulation was helpful in finding a practical compromise between the desire for large quantities of natural light and the requirements of a pleasant climate.

sentation migrated from the drawing paper to the monitor, yet the drawing on the monitor's surface still remains two-dimensional. Designing in virtual spaces is unrealistic and not at all desirable. Thus, architects, engineers and software developers have to develop solutions that improve the possibilities of three-dimensional drawing and construction in an ordinary environment.

Three-dimensional representations are able to contain more information and offer more exchange possibilities between the various professions. The fact that the intuitiveness of the design will improve, particularly in the area of light, is a welcome additional aspect.

Renderers take up a certain space in design firms (*3Dstudio, softimage*, in the area of light in particular: *Lightscape, Radiance, Alias Wavefront, Accurender*). They "visualize" the designs. At present, their use is not economical as convincing "photorealistic" presentations require much work and preparation time. The adaptation of existing images by means of image processing applications *(Photoshop)* is much simpler. Highly developed scanning technology allows for the digitalization of practically any (flat) model. Although the post-processing of the digitally stored image is still time-consuming, the "construction" of the "façades", i.e. of the scene of a computer animation, has already been eliminated. And once the images have been stored, they can be used over and over again in various computer environments.

Depending on the type of work, the simulation applications that imitate the states of buildings on computers are often much more sophisticated in their operation and their goal. As a rule, they are not integrated into the continually evolving CAD programs for the preparation of drawings and are only used all the way into the construction phase by very few designers.

The numerous individual programs to calculate of artificial light in rooms, which also simulate (static) states of buildings, are still widely used but are already antiquated. 10 years ago, practically all major luminaire manufacturers began to offer software for determining the illuminances of their luminaires in interior spaces. Over time, more and more features were added to these programs, including the furnishing of the rooms, the calculation of the portions of daylight and simple renderings. Soon, the applications were distributed free of charge. In their proprietary form, they are a marketing instrument of the respective manufacturer. These calculation programs will hardly promote good design. Finally, the paths of data transmission between designers and clients still need to be discussed. The old blueprints are more or less worn-out; the firms receive drawings on paper as plots. The distribution of diskettes in various forms is likewise no longer customary and the direct transfer of a drawing from one computer to another (via modem or ISDN) is being replaced by the use of FTP (= File Transfer Protocol: the user transfers the files via the Internet directly to another server) as well as by e-mail via Internet service providers (the drawings are first compressed). This now usually works without problems. The type of Internet access generally provided in Germany still sets limits on exchanging of data. Unless a firm has its own webserver with a leased line, transmission (via conventional telephone lines or ISDN) can be rather slow.

The Internet will continue to gain in importance. For lighting design firms this may mean that they will soon communicate their plans on-line. The general transfer performance of the net is still insufficient, since the CAD resolution on the monitor is (and must be) very high. It is not yet possible to transfer the data without longer delays and problems in a generally compatible way (e.g. by means of browsers). A quick solution, and thus a way into this technology, might be offered by local conversions of the CAD formats, into VRML formats, for example.

While "on-line design" will soon be generally feasible, at present it is not yet possible to say precisely what influence this will have on the design and quality of buildings. One Internet trend, however, has already taken root in large projects: clients and/or project leaders try to set up software tools around project servers, which must be used by all project participants. The often substantial costs for hardware, software and training are passed on to the designers in the contract award process. The idea of the compatibility of expert software is lost with the forced use of tools concentrated around one manufacturer, as these tools consist of standard software, which is useless to specialists. With sufficient know-how, tools linking independent software applications can be assembled using current exchange formats.

12

13

Detail

Construction Documents

In 1996/97, *Hapag Lloyd* of Hamburg planned to renovate its large building at Ballindamm and to make alterations to suit their new requirements. Over the course of the years, numerous little modifications had turned what had formerly been spacious and bright rooms into a maze of gloomy little "boxes". The architects of Gerkan, Marg and Partners proposed to restore the succession of halls on the ground floor, to revive old color findings from 1928 and to supplement these in some cases with modern materials. Formerly, two large halls had been illuminated almost exclusively with daylight; now the proposal was to install artificial lighting resembling daylight above the glass ceiling for the darker periods of the day. The photos show the former booking hall for America and the middle hall behind the entrance hall, which was situated between the booking hall for America and the booking hall for Asia. Today, the America hall is used as a partitionable conference area, while the middle hall is a spacious entrance hall and waiting area. The Asia hall has been converted into a cafeteria. The lighting concept provided for the reintroduction of much daylight into the rooms. A daylight simulation revealed that, due to the tall structures surrounding the atrium, only small amounts of direct sunlight fall onto the glass ceiling.

Climasol 66/38 sun protection glass was chosen for the outer glass shell, while the dust ceiling was equipped with multilayer glass with an inserted double matted film so that the roof trusses above would not show through. The basic idea was to enhance the spaciousness the architects had restored by making as few lights visible in the halls as possible. Sufficient brightness was to be produced by fluorescent lamps above the dust ceil-

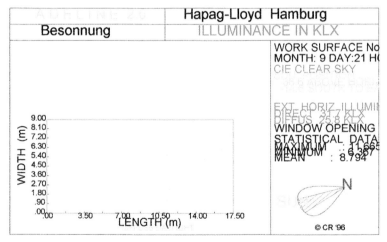

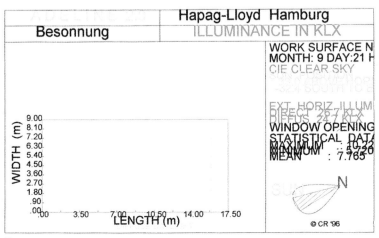

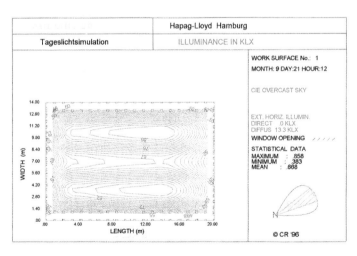

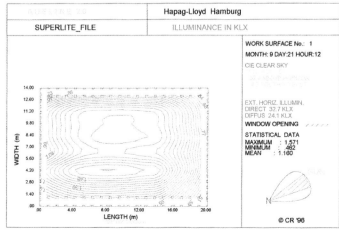

15   The newly designed area on the ground floor indicating
     the positions of the luminaires in the floor plan ...

16   ... and in two sections.

ing. A refined type of light was to be supplied in the conference area through built-in floor lamps illuminating the wire mesh, and through pendant downlights above the dust ceiling which would project warm "sunlight" downward. In the section, the drawing shows the positions of the luminaires and the directions of light. Since, starting from the entrance, there is a succession of ceilings of various heights, these rooms would also be equipped with various types of light so as to enhance the special experience of the daylight in the interior of the building.

Finely fashioned individual luminaires were hung in the entrance and reception area corresponding to the historical luminaire positions. Side rooms such as hallways, anterooms and washrooms were to receive simple downlights.

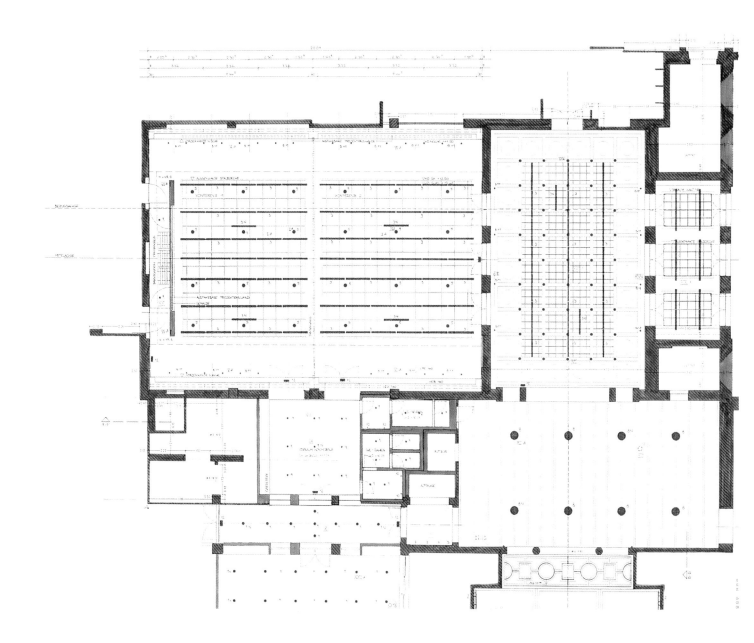

This design design formed the basis for the construction documents. It had to do justice to the existing building structures and had to be carried out in coordination with a general contractor. General contractors reduce the planning services of architects and engineers. The drawings were executed in precise detail and an accurate "luminaire book" was put together. Luminaires which at previous stages were simply called "downlight, low-voltage halogen incandescent lamp" now became:

Downlight

QT 12 50 W / 12 V

ERCO

89197

and the "batten with fluorescent lamp" (No. 3) above the dust ceiling now became:

Batten Lamp

T26 58 W

SITECO

5LJ 1800–7TW

The luminaire book and the plans drawn to a scale of 1:50 constitute the planning and final working documents for the project. The luminaire categories and their wattage are listed in the legend on the drawings, in particular as a guideline for the building technician/electrical engineer who must plan the wiring diameters. The precise technical information together with an illustration of the luminaire, its specific features with regard to electrical and lighting technology, its dimensions and installation options are all provided on the respective page of the luminaire book. At the beginning of the luminaire book, there is a list of all luminaires with their particulars regarding installation locations and quantities. An additional index in tabular form facilitates the allocation.
CAD applications are of great help in managing luminaires. Since every luminaire is registered in the program, tender specifications are easily generated.
In the course of the project, the plans and the luminaire book undergo certain changes. Following consultation with the architect, the lighting designer presents the luminaires to the client. Records are kept of these presentations. The following is an excerpt of such a record concerning the lighting concept:

"Hapag Lloyd, Ballindamm"
Note for the Files

Participants:	......	*Hapag*	*Lloyd*
	......	*Hapag*	*Lloyd*
	......	*Hapag*	*Lloyd*
	......	*Allianz*	
U. Brandi	*Büro*		*Brandi*
	......	*gmp*	
	......	*gmp*	
	......	*gmp*	
	......		

Subsequently, gmp (Gerkan, Marg and Partners Architects) explains to the client the various implementation options for the glass of the dust ceiling, using original samples. These represented various degrees of transparency and coloration:

1. *Multilayer glass consisting of 2 x 4 mm float glass, clear with 1 layer of film, light mat*
2. *Multilayer glass consisting of 2 x 4 mm float glass, clear with 2 layers of film, light mat*
3. *Multilayer glass consisting of 2 x 4 mm white glass, clear with 2 layers, each consisting of 1 layer of film and 1 acrylic layer of a thickness of 3 mm, RHÖM 012*

Glass samples 1 and 2 are common types of multilayered glass which feature a light green tone. Glass sample 3 is a special type of glass which, due to its color rendering quality, is used, for example, in museum construction. Here one can only make out a white coloration. In order to block the view or the recognition of the roof structure from below, gmp proposes the use of glass number 2, that is, the glass with 2 light mat layers of film. The client emphasizes that he wishes to prevent a plain view of the ceiling construction or any distinct reflections of this construction.

The daylight simulation undertaken by Mrs. Brandi demonstrated that changes in the light conditions of the sky due to changes in weather conditions can be discerned in the conference room and is desired by the client as well. On this basis, the decision is made to continue to work with glass number 2.

17 This excerpt from an illustrated luminaire book
provides some formal representations of the suggested
luminaires in their future surroundings. This type of
illustration also can be helpful in increasing the acceptance of the plan and its result.

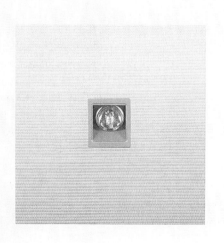

At this point, the light simulation is presented, which demonstrates an artificial lighting system in the ceiling space. It is shown that the general illumination with fluorescent tubes is not discernible and that only diffuse light passes through the glass.

Various colors of light are also simulated to illustrate the different effects of "warm light" and "cold light". Point lighting, by contrast, is marked by distinct light circles visible on the "dust ceiling". These lend an evocative atmosphere to the room.

These light variations should be quite pronounced so as to offer a variety of illumination options for different uses. This simulation gains universal approval among the participants so that planning can proceed in this regard as well.

The next item on the agenda is Mrs. Brandi's presentation of the floor luminaire and the recessed ceiling luminaire for the hall. The purpose of the built-in floor luminaire in the conference room is the illumination of the wall design with its V2 A steel fabric, which requires light to display its special elegance and reduce its technical character.

This luminaire was also intended for the main hall in order to provide more refined illumination options for that space as well.

Hapag Lloyd recognizes the value of these luminaires for the wall surface in the conference room and agrees to that part of the proposal. The luminaires for the hall, however, were discussed critically and it was decided to do without them.

Instead, the proposal for the main hall, illustrated by means of a sample luminaire, of inserting recessed spotlights into the circular hollows at the front of the ceiling, which would illuminate the surface of the wall and be fitted with a glass ring so as to leave the light source visible, was met with approval and scheduled for further planning.

The ceiling luminaire of the transverse hall was sampled on site. Participants realized that the lamps may be too strong or that the glass must be substantially more frosted. Moreover, the luminaire must be hung lower and the canopy must be reworked.

All participants are so pleased by this luminaire that they agree to pursue these specifications and keep the luminaire in the planning process."

Once the client has reviewed and passed the formal and technical issues in outline, technical subtleties such as the switching and control options of the lighting system are coordinated.

In the Hapag Lloyd construction project, the luminaires above the dust ceiling had to be installed in a special manner in order to prevent their collision with the moveable maintenance platforms. One of the questions is documented in the following passage:

Project : Hapag Lloyd, Ballindamm, Hamburg

Dear Ms. Brandi,

We have received the drawings of the lighting design. Upon inspecting them, we noticed certain items which would have to be adjusted or changed. In this regard, we have already reached an agreement with Mrs. ...., gmp, by telephone.
The points to be discussed are the following:

Large Skylight
The emergency lighting installations indicated in the enclosure must be shifted in the direction of the arrow to such an extent (approx. 0.6 m) that they, like the other luminaires, allow for the passage of personnel over the transverse fall-prevention installation (cf. p. 3).

Small Skylight
The plan provided for a lengthwise fall-prevention installation in the ridge area. Since, however, a stretch of lighting is suspended in this area, with luminaires reaching 1.8 m in length, an unobstructed movement of personnel in the transverse direction cannot be guaranteed throughout with a catwalk width of 0.6 m. For this reason, two fall-prevention sections have now been planned, as sketched in the enclosure.

Work in the skylight with the inclusion of the lighting fixtures is now possible in principle. Unfortunately, the securing ropes intersect the emergency lighting or its suspension cables.

A temporary suspension of the emergency lighting fixtures directly underneath the roof structure for the duration of the construction work could remedy the situation (cf. p. 5). If there are no objections to this proposal from your side, the planning can be regarded as adopted as far as we are concerned.

Please let us know your views on the points mentioned above as soon as possible, so that we can pass the modification on to the firm executing the work, which has already been commissioned.

With kind regards, TAW

21 These ladders are standing on a room-sized scaffold approximately 4 m above the floor of the hall. The glass panes have been removed, the old luminaire wiring has been exposed. In the background, we see the bare front wall which has already been sanded off; above, the new roof construction is visible through the scaffolding.

22 The scaffolding has been partly removed, thus opening a view of the glass roof (straight structure) and the tracks for the bare fluorescent lamps suspended below. The frosted glass at ceiling level has not yet been instal- led. Part of the concrete-wood structure has already received an undercoat, and new wires have been laid.

18 This is what the roof area above the hall looked like.

19 The red color of the wall was added later, making the room darker than it was originally. Daylight entered through the glass ceiling and bare incandescent lamps masked the intersecting points of the supporting concrete-wood structure.

20 A detailed view of the concrete-wood structure from above. New wiring will have to be installed in this area.

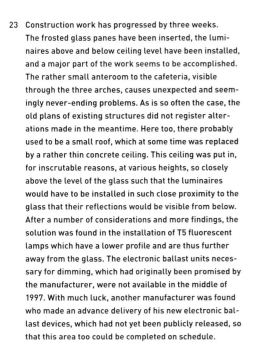

23 Construction work has progressed by three weeks. The frosted glass panes have been inserted, the luminaires above and below ceiling level have been installed, and a major part of the work seems to be accomplished. The rather small anteroom to the cafeteria, visible through the three arches, causes unexpected and seemingly never-ending problems. As is so often the case, the old plans of existing structures did not register alterations made in the meantime. Here too, there probably used to be a small roof, which at some time was replaced by a rather thin concrete ceiling. This ceiling was put in, for inscrutable reasons, at various heights, so closely above the level of the glass such that the luminaires would have to be installed in such close proximity to the glass that their reflections would be visible from below. After a number of considerations and more findings, the solution was found in the installation of T5 fluorescent lamps which have a lower profile and are thus further away from the glass. The electronic ballast units necessary for dimming, which had originally been promised by the manufacturer, were not available in the middle of 1997. With much luck, another manufacturer was found who made an advance delivery of his new electronic ballast devices, which had not yet been publicly released, so that this area too could be completed on schedule.

24 The hall is finished but not yet furnished. The incandescent lamps create a brilliant accent against the diffuse daylight. The first design concept did not provide for the faithful restoration of the grid pattern of incandescent lamps. These points of brilliant light were supposed to be "cited" in a row by the back wall and provide additional illumination of the wall. In retrospect, the chosen path seems to be the right one.

25 The small original luminaires had been replaced by metal cylinders with incandescent bulbs. These have been removed together with the wiring, and the lacquer coating has been partly sanded off.

26 Incandescent lamps in porcelain sockets correspond to the original light points in the ceiling. Here only the fluorescent light above the glass level is switched on.

27 When the light points are switched on, the luster of the delicate golden strip is nicely visible.

88

28　These are the lateral hollow channels of the large roof area above the conference rooms.

29　The glass ceiling was no longer functional, since an additional plaster-board ceiling had been put in below.

30　The new roof is finished and glazed, and the battens are installed. It was not possible to install the luminaires as continuous strips of light: they had to be suspended individually at great cost.

31　It was necessary to ensure that the maintenance platform for cleaning the glass surfaces and exchanging the lamps could be moved at a right angle to the luminaires, between luminaire and glass ceiling. At the same time, the securing rope of the installing personnel attached on top would have to be free to move forward unimpeded between the luminaires. The pendant downlights for the "suns" have not yet been installed.

32 Details of the fastening hardware for the luminaires. For warranty purposes, the roof structure could neither be drilled nor could anything welded on – screw clamps were used instead.

33 Core drilling in the existing concrete floor of the conference hall created the spaces for the installation of the recessed floor luminaires.

34 The installation of recessed floor luminaires is never entirely without complications, whether in the case of existing floors or floors to be newly constructed. There are various types of installation. In this case, the housing is substantially larger than the opening of the luminaire.

35 Switched on, the luminaires create reflections on the metal texture behind them which appear differently from every viewing angle.

36

37

38

40

39

36 General lighting in the conference room: the large conference room is gutted, the roof, the level for the interior glass ceiling and the lateral hollow channels have been restored.

37 The hollow space under the roof provides room for the new lighting system: as daylight becomes faint, the uniform light from dimmable fluorescent lamps is added.

38 A brilliant light is created when the 24 "sun downlights" are switched on, in addition to the fluorescent lamps or by themselves. With their warm incandescent halogen light, they enhance the festive mood or evening atmosphere in the room.

39 The projection wall is visually detached from the back wall of the room due to the fact that it is illuminated from behind.

40 Craftsmen work in the roof area until the final moments, while painters are already whitewashing below.

41 Various light settings provide different atmospheres to the conference rooms.

3

42 The space can be divided into two. This is why every circuit is duplicated.

43 Part of the succession of representative rooms in this building is the entrance area with the porter's counter and the luminaires by André Putmann, which illuminate the ceiling above and whose large shades are themselves illuminated. These few visible luminaires also illuminate a reception room with its small set of conference furniture and a bar.

44 As intended, the client was presented with rooms which again radiate the spaciousness and brightness they formerly possessed.

Award of Contracts

Preparation and Participation

The results of the lighting designer's design development and construction documents is described in detail while preparing the contract awards. Frequently, at this point, the construction documents will have been carried out only in a rudimentary fashion (just to the extent that a luminaire catalogue was drawn up). The construction documents proper are then completed during the construction phase. Such a planning process running parallel to construction can be marked by numerous changes and step-by-step services, since important decisions are made only along the way. The more precisely the award of contracts is the more agreeable and smooth will be the further course of the project. The work of the artificial lighting designer usually describes the luminaires and their accessories such as glare shutters, filters, lighting tracks or lamp poles. Daylight elements are frequently taken over by the architect in his tendering after consulting with the lighting designer.

Until a standard for the European Union goes into effect, the division of the cost categories for the completion of a construction project in Germany effectively is still regulated by the German standard DIN 276. Lighting installations can be found under item 4.5.n under the heading of "high-voltage current installations". This category is divided into:

4.5.1.0	General Lighting
4.5.2.0	Special Lighting
4.5.3.0	Emergency Lighting
4.5.9.0	Other Lighting

Tender Specifications

The tender specifications "Electrical Services" may include the lighting installations as an independent section (also called a "lot"), as far as accounting is concerned.

In this case, the electrical engineer receives the documents of the lighting designer. There are the general and technical preliminary remarks for electrical services for the tender specifications, and there may be additional preliminary remarks of the lighting designer regarding specific luminaires. The other option is a separate "Luminaires" tender and, if necessary, a separate tendering process (since, for example, luminaire installation takes place long after electrical installations.)

Lamps differ from other items required during construction: while one can issue tendering for 10 meters of baseboard or 100 cubic meter of concrete without reference to a manufacturer, this is difficult in the case of luminaires. With standard products such as battens for bare fluores-

cent luminaires or simple louvered luminaires, for example, this is plausible. Yet already with built-in downlights, which all look the same at first glance, there are subtle but crucial differences in the quality of the material, photometric values and the visual quality of the exposed installation rings. Many clients put the luminaire actually proposed by the designer out to tender. Public clients, on the other hand, require a description of the luminaires without reference to a manufacturer: they permit the phrase "model product XY manufactured by Z"; but require the addition of "or equivalent". The designer later verifies the equivalence of alternative luminaires.

Tendering

Tendering may be subject to various conditions. In the case of large sums, public clients in Germany, for example, must issue tendering in Europe, while federal, regional, or invited tendering are conducted for smaller amounts. Only in cases of extreme time pressure and small contracts the public client has the right of awarding a contract privately, that means, without a call for tenders.

Analysis and Assessment of Tenders

The designer verifies the originals of all offers received on time by the client for completeness, correctness of content and calculation, and checks each item using green checkmark. The complete tender specifications contain a certificate of verification. Sometimes an offer is not verifiable. In that case, the lighting designer makes a note stating the reason, such as lack of clarity or incompleteness. It is also important that tenders be comparable. If one of the tenderers offers the requested high-quality luminaires at consistently higher prices, and another offers cheaper alternatives across the board, they are not comparable. In the case of larger advertised tendering, the designer prepares a price breakdown by comparing every item of every tenderer in a table together with the sum total. The price breakdown shows very clearly how convincing or plausible a particular tender is within the range of all tenders. If there are items the prices of which are conspicuously higher or lower than the prices of others, the obvious thing to do is to see whether something has been misinterpreted.

Meeting with the Tenderer

The client decides which tenderer to invite to a meeting. The special engineer may conduct the meeting even without the client, as the meeting often serves only to remove misunderstandings or to ask the tenderer to complete or explain things. The designer and the tenderer sign the minutes, which may become an annex to a possible contract.

Award Meeting and Negotiation

The award meeting which the client, supported by the expertise of the planner, holds with the tenderer constitutes the second stage; in separate discussions, the client asks the tenderers about their calculations in order to negotiate the price. The tenderers give information regarding the history of their firms, demonstrate their economic strength, and name references. The lighting designer explains technical issues, mentions possible past experiences with the respective firms and states his/her view regarding the likely further course of construction. Once some tenderers have caught the interest of the client, the client either invites them to tender negotiations or awards the contract to the best tenderer without further negotiations. Clients have different styles, with some, clients following well-established rituals. The designer is not necessarily present. This depends on the wishes of the client. It is not the task of the specialist designer to participate in price negotiations or to evaluate prices. Of course, he must not pass on what he learns about the tenderers in the negotiations to the outside.

Annex

If, following the commissioning of a firm, modifications are made in the planning – for whatever reason – and different types of lamps or quantities of luminaires are required, the client will request a revised tender on the basis of a list of lamps drawn up by the designer. The supplementary bid will list possible reductions and increases, and must have been approved, by the client before the contractor may order new luminaires. In some projects, the annexes reach almost similar quantities to those negotiated in the main contract. Large annexes are unfavorable for the client; theoretically, he can also negotiate, but practically, he will hardly seek the competition of a further contractor on his construction site.

Construction Site Operations

Construction Supervision

Life on the construction site follows different rules from life in the "warm and cozy" planning office. Every appointment on the site can be a new lesson. Frequent visits to construction sites are advantageous not only for novices, for benefits can be drawn not only with regard to the current project, but also for all future projects. The principle we followed in the chapters of preliminary inquiries, design development, construction documents, and tendering procedures – of explaining the individual phases of a planning process by means of examples – cannot be applied with the same success in the chapter on construction supervision.

Hence, this chapter will focus on errors, on their causes and consequences. All errors arising from this as well as from preceding planning phases will now be revealed to their full extent. These errors are not necessarily the deficiency of the lighting designer, since all participants contribute in equal measure. The best guarantee of a flawless construction phase is good construction documents and tendering procedures. As with a set of instructions for using a technical device, the individual functions of the planning and construction process can be examined and errors can be located and corrected.

Communication

The designer's most important means of communication is the drawing. Apart from their content, the quality of these drawings can vary a great deal. Symbols, legends, measurements, additional information, directions of spotlights, references to details or sections and connections to other details or other areas may at first glance be either illegible or puzzling. Lighting designers are very specialized professionals, and they cannot expect always to encounter electricians who are specialized in the installation of lighting and lighting control systems. Designers should provide comments or references regarding special devices or devices which are new on the market such that the electrician may obtain the specific information needed. Further: The plan never (or only upon the express and documented wish of the client or project manager) passes directly from the lighting designer to the construction site; it passes through the hands of the architect as well. This is the only way of ensuring that the craftsman has the current and agreed version of the plan at his disposal.

Communication of Plan and Text:

·Not clear	→	Error
·Clear, but electrician does not understand it	→	Error
·Clear, but old version of plan was used	→	Error

Communication, verbal, on-site

All of the three cases above lead to error. A clarifying talk on the construction site can act as a countermeasure to such confusion. If the talks take place at a construction meeting, minutes will be kept. If individual consultations are held between the lighting designer and craftsmen and relevant issues are determined, both sides will cover themselves by means of notes, which one of the participants draws up and the other countersigns, provided there is agreement. While it is difficult to strike the right tone in this type of communication, it is also the secret of good project supervision. Every individual will develop a distinctive personal style. Designers and craftsmen are most likely to achieve their common goal if they accept each other and do not confront each other with arrogance. The consciousness of mutual dependency should lead to rational action; power games are damaging to both sides. Friendly cooperation is fun, it motivates both parties, and in the end, one can be pleased with the collective result.

Communication: verbal, on-site:

Not clear	→	Error
Clear, but not sufficient from a formal point of view	→	Error
Communicates (minutes), but lack of objectivity, no willingness to cooperate	→	Error

Other Trades

Who is responsible for what? The interface to the other trades must be clearly determined, be it at the level of designers or of craftsmen. Especially in the case of lighting installations, this must be settled already at the planning stage: ideally, the interface to the electrical engineer is the outlet of the wire, while the luminaires are the responsibility of the lighting designer. Here, things can begin to get complicated, for some luminaires already feature a short piece of wire installed by the manufacturer, while others do not. Sometimes the emergency lighting is planned by the lighting designer, sometimes this is done by the electrical engineer.

Aside from electrical installations (wiring, switches, controls), other related trades are ceiling construction (plaster board ceilings with openings for recessed luminaires), metal work (if special fittings are needed for mounting on steel parts) and painting (if something is to be lacquered in the same color as the lamps). There can be various assignments, depending also on the size of the construction project and the extent of the work of the individual trades.

Interface with Other Trades:

Not clearly determined	→	Error
Determined, the wrong preparatory work was nevertheless done	→	Error
Determined, but there was no or flawed temporal coordination	→	Error
Determined, but temporal coordination was not maintained	→	Error

Construction Sites

Construction sites which are difficult to access, on which there exists little or poor storage space, or which include buildings still in use during construction, thus offering only short periods for carrying out construction activities, add to the difficulty of project execution and supervision. In the case of old buildings, there might be a belated discovery that plans of existing structures were false and that the renovation planning built on false assumptions. This discovery is made repeatedly, for example, with regard to the structures above suspended ceilings in the renovation of shopping centers.

Conditions of Construction Site:

Crowded	→	Error
Not crowded, but difficult to reach in terms of transportation	→	Error
Not crowded, but poor storage spaces	→	Error
Attention to ongoing activities is required	→	Error
Only small windows of opportunity for construction work	→	Error
Plans of existing structures were incorrect or incomplete	→	Grave sources of error

Clients, Users and Designers

With some projects it is unavoidable that decisions are made only during construction; with others, new requirements are constantly set. Frequently, an investor finances a building without knowing who the future tenants will be. In some projects, there is a lack of discipline, in others, possibilities for real improvement are discovered at a late date. Somewhere else, funding gaps may force last-minute modifications. Whenever something like this happens, the lighting designer should not allow himself to be pressured into rash modifications of plans in his work. Everyone requires time for reflection at the office far away from the construction site to be able to consider every consequence of the change.

Clients, Users and Designers:

New requirements and desired changes affect the construction site	→	Error
Samplings lead to rash decisions	→	Error

Deliveries

The craftsman is dependent on his suppliers. Today, luminaires are frequently manufactured only upon ordering, and the logistics between manufacturer and end user are of varying complexity. Unfortunately, the saying often proves true: Anything that can go wrong, will go wrong. Some clients decide to "provide" the luminaires. That is to say, they buy the luminaire and the installation accessories directly from the manufacturer or wholesaler and then buy the installation service from the electrician. At first, this route is often more cost-effective; things get complicated for these clients, however, when warranty issues arise. Then they are confronted not with just one but with two or three responsible parties, each of whom attributes the deficiency to the other.

Deliveries of the Lamps:

Wrong product	→	Error
Right product, but defective	→	Error
Right product, but available too late	→	Error
Right product, but wrong/defective/absent lamp	→	Error

Scheduling

It is not always possible to follow a tried and tested order of events. It is true that lamps should be installed after the painter has been on the construction site. On the other hand, heavy scaffolding should be used before the floor is put down. Although the architect is responsible for the correct order of events on the construction site, the specialist planner should nevertheless be well informed in this regard.

Scheduling

Incorrect order of events	→	Error
Decision in favor of less than optimal products	→	Error
Decision in favor of less than optimal methods	→	Error

Funding and Solvency

In the case of public construction projects, the client must opt for the lowest tenderer, while in the case of private investments, the client is free to choose. The private client, of course, will also aim to purchase the service at the best price possible, but because of the private allocation, he also has more options.

Nevertheless, the "price war" may be so fierce that it will have to be paid for dearly on the construction site. Craftsmen are usually not rewarded on account of their conscientious and proper work, but rather for having cut costs in all possible places (costs of material and wages are being most promising). Only a high or commensurate quality requirement on the part of clients and designers can stop or slow this downward price spiral.

Difficulties in Funding

Cheap material	→	Error
Unqualified trade contractors	→	Error
Too much time pressure on tradesmen	→	Error

Dealing with Faults

With so many possibilities for faults, there will be no construction site without problems. Once a problem has occurred, the question arises how the people involved deal with it. This varies greatly from case to case. Experience shows that the client has a great deal of influence on how faults are dealt with. In cases where the client has driven down the price and is only waiting for his contractors to make mistakes so that he can drive the price down even further, his engagement will not be focussed on damage control but rather on shifting responsibility. If a client deals frankly with contractors and contributes substantially to damage control, practical and good solutions will be found. Thus, a personally com-

mitted client is a great asset for a construction site and hence for the finished building. In such projects, the participants also display a great readiness to support one another rather than cause problems.

Minutes, Notice of Impediment and Notice of Deficiencies

Anyone involved in deficiencies and delays should pursue two aims: He should work towards removing the deficiencies as quickly as possible. The longer it exists, the more firmly it establishes itself in people's minds. Even if the lighting designer is not responsible for the deficiencies, but for example the tradesman, the site engineer has to inspect the work of the tradesman and has to care for the proper execution of the work in the interest of the client. A site engineer who tolerates a deficiency is not fulfilling his contractual obligation as a project supervisor.

The first legal means to demand correction of a deficiency is the minute which names the deficiency, the person responsible and completion date. An admonition is made if the minutes have no affect. In this case, the lighting designer proposes a formulation of the justification to the client. He does not admonish the executing firm, as he has no contractual relation with this firm. Only the client (or the project manager as the client's representative) may threaten consequences if the service demanded is not rendered on schedule. Normally, the client has the option of withholding payment and of entrusting other firms with the repair at the contractor's expense. This route is costly and annoying for everybody, and is avoided if possible.

The next step would be a notice of impediment. With a notice of impediment, a party involved in construction or planning officially announces that another party is impeding the realization of its service on schedule. The notice is handed to the client, who asks the accused for a statement. If a notice of impediment is justified, the responsibility for a delay no longer rests with the party hired to perform the service but rather with the party impeding. On a poorly functioning construction site, the various parties can virtually "bombard" each other with notices of impediments, and significant work is delayed. The search for a cooperative solution will always pay off in the end. Nevertheless, to protect one's own interest, it is advisable to draw up a (at a well considered time) a written notice of impediment if it is not possible to succeed in another way and one's own deadlines are jeopardized. Clients are right to hold lighting designers who do not express themselves correctly partly responsible for delays.

Acceptance Record, Deficiencies List

Finally, the acceptance record documents the state of the services accomplished; ideally, this happens once the work is completed (there are exceptions, if, for example, a small part of the work can only be per-

45 Through a railway track, the ballast of which has been completely removed, one gains a view of a lighting sample at the Friedrichstrasse railway station in Berlin. Yellow light falls onto the pillars of the mall on the ground floor.

46 A mock-up room (at *ERCO*) with adjustable ceiling height can stand in for a model room. It aids the lighting planner in illustrating his vision of the light atmosphere to the client and the architect and to test his ideas.

formed following a new delivery, or if parts of the building are ready for operation). There may be a preliminary acceptance of a part of the project; this record becomes part of the actual acceptance of work. The acceptance record forms the basis for the rightful (final) invoice of the electrician; if the record does not list any deficiencies or reservations, the electrician may issue the invoice as agreed. Clients and contractors have various ways of dealing with deficiencies. Deficiencies will lead to a reduction in the purchase price or must be corrected within a predetermined period. If the deficiencies are so numerous or so grave that the client refuses to accept the work, a new acceptance date will be set. It is in the interest of the lighting designer that deficiencies are actually corrected, for after all, he had planned the lighting system without them. He, as well as his client, will eventually be judged by what was actually built, and no one will ask whether this deviates from the plan. The lighting designer should insist that the deficiencies be remedied as soon as possible, since a project that is completed will quickly fade from the consciousness of designers and tradesmen, and it will be difficult to reopen the case.

Usually, the designer will have seen the lighting system long before the official acceptance of work and will have verified that all the light conditions correspond to his original vision. When everything is just as designed or when expectations are even exceeded, these on-site impressions are some of the most beautiful moments of the profession.

Samplings and Lighting Tests

On-site samplings constitute the best method for determining whether the desired light effect is achieved and for conveying to the client a concrete idea regarding the future lighting scene.

Frequently, clients and architects want to see a sample of the proposed luminaire in order to examine its shape, size and surface quality. The presentation of sample luminaires in isolation at the meeting table is of questionable value. In such a situation, the luminaire will usually appear larger than in the actual installation situation, for example, under a ceiling. Looking at a luminaire without seeing its lighting effect in a certain room leads one to concentrate on its appearance rather than on its proper function. Hence, it is much better to conduct samplings and lighting tests on site, in the case of existing buildings, or in a prototype room, in the case of new buildings. This may be quite costly. For the two railway stations Alexanderplatz and Friedrichstrasse, the two lighting designers in each case spent a week on site to supervise installation work and to make necessary preparations: ordering the luminaires, preparing the drawings for the sample area, settling on provisional luminaire fixtures etc. Sampling is not part of the basic services according to the HOAI. As a special service, it may be invoiced at an hourly rate.

Fundamentally, there are two possible situations for samplings:

· The client has already decided on a certain luminaire and would like to verify its lighting effect.
· The client lets several manufacturers compete against one another and makes a decision on the basis of lighting effect, price, and appearance of the luminaire.

It is surprising to learn how much can go wrong during sampling: hence, it is customary to inspect the installed luminaires together with the electricians before presenting them to the client. All sorts of mishaps can occur:

Mishaps during Delivery

The wrong type of luminaire, the wrong model, or the wrong accessories are delivered; the luminaires are poorly packaged and therefore defective, they are delivered at the wrong time or to the wrong location and hence are lost on the construction site.

Mishaps during Installation

Luminaires are installed in the wrong place, they radiate in the wrong direction, or the circuitry is mixed up; luminaires have been assembled in the wrong way, they are dirty, crooked, or the electricity is not hooked up. If the lighting designer is present during installation, he still has the chance to correct the worst mistakes.

This listing of the possible mishaps is not meant as a reproach of electricians. Admittedly, some luminaires are constructed in such a way that they can hardly be installed without precise instructions. There are so many types of luminaires that it is incumbent upon the lighting designer to furnish precise details ahead of time. The manufacturers, who naturally have an interest in a successful sampling, go to various lengths to support lighting planners and electricians. The extent of their support is not necessarily dependent upon the volume of the expected sale but on the individual manufacturer. At times, regional branches differ in their service and level of commitment. The commissioned electrician or the "resident electrician" of the client conducts the sampling. He orders the sample luminaires on instructions from the lighting planner, procures the lamps, and installs the luminaire. If, at the time of sampling, an electrician has not yet been engaged in the construction project, the lighting designer may personally order the sample luminaire which the manufacturer should deliver, if possible, ready for connection with cable and plug. Along with the sample, the lighting designer will receive an invoice, which will be credited upon return of the sample luminaires within a certain period (1–3 months).

Sample luminaires may no longer be sold as new luminaires and the handling of such test lighting is a great expense for all involved. Not least for this reason, the luminaires should be carefully selected and not too many alternatives should be sampled. It is best to show the client two or three of one's favorite alternatives instead of a confusing multitude.

4 EXAMPLES

DESIGNING
WITH LIGHT

2

3

1 *Tokyo International Forum*: Even a ceiling can be turned into a façade and can determine the exterior effect of a building from afar...

2 ... as well as from nearby.

3 Glass façades offer many possibilities for giving a building presence in its surroundings at night. A clear choice is the homogeneous light pane of the *Hotel Poluinya*.

Façades

Every lighting design of an interior space with windows is at the same time the lighting design of the façade. The viewer of a façade in the evening can make out what there is behind. By means of spotlights, the shop window draws attention to the goods offered for sale. The office building transforms itself from a completely lit façade into a mosaic of those rooms in which people work long hours. Vertical elements, such as stairways are usually distinguished by a different color of light and different intervals of illumination. Entrances are set apart by additional light. Observing façades can give one the impression of watching a film in slow motion. Generally, large surface glass façades are distinguished from apertured façades with individual windows.

Glass façades shine light from the inside outwards like a lantern; a nice example of this is the *Gedächtniskirche* (Memorial Church) by Egon Eiermann in Berlin. Through the blue glass brick, the viewer just makes out a glimmer and sparkle. The light is not distributed over large diffuse surfaces, rather, it shines selectively and partially directly through the façade. The glass brick façade of the *Hotel Poluinya* in Hokkaido, Japan, creates a very different impression. Behind the façade, there are two long corridors, the back walls of which function as diffusely reflective surfaces. In a lighting slot facing the wall in the suspended ceiling, there is a series of lights with fluorescent lamps combined with low voltage halogen lamps, which, apart from supplying the functional lighting via the reflection of the wall, also cause the façade to shine. Such a lighting slot should throw a light as uniform as possible onto the wall. The sockets themselves, which meet at the ends of the lamps, would cause dark spots if the luminaires were positioned too close to the illuminated wall. The lighting channel in the *Hotel Poluinya* is 15 cm high and 11 cm wide. The fluorescent lamps are situated at a distance of 8 cm from the wall and are shielded below through a projection of the suspended ceiling.

Modern office buildings as well shine from the inside to the outside through their glass-covered façades. Beautiful examples from the 1960s are the *Unilever* high-rise in Hamburg which features a band of light around the building created through the illumination of one of the upper stories and the *Mannesmann* high-rise in Düsseldorf, the illuminated windows of which create a seasonal sign for Düsseldorf in the shape of a Christmas tree. After approximately 30 years, the lighting systems in these buildings had to be rebuilt. While the original bulkhead luminaires also threw their light diffusely to the outside, the new mirror screen luminaires throw their light directly downwards, while the floor and the tables in turn reflect the light to the ceiling such that only a reduced glimmer penetrates to the outside. For this reason, the *Mannesmann* high-rise was equipped with additional downlights in the window area which illuminate pillars behind the façade, thus presenting the building at night. Indirectly lit rooms look brightest from the outside since ceilings are visible from many angles. The *Tokyo International Forum* shows its illuminated ceiling construction far into the distance and thus stands out in the midst of an area of high-rises where the nearby main railway station is the only low-rise building. Up close, from the publicly accessible interior courtyard, the façade appears uniformly backlit, since from this perspective, the illuminated walls and the ceiling construction are visually drawn together.

Façades with brightly lit windows appear as black silhouettes, sharply contrasting the windows. Other buildings have an additional floodlight illumination from the outside, often completely replacing a light shining from inside to the outside. For a time it was fashionable to floodlight city halls, churches and other buildings from some distance – head-on and wholesale – one building often competing in brightness with the next. Nowadays, a subtly differentiated floodlight illumination of the façades of surrounding buildings is used to create a special atmosphere in pub-

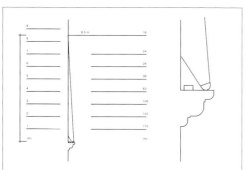

4 Luminaires mounted on the cornices of the façade create this soft light for the *Louvre*.

5 The *Louvre* is not flooded head-on. The façade appears three-dimensional and has almost a mysterious air with the illuminated windows .

102 lic squares, for example. A building is no longer considered in isolation; urban spaces are alive even at night.

Through an extensive floodlight illumination, the façade of the *Louvre* would have lost its plasticity; thus it was decided to install minuscule luminaires on the cornices and ledges of the façade. Not only this made fine adjustments to the lighting effect possible to match the light from the windows, it also eliminated the need for luminaire poles or large floodlights on opposite roofs. The profile spotlight used is equipped with Xenon incandescent lamps (5 W and 8.5 W, life of 20,000 hours). A parabolic channel reflector serves to direct the light. The transformers up to 300 VA are installed separately. Some luminaires radiate upwards, others downwards.

Light is shone upon the façade of the *Deutsches Schauspielhaus* in Hamburg with similar subtlety, although in this case the effect is realized via a technology using end-emitting and side-emitting fibers.

The golden lettering "Deutsches Schauspielhaus" receives light from two light sources with metal halide lamps, each feeding eleven strands of fiber glass. The light sources are located in the attic of the building, where they are easy to maintain. Special attachments direct the ends of the fibers, which penetrate the wall in 22 small holes, onto the lettering. The edge of the roof, the arch of which is revealed by a change of light from bright to dark, is formed by a strand of fiber glass emitting blue light generated by a light source fitted with a metal halide lamp.

Checklist

Prior designing a façade illumination the surroundings should be studied carefully:

· Which buildings are illuminated in the neighborhood?
· How powerful is the street lighting?
· Are there surfaces of water which reflect the building?
· Will the light disturb the residents, or is a permit required for the system?
· Is it possible to block other, interfering sources of light?
· Does it even make sense to illuminate façades in a medieval town, where in former times it used to be completely dark?
· How does the building appear during the different seasons or with the variously colored foliage of the surrounding trees and shrubs?

6 With a blue line of light at the roof, the *Deutsche Schau-spielhaus* in Hamburg presents itself in a subtly differentiated way between brightly illuminated hotels across from the main train station.

7 A historical entrance in Berlin was fitted with a glass door. Scarcely visible uplights enhance the light of the original chandelier.

8 The bright ceiling continues in the passage way to the offices in the courtyard.

In the illumination of façades, the operator will place high value in economic efficiency and uncomplicated maintenance. Otherwise, there is the danger that after a while, the illumination system will no longer be serviced and consequently no longer be operated.

Entrances

Entrances receive the visitors of a building. Usually emphasized in the frontal view of a building, entrances signal the style and the way of life of the inhabitants or the image of a firm. Entrances form the transition between the bright exterior space with daytime illuminances between 10 and 100 klx and the darker interior space with illuminances between 50 and 500 lx. At night, the light situation is reversed: inside the building it is 100 to 1000 times brighter than outside. The light for entrance areas must harmonize these transitions in a meaningful way – in the glass-covered entrances of administrative buildings just as much as in the case of shopping arcades and malls.

The *Bürgerhaus Uhlandstraße* in Berlin receives its guests with a grand gesture of splendor and wealth and with a magnificent chandelier. This chandelier was originally the only source of light, the current lighting concept discreetly adding several indirectly radiating luminaires. The luminaires for halogen incandescent lamps are reduced to the minimal size and are thus hardly visible. The walls and ceiling of the passageway to the courtyard were intended to be as bright as possible in order to give the entrance a public appearance to the back offices.

In a different way, the luminous structure catching the eye of visitors in the entrance hall of the *RWE high-rise* in Essen is also a chandelier. The various ceiling sections formed between stairs and galleries cross each other in such an elegant way that – framed by downlights – they turn into a three-dimensional object of light.

At the same time, the openings and curves permit views into the upper levels and thus facilitate orientation within the building. A simple way of making an entrance recognizable from the outside is by means of light falling through a glass door. If the color of the light is warmer than that of daylight, a great difference in the degree of brightness will not be necessary.

9

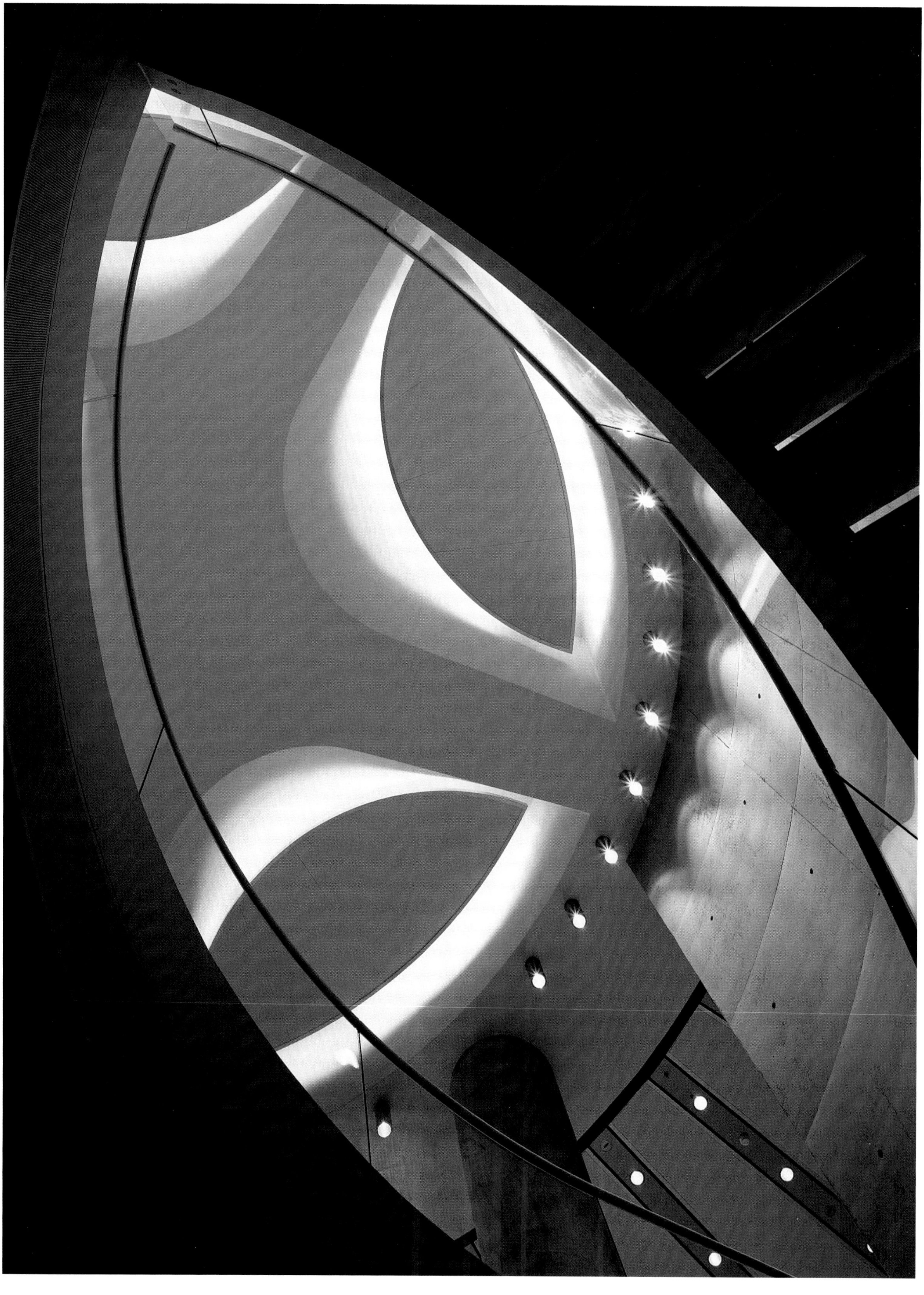

9 The ceiling itself is an object of light with a soft outline.
   The circle of surface-mounted downlights floods the wall
   surfaces.

10 An austere halo of lighting tracks with individual downlights frames the natural ceiling openings.

This effect is observed by visitors in the entrances to the individual galleries of the *Museé de l'art contemporaine* in Strasbourg. The entrances open towards the central, glass-covered hall and throw the warm light of halogen incandescent lamps from inside onto the floor of the hall. Former army barracks now house the new head office of *Adidas*. A new building connects the two long office sections. On the first floor, below the executive floor, there is the entrance hall. The transparent hall already reveals itself on the outside to the approaching visitor. The hall is easily surveyed due to the reflection from the light wood floor. Three utility tracks pass lengthways through the ceiling of the hall: two air conditioning elements and a lighting channel which integrates compact fluo-

rescent lamps TC-L 55 W for general lighting as well as directional spotlights with halogen incandescent lamps for exhibition items. During the day, the compact fluorescent lamps permit an energy-saving permanent illumination. For events in the evening, users switch off the fluorescent lamps. The halogen incandescent lamps then create a festive, brilliant atmosphere. The reception counter has an additional light for the workspace. Asymmetrically radiating recessed downlights illuminate the interior walls of the solid vestibules. The light enhances the functional and fresh impression of the space making it suitable for colorful exhibits and events.

11 Brightness and color of light can mediate or mark
a contrast between indoors and outdoors.

12 The indirect light on the executive floor of *Adidas* carries
a bright and friendly atmosphere to the outside.

13 The two lighting components are integrated in a utility
channel: soft general light from fluorescent lamps and
directable halogen incandescent lamps for exhibits.

14 In the medical technology factory *B. Braun* in Melsungen, it was possible to create very distinct light atmospheres through the modification of a single luminaire (a simple protective tube luminaire). The bare luminaire on a bracket ...

15 ... the vertically mounted wall luminaire ...

16 ... and the reflector luminaire on the ceiling. In spite of a low budget, a varied lighting design was achieved.

Hallways, Stairways, Elevator Foyers

Hallways frequently feature a suspended ceiling concealing technical installations. They can be located in the interior, e.g. between two rows of offices, or on one side of a building, where they are supplied with daylight. In modern office buildings, hallways are between 1.50 m and 2.50 m wide. Sometimes they are structured through pillars or supports; in hotels or hospitals, hallways have widened and narrowed areas.

The lighting concept for a hallway derives from the concept for the building as a whole.

In the building complex *B. Braun Melsungen* there is a hallway with various sections: the connective passageway leads from the administrative offices along the multistory car park through green spaces to the production facilities. This walkway is brought into prominence: from the outside, the walkway leans on tall supports against a rough concrete wall. Inside, the user walks through various sections. In the foyer of the administrative building, the connective passageway begins quite unspectacularly as a rectangular concrete case. It is narrow and high and has light openings on both sides in the upper region which are directed in different ways. In the morning, when the employees arrive, daylight is let in from one side and in the afternoon from the other side. The sunlight is diffusely reflected by the reveals of the openings which are set at an angle. Below these windows there is a row of bare fluorescent lamps (T26, 18 W) which illuminate the entire space. Since they are not mounted directly on the ceiling, these lamps form, visually speaking, a second plane. This hallway leads in an offset way into the free-standing passage that faces the outside. The abundant daylight is reflected by the floor. Apart from that, the passageway represents only a protection against the weather and not a closed off room. The rhythm of the architectural axes is continued in the artificial light design. Unspectacular transversely mounted corrosion-proof luminaires are found here which appear again in other places in different arrangements. In this area, the luminaires are installed at a lower level and have a reflector which simultaneously serves as a shade. One of the overriding goals of the lighting plan was the limitation of the number of types of luminaires. Nevertheless, for each space, various atmospheres of light can be achieved with one type of luminaire, as can be seen here in the case of the stairway. If hallways are reduced to their minimally required dimensions, the lighting designer will not want to disturb their profile through protruding or hanging luminaires. Hence, he will often look for built-in luminaires which are integrated into the wall or ceiling.

In the buildings of the *Forum Elbflorenz* in Dresden, the hallway luminaire specifically designed for this project fulfills several requirements:

18

Installation Depth

· Although there is a suspended ceiling, the space above is filled with other types of technical installations leaving an installation depth of only 8 cm for the luminaires.

Portion of Indirect Light

· In order to illuminate the ceiling itself (and thus make it appear higher), the frosted glass tube is set lower and made visible as the proper source of light.

Reduced Number

· A relatively high luminous flux was realized by means of a relatively small luminaire (2 x 18 W) in order to achieve larger distances between luminaires and a relatively low quantity.

These hallway luminaires for basic illumination are combined with accentuating, narrowly focused downlights so as to unite a uniform bright-ness with a pronounced rhythm of light. These luminaires are positioned on axes in order to enable the installation of dividing walls. In the foyers of elevators, downlights are directed as spots on the company signs. The elevator foyer at *B. Braun Melsungen* is enlivened through its color. The exposed concrete is glazed blue. The luminaires are fitted like portholes with a round pane of glass and a steel cover ring. The light of the metal halide lamps is white as daylight and enhances the color effect. In the adjacent blue stairway, the same type of light illuminates a metal sheet mounted under the ceiling. Here the light effect is even stronger.

In hallways, elevator spaces and stairways, the duration of the required artificial lighting depends on the presence or absence of daylight. Fluorescent lamps or compact fluorescent lamps are usually the suitable means of illumination. Wall luminaires are often equipped with lamps ratings of 18 W. In the hallways of hotels and hospitals, reduced night lighting is practical. In hospital corridors, luminaires should not blind patients who are transported in beds. A lateral arrangement of ceiling luminaires or wall luminaires is suitable for this purpose. In hotels, this

17 Hallways often house tremendous amounts of air-
conditioning and sanitary installations.

18 Suspended ceilings hide these from view.

19 The remaining space above the ceiling often only allows
for luminaires of limited installation depth.

20 The hallway lamps of the *Forum Elbflorenz* in Dresden
protrude somewhat from the ceiling, ...

21 ... their installation depth measures merely 8 cm.

22 Positioning downlights in exposed concrete such as
in the elevator foyer of *B. Braun* at Melsungen is quite
challenging in the ceiling ...

23 ... and in the walls, both in terms of planning and
in terms of execution.

type of lighting likewise provides additional comfort. Hallways and stairways frequently serve as escape routes. The necessary lighting for this purpose can be ensured by additional luminaires or by some of the luminaires designed to provide general illumination.

The illumination of stairways can follow various principles. The installation of surface-mounted luminaires on the level sections of the ceilings above landings or half-landings and of luminaires on the walls is common and technically simple.

In the stairway of the *Norddeutsche Landesbank* in Hamburg, wall luminaires continue the indirect illumination installed in the elevator foyer. With any indirect lighting system in stairways and halls featuring open spaces and galleries, there is the danger of a strong blinding effect when looking into the luminaires from above. This requires a thorough investigation of the lines of vision and their relations during designing.

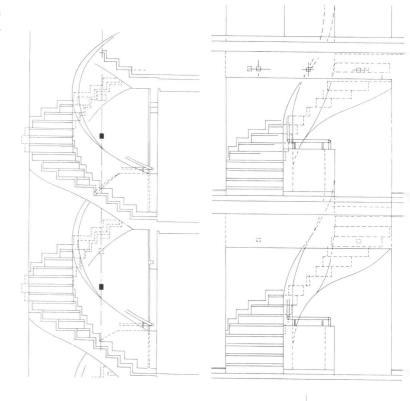

24 The square built-in wall luminaires of this elevator foyer, which almost give the impression of ornamentation, illuminate the ceiling, ...

25 ... a principle that is continued in the stairway with a surface-mounted wall luminaire. The curved bottom views of the stairs give the appearance of a sculpture.

26 The art of the lighting designer is to create lighting with soft transitions avoiding busy cast shadows.

27 When drawing luminaires in floor plans and sections, it is easy to forget that the user might be blinded, looking into the lamps from above.

28 The distinctive technical feature in this case are the recessed downlights built into the sloping bottom view of the staircase, which radiate light vertically downward.

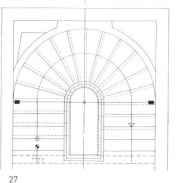

The installation of luminaires in the bottom view of the stairs is technically more involved. In the case of the office building *Heidenkampsweg* in Hamburg, the square built-in luminaires are special designs which were inserted into the recesses provided in the concrete. They are covered with frosted glass, emitting a diffuse light.

In the administrative building of the *Grola*, Bremen, directly radiating downlights were installed. In order to shine directly downwards, they had to be inserted into the concrete of the staircase at an angle. The round staircase at the *Bahnhof Alexanderplatz* connecting the ground floor with the subway level is an important junction of the train station. Any surface-mounted luminaire would have spoilt the view in this clear space. Hence, flush recessed wall luminaires without frames were used to illuminate the ceiling. The free-standing staircase can readily be brought into prominence.

The austere downlights in the ceiling element of the *Norddeutsche Landesbank* retrace the surface area of the staircase on the ceiling and throw light from above onto the steps.

The recessed point source wall luminaires of the *EXPO Café* in Hannover retrace the curved line of the staircase, while additional downlights provide for the illuminance of 100 lx required on staircases.

The staircase of the *Syltquelle* in Rantum receives a sided light from small halogen spots and projects a varied play of light and shadow onto the perforated sheet metal shade.

The grand conception and the light atmosphere were important aspects in the considerations for the illumination of the elevator cabin of the hotel *Forum Elbflorenz* in Dresden. The cabin is illuminated quite lavishly. The soft canopy of light radiating diffusely over a large area as well as the glass backlighting of the cabin wall originate from fluorescent lamps. The lamp behind the green printed glass had to be fit into a very tight space on the exterior of the cabin. For replacing, the lamp is accessible from the interior of the cabin. Small downlights – positioned in the corners of the elevator cabin to not radiate unpleasantly onto the heads of the users – bring brilliance and an intimated depth into the small space.

30 This staircase with its round landing leads from the underground train to a shopping mall level. Large amounts of light under the ceiling mediate the relation to the upper world.

31 Consciously designed sharp-edged shadows create a unique geometrical play of light.

32 In places where the open airspace above a staircase is not to be disturbed, luminaires radiate out of the ceiling. An arrangement above half-landings makes maintenance relatively easy.

33 The elevator car with backlit walls appears larger than a car with dark walls.

34 At the *EXPO Café*, downlights above the staircase complement step luminaires in the walls.

31

32

33

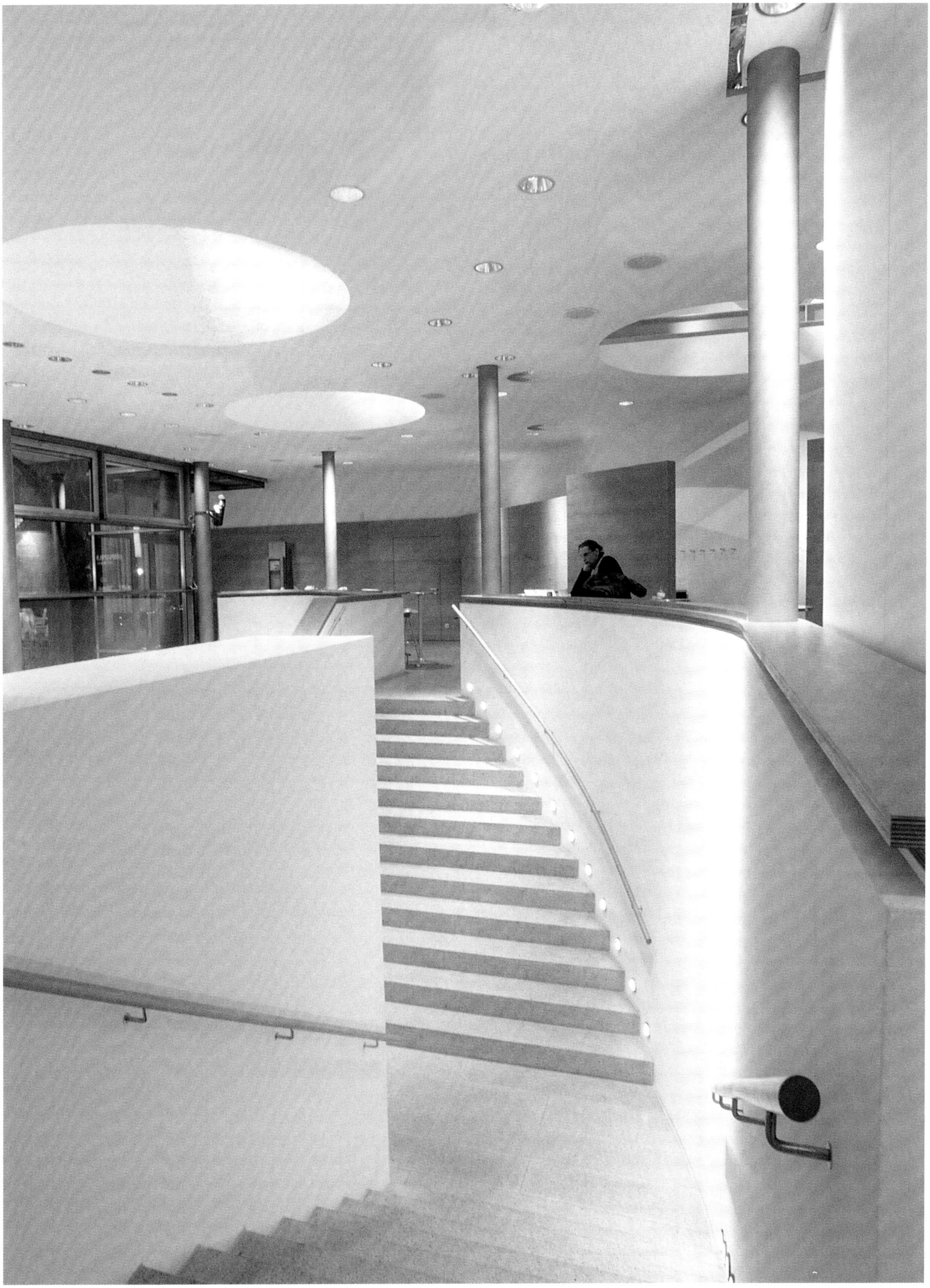

Offices

Today, office spaces are mainly designed as individual work spaces or for two to four people. There are practically always computer monitor work spaces requiring illumination without glare and reflection. As far as the light distribution is concerned, there are several options. The requirements can be fulfilled by means of direct light (e.g. through louvered luminaires), indirect light (e.g. through ceiling washers), or a combination of direct and indirect light (e.g. uplight with desk luminaire).

Light radiating from ceiling luminaires or reflected via the ceiling counts as general lighting. It creates the necessary basic illumination in the room. It may be replaced by work space oriented general lighting or supplemented by individual work space lighting.

The German standard DIN 5035 (Part 1,2,7 and 8) as well as the monitor work regulation (Bildschirmarbeitsverordnung) and the industrial safety act (Arbeitsschutzgesetz) lay down the requirements for monitor work stations.

The visual tasks are various: a person's eyes move from the monitor to the keyboard, to the document and into the room. They must adjust to various degrees of brightness (adaptation) and distances to objects (accommodation). In between, the eyes concentrate on the monitor. In order to avoid additional strain on the eyes, interfering reflective glare on the monitor, the keyboard and the document must be avoided.

The first precondition is the correct orientation of the monitor workplace to the window. The monitor workplace should be at a right angle to the window so that employees are looking at the monitor parallel to the window. If the monitor were in front of the window, the sky's luminance in the window would create too much of a bright contrast to the monitor. If the monitor were positioned the employees had their back to the window, the window would possibly reflect on the monitor.

35   In spite of the purely direct illumination, the ceilings appear bright from the outside: the lightly colored tables and the floor reflect sufficient amounts of light.

36   The facade filters the daylight and conversely allows artificial light to pass to the outside.

37   The ceilings inconspicuously house the various technical functions.

38   Every element can be opened. The luminaire folds down with the panel.

International standards and guidelines require 500 lx as a mean illuminance. This mean value is to be maintained at the work level of the desk (0.85 m above the floor) throughout the room or in the area in which monitor work spaces are situated.

DIN 5035 distinguished between daylight oriented work spaces and other types of work spaces, while the monitor guideline of the European Union (EU) requires illuminances of 500 lx for both situations. And while DIN 5035 demands that the required mean illuminance be maintained throughout the entire room, the EU monitor guideline provides for the mean illuminance only in the work area.

The EU illumination guideline additionally stipulates that the reduced vision of older people must be taken into account by means of additional lighting (e.g. table luminaires). In this regard, however, no specific illuminances are prescribed. The luminances, i.e. the brightness distribution of the illuminated surfaces in the space, should be balanced. Binding values are not mentioned. Too much monotony is just as tiring as too much brightness contrast.

Direct Illumination

At first glance, the direct illumination of surfaces without light absorbing interflections seems to be the most economical method. The stringent requirements on glare or luminance limitation, however, have led to the situation that on account of their mirror screens, directly radiating luminaires now have lighting efficiency factors between approx. 50% and 70%. With limited radiation angles, it is not easy to ensure a uniformity of illuminance throughout the room. Direct illumination only reflects little light via user surface and floor so that rooms with little daylight could seem gloomy and as though they had low ceilings. As far as the client is concerned, low purchase costs often speak in favor of direct light; a built-in ceiling luminaire with a 58 W fluorescent lamp costs approximately half as much as a pendant luminaire with a visible housing. When installing a luminaire, however, one should not overlook the higher costs in a different trade for the construction of a suspended ceiling. Directly radiating luminaires must not be installed exactly above the desk, but must be offset to the side to get no reflections on the keyboard or on shiny documents lying flat on the table.

A good example for the principle of a pure system of direct illumination for offices is the head office of the *Götz GmbH* in Würzburg. The building with a square floor plan and a large atrium accommodates open-plan as well as individual offices. Much daylight enters through its dual glass façade. Slats in the upper area of the windows reflect diffuse daylight into the interior of the building, while the slats in the lower area provide protection against glare. With such a favorable proportion of daylight, even into the inner reaches of the rooms towards the atrium, a pure system of direct lighting is practical. The ceiling height of 4.10 m allowed for a 0.60 m high installation area above the 2.50 x 2.50 m grid of the suspended ceilings. Each ceiling element specially developed for this project contains one built-in downlight. There are cooling grid ceiling elements adjacent to the façade and the atrium which are porous enough not to interfere with the function of the energy storing solid ceilings. 3 TC 24 W downlights with louvered cells against glare provide general illumination. Through their fabric cover, the interior ceiling elements take on acoustic and natural light-reflecting functions. Ventilated downlights with 3 x 26 W provide light conforming to the requirements for monitor work spaces.

Illumination with Secondary Sources

An early example of an office building in which work is done consistently on computers is *Lloyd's* in London. The colored exterior illumination of the building leds to many discussions in the city. The open offices are arranged around a large hall which supplies the inner areas with some daylight from above. With favorable positions of the sun, direct sunlight even enters all the way down onto the large ship's bell which is a central element of the hall. In both directions, joists form squares under the ceilings. One luminaire is mounted in the center of each square, on the elevated ground floor as well as on the upper stories. The lighting designer developed the luminaires especially for *Lloyd's*. The circular lamp of these secondary spotlights is shaded towards the bottom and emits its light downwards only via the large mat anodized reflector. This results in luminances below 200 cd/m².

Direct/Indirect Illumination

The head office of *Pihl & Sons* in Lyngby, Denmark, is located in a building with a repertory of clear forms reminiscent of the 1920s. The generously glazed façade of the entrance hall stands in contrast to the closed western façade of the office which allows measured amounts of daylight fall into the rooms through window openings and slots just below the ceiling. The offices are transparent towards the interior and open towards the access-providing galleries and staircases. The discipline expressed in the selection of a limited number of building materials is also maintained in the small number of luminaire types: The basic element in each case is the T 26 fluorescent lamp which continually reappears as a linear graphical building block: as individual light slots in the ceiling element of the foyer, in the lower edge of vertical daylight reflectors under the skylight and as pendant luminaires in the offices. The indirect portion of light provides extensive illumination of the ceilings. With the direct portion of light, the offices are sufficiently illuminated. The arrangement of the luminaires in a perpendicular direction to the window is unusual and only possible because the direct portion of the light does not exceed approx. 30% of the total quantity.

In the *Bundesministerium für Verkehr* (Federal Department of Transportation) in Berlin, the challenge was to combine the stringent illumination requirements for computer monitor work spaces with further aspects: a design appropriate for the historical buildings and a high energy efficiency. In Berlin, the Federal Department moved into a former building of the *Museum of Natural History* on Invalidenstraße with its new extension. The typical floor plan of the old building features a spacious central hall with surrounding galleries and "smaller" rooms oriented towards the exterior façade.

Separated by dividing walls, the latter now serve as offices. The new dividing walls are only 2.30 m high and glazed above to show the entire vaulted 5.70 m ceiling of the entire long space. The lighting designers supported the architects in their goal of combining together the spaciousness of the old room and the intimacy of the new single offices. The combination of indirect light against the vault (large room) and direct, concentrated light on the desks (small room = office) seemed to realize the goal in the best possible way. In addition, the illuminated ceilings create a bright exterior effect of the windows in the massive façade. Two rails running parallel to the window, which were also used structurally, offered the possibility of installing, among other things, two directly radiating built-in fluorescent luminaires and a batten directed towards the ceiling and likewise fitted with fluorescent lamps. An energy commissioner was in charge of testing all of the installations within the building for their economic efficiency. In accordance to his requirements, a typical office space of approx. 16 m² with a 4 x 54 W share of direct light

43 44 45

46   Good indoor lighting design incorporates consideration of the exterior effect of a building from the beginning.

47   Daylight dominates the office space. Two types of luminaires create direct artificial light: ...

48   ... linear fluorescent luminaires and downlight.

49   The ceilings and hence the rooms may be divided along any of the ceiling panels.

and a 2 x 54 W share of indirect light for the illumination of the ceiling. Upon the express wish of the user, the illuminance does not conform to the EU guideline but rather only measures 300 lx. In spite of the black walls, the required maximum value of 8 W/m² on average was clearly undershot with 6.02 W/m². This is especially due to the high efficiency of the luminaires with the T 5 fluorescent lamp.

The façade of the *RWE* high-rise reveals its internal structure particularly through the lighting effects. The basement is presented differently than the bright foyer. The office floors are differentiated from the conference and technical installation areas. The circular floor plan of the high-rise divides the ceiling level into radial segments. Since a modular dividing wall can be installed along every axis, this requires that every space between two axes be illuminated autonomously. Therefore, a channel for technical equipment was installed at the center of the ceiling elements which accommodates the lighting and other functions in a systematic and discreet way. Two kinds of light complement each other: the soft light of the secondary luminaire equipped with standard fluorescent lamps and the direct light of the downlights fitted with compact fluorescent lamps. The back wall shows the vertical course of light. One can also make out the varying illuminances. While there is a high degree of illuminance in the area of the desks, only the downlights illuminate the area of the shelves.

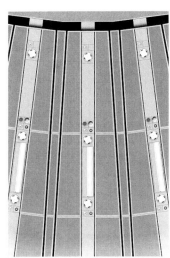

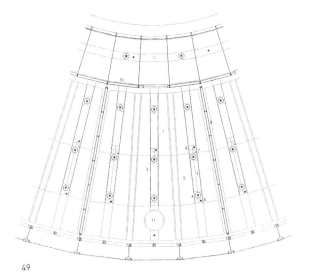

Conference Rooms, Auditoriums and Concert Halls

Conference rooms, auditoriums and concert halls have comparable illumination requirements. Different usage situations require different light settings: slide presentations or other types of projector presentations take place in a darkened room with illumination for taking notes; a lecture without projections takes place in a room with mean illuminances between 300 and 500 lx. In the case of concerts, the orchestral space requires illuminances of up to 750 lx. For soloists, additional stage spotlights are needed. Conference rooms in administrative buildings or hotels have partitions to devide a large room into, for example, three small rooms. With the help of lighting consoles, light must be adjustable to each of these situations.

The *Tokyo International Forum* houses a conference center. From the publicly accessible central hall, visitors may enter auditoriums, a large exhibition hall, theater and concert halls, a mall with shops and restaurants, and an interior courtyard with trees. Three components create a subtly differentiated and pleasant light in the hall: spots installed on the interior side of the façade illuminate the bulging Zeppelin girder on the roof and also represent the Forum to the outside in a distinctive way. The galleries receive light from their ceilings: in a technically very neat and elegant way, each ceiling element accommodates an acoustically active, perforated field and a downlight equipped with a halogen incandescent lamp. In front of the elevators and on a ramp, these built-in luminaires function as asymmetric wall washers. On the first floor, where the overhang of the upper gallery is missing, the principle is reversed: Built-in floor luminaires create an atmospheric sided light on the curved timbered wall. Linear fluorescent lamps integrated into the glass banisters generate the light on the bridges as well as on the partitions to the exhibition hall and on the reception counter on the first floor. From a European point of view, such a large number of halogen incandescent lamps is astonishing in terms of the costs of energy and maintenance. Over 100 downlights below each of the four galleries and the built-in floor luminaires already consume approx. 30 kW. The decision in favor of lamps with such high energy costs is representative of the grandeur and superior quality which was applied to the entire building. When a guest steps into one of the halls accommodating up to 5000 people, the interplay of light and materials creates a particular atmosphere and gives each hall its own distinctive character. The electrical engineering of the ceiling is the same. Here as well a halogen incandescent downlight is integrated into each of the metal ceiling panels as in the undersides of the galleries. In addition, there is the classical stage lighting on the spectators' bridge. The hall with the timbering on the walls, whose lively graining is nicely accentuated in the light of the laterally arranged wall washers, looks warm, almost cave-like. The hall with the back-lit glass side walls presents itself cooler, more technially and neutral. The fluorescent lamps mounted behind the white translucent glass can be dimmed in order to create soft light transitions throughout the space.

In the auditoriums of the *Technical University Chemnitz*, the character of the light changes on account of timbered side walls and a metal ceiling with built-in skylights. While the metal ceiling has a relatively bright appearance during the day, it appears dark in the evening or when the hall is dimmed. Each square metal panel contains a downlight which, equipped with compact fluorescent lamps, creates sufficient lighting for the lectures. Since the very tight budget did not permit dimming of all the luminaires, only every second luminaire is dimmable. Thus, if users want to dim the lights slowly, every second row needs to be switched off first and then the remaining luminaires dimmed down to the desired level. The stage area was equipped with an electrical track with flexible spotlights at various angles of radiation.

With all these switching options, the designer should not forget to keep their operation simple. A clear operating instruction table will help the lecturer quickly switch to the desired light setting. With the appropriate control system, light settings can be programmed ahead of time and then must only be named. The setting "slide presentation", for example, causes the blinds to be lowered and the lamps to be dimmed to 0%, with only the reading light of the lecturer remaining. A setting "lecture" would switch on all of the lamps in order to allow the audience to take notes. Many other combinations are possible and depend only on the number of available circuits.

In *St. Katharinenkirche* in Stendal, concerts and international music forums have been held since the church was renovated. The brick Gothic church was not designed for concert usage and thus new requirements were placed on the acoustics and the lighting system. In order to avoid cluttering the spacious interior of the church with various kinds of ob-

50 The basic illumination is complemented by luminaires directing light onto bridges and galleries. This functional differentiation also structures the space visually in a harmonious way.

4
125

51   The illuminated bulging roof trusses have become
     a symbol of the *Tokyo International Forum*.

52   The light character of the glass façade changes from
     day to night.

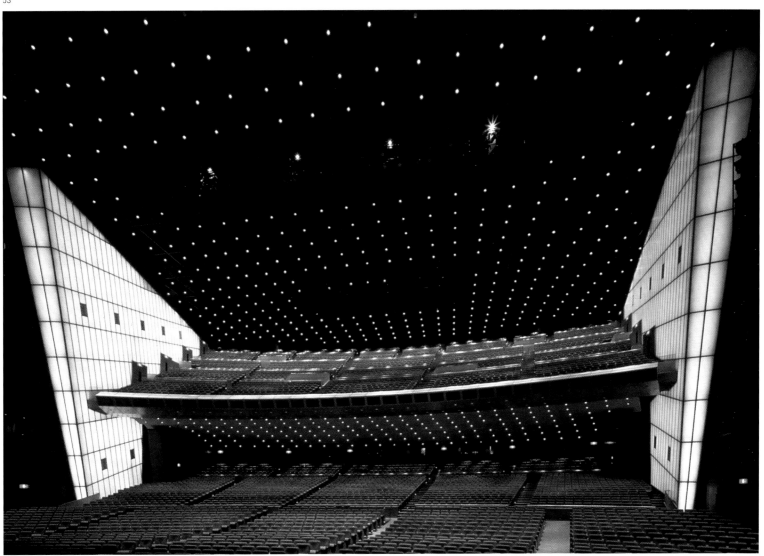

53 Downlights illuminate both convention halls. The vertical surfaces provide their distinct features: the back-lit glass wall ...

54 ... or the illuminated wooden wall.

128

55 This auditorium at the *Technical University of Chemnitz*
    makes effective reference to daylight.

56 auditoriums require light for various usages: daytime
    lectures, slide shows and overhead presentations in a
    darkened space, or improvised theater or concert per-
    formances. The lighting systems should have various cir-
    cuits, at least one of which should be dimmable.

57 Both auditoriums stand freely at the center of the foyer
    of the building. The bottom views of the slanted ceilings
    appear as light objects.

58 Each structural component seems separated from the
    others and appears in a different light. The light
    enhances the effect of the strong colors.

jects, the luminaires were integrated into the acoustic elements. 30 m² of acoustically active surfaces were needed in addition to the surface installed underneath the gallery. Any horizontally installed light element would have destroyed the splendid view into the church's vaults. Therefore, the elements were mounted vertically and are relatively long and narrow. The precise proportions were verified and adjusted by means of a model. The 16 luminaire elements now have a size of 2.90 m x 1.00 m. Constructed like a sandwich (the acoustic material is mounted between two perforated metal sheets), the elements trace the respective crossing in the church's architecture. The integrated luminaires are located in the upper and lower edges of the element. Four of them create a direct illumination, while two create an indirect illumination, which are controllable independently of each other. The dimmable halogen incandescent lamps generate a warm and atmospheric light of maximally 200 lx. They feature a wide beam upwards and a narrow beam downwards. The comparatively limited use permits the installation of lamps with a relatively short life. Since the seats are not fastened, a simple rolling scaffold can

be wheeled under the light elements for maintenance. The exchange of lamps at great heights is more complicated if the floor below is not leveled, as in rising auditoriums and theaters, therefore, the ceilings are often passable. The idea of lowerable light elements is very difficult to realize wherever the audience is located underneath the lamps. Large safety devices disturb the visual impression and are expensive.

The modern, slightly protruding gallery integrates small halogen incandescent downlights in its underside. Behind the acoustic reflectors in the area of the stage platform, ceiling washers complement the light from the panels. The music stands of the musicians are individually illuminated.

The conference room of the *Hongkong-Shanghai Bank* differs from the projects so far described; it is a single purpose conference hall with a limited capacity. The room has a representative function for the bank. The furnishings including the luminaire have been specifically designed and manufactured for this purpose. A reserved general illumination through PAR downlights on the 6-meter high ceiling contrasts charmingly with the spectacular pendant luminaire. Its housing, in section like

59 Artificial light and daylight work together, with halogen incandescent lamps creating a warm effect in the bright vaults.

60 The model illustrates the effect of the light and acoustic elements on the space.

61 The vertically suspended panels produce festive light and good acoustics.

62 The light and acoustic elements trace the diagonal lines of the cross ribs.

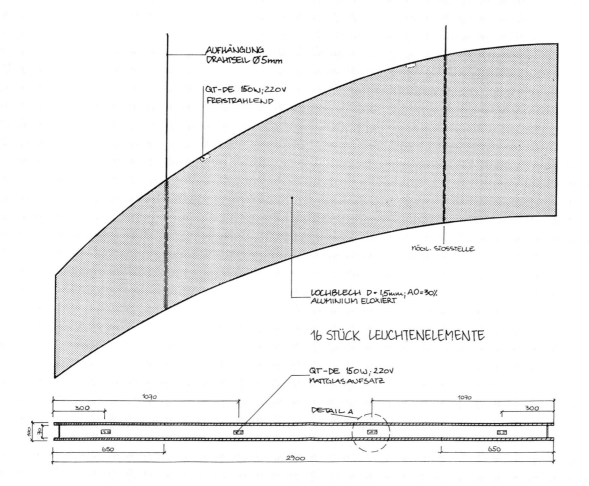

AUFHÄNGUNG
DRAHTSEIL Ø5mm

QT-DE 150W; 220V
FREISTRAHLEND

mögl. STOSSTELLE

LOCHBLECH D=1,5mm; AO=30%
ALUMINIUM ELOXIERT

16 STÜCK LEUCHTENELEMENTE

QT-DE 150W; 220V
MATTGLASAUFSATZ

DETAIL A

1070
300
1070
300
650
650
2900

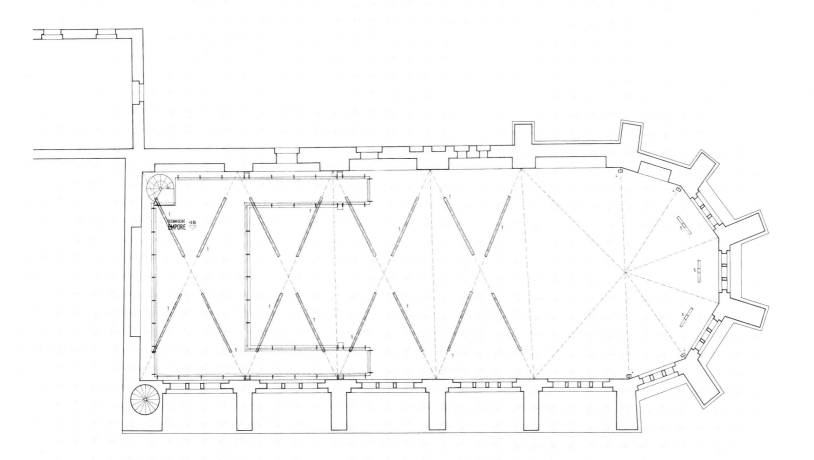

TECHNISCHE
EMPORE -3.95

the wing of an airplane, consists on its underside of a segmented prism lens. Above the lens, 570 halogen incandescent lamps shine on to a reflector installed on the upper side of the housing. They create a soft general light in a horizontal (towards the table) and in a vertical direction (towards the faces of the meeting participants). The prisms spread the individual light points of the small lamps and change the character of the light depending on the angle of vision of the viewer: from a soft illumination all the way to a brilliant glitter. Pairs of directional spotlights with good glare protection are recessed in the inner ring of the chandelier and illuminate the neighboring work space well, from the right side and from the left. Switches for these luminaires are found at each seat under the table top. In various stages of the development of such special luminaires it is important to conduct lighting tests. The course of the light rays is readily visible if smoke or fog is created in a dark room.

In the *Panasonic Data and Communications Center* in Tokyo, employees and guests meet in one section of the large atrium. Softly demarcated islands of light, an intimate silence around every table – almost paradoxical in this gigantic hall: 104 reflectors, threaded in two lines like chains of pearls under the roof, reflect spotlights emanating from halogen incandescent lamps downwards. During the day, the daylight, which is captured in a clever way, especially in winter, and the warm accentuated artificial light complement each other.

63 Another luminaire which was specifically designed for a particular room in coordination with its furniture is the large chandelier in the meeting room of the *Hongkong-Shanghai Bank.*

64 The test at the manufacturer's facility already gives a good demonstration of the precise and at the same time atmospheric light settings.

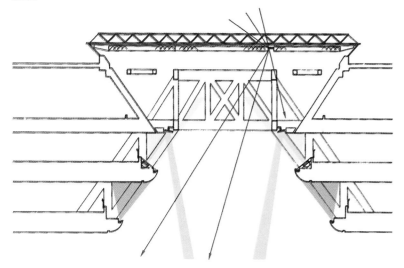

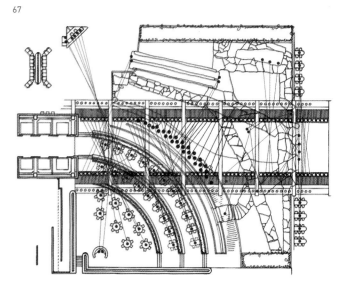

65 In the steps of the skylights of the *Panasonic Data and Communication Center*, redirecting mirrors take the light from upwardly directed spotlights ...

66 ... into the common areas on the first floor.

67 Even over large distances, precise islands of light can be created by means of narrow-beaming spotlights.

Restaurants, Bars and Cafeterias

Restaurants are places where, apart from good food, the atmosphere is most important. Hosts create a pleasant atmosphere by means of good light and good acoustic conditions. These influences are probably more important than the architectural setting. Restaurants also differ with respect to their opening times, whether they can be visited only during the day, only at night, or both, during the day and at night. Everywhere, however, guests enjoy observing and being observed. The restaurant's dining room is like a stage on which people may show themselves "in the proper light". Some restaurants offer a view from outside, others are withdrawn or introverted. To a lesser degree, all of this is true of cafeterias as well.

The dining room of the Italian restaurant *Marema* in Japan has a ceiling height of 6 meters and is almost entirely enclosed by glass walls. Like airy projection surfaces, lengths of material cover part of the large glass front for luminous and acoustic effect. Between the suspended ceiling and the bare ceiling, spotlights throw light onto the projection surface. The light changes color and brightness in a slow and steady rhythm. Simple patterns or graphical symbols enliven the surface and change the atmosphere in the room. For the illumination of the tables, the lighting designer availed himself of a trick: one candle does not supply sufficient light, but it creates a "cozy" atmosphere. Directional spotlights in the ceiling, slightly dimmed and directed onto the candles, imperceptibly reinforce their light.

In the restaurant *Nil* in Hamburg, candles characterize the light atmosphere. The large candelabrum forms the focus of the restaurant and creates warm reflections with its central golden sphere. The airspace connecting the upper level with the main floor of the relatively small restaurant is almost completely filled. By now it has become a regular evening ritual for the waitresses and waiters to climb onto the bar and light the candles and to extinguish them at closing time from the gallery by means of a candle extinguisher.

The *Schiffergesellschaft* in Lübeck is an old established restaurant known far beyond northern Germany on account of its tradition and good cuisine.

The restaurant was originally the "club house" of the Skippers Society, a union of Lübeck captains. The room is dominated by long, precisely lined-up benches. Most of the furnishings stem from the early history of the house. They were, of course, supplemented and renewed in accordance with the needs and the technical possibilities of the respective period. The electric lighting was added carefully and with sensitivity, of course, in various styles. Along with many ship models, there are splendid lanterns hanging from the ceiling. Covered with dyed animal hides, these lanterns have turning silhouettes of ships and fish inside, propelled by the heat of the lamp.

The dining room of the Skippers Society resembles a museum: the walls are decorated with the society's own oil paintings. They were restored in 1998 and were supposed to receive their own light. The decision was in favor of filigreed, modern luminaires with wide-angled optics which distribute the light of the halogen incandescent lamps over a wide area. A lighting test with three sample luminaires showed the suitable quantity of light: too much light would disturb the atmosphere of the room. The new lamps discreetly fit into the historic space.

In practice, it is not always possible to position tables precisely underneath the pendant luminaires planned for them. Hence, general lighting which illuminates the room evenly is often suitable, since it also allows for flexibility in the arrangement of tables.

In the cafeteria of the *Grola* in Bremen, which in spite of its large area only has a standard height, the ceiling is visually heightened by indirect light from the luminaires. With its downlights, by contrast, the suspended ceiling of the room housing the ventilation equipment appears lower. Thus, the room is divided into two different areas: a traffic zone and a dining area. The high-voltage tungsten halogen lamps are staggered to make the light in the room uniform even with a minimal number of luminaires. These luminaires are dimmable. In the evening, this emphasizes the built-in floor luminaires of the roof terrace which integrate the terrace into the visual space of the cafeteria.

The refectory or *Mensa* of the national *Berufsbildungswerk* in Staßfurt, a vocational training school for handicapped youths, received luminaires which can follow the variable positions of the tables. They are in fact industrial work space luminaires installed upside down on the ceiling. During festivities, they are pushed upwards and out of the way. During refectory mealtimes, their light is directed onto the individual tables. The luminaires in the corridor area radiate against the ceiling to provide indirect illumination.

Cafés and restaurants should not only create a special atmosphere inside but also make an impression to the outside.

The *EXPO-Café* in Hannover presents itself to the outside by flooding the walls behind the glass façade with extensive light in accordance with the time of day and the degree of brightness outdoors. The architects did not want to disturb the calm airspace with pendant luminaires above the bar. Hence, four narrow beaming downlights were used to transport light 6 meters downwards, where it forms a series of light circles with a diameter of about 0.5 m.

Since for gastronomers it is important that the chosen light is favorable to their guests' appearance, the architectural effect of the light must fre-

68 Narrow-beam downlights produce light on the tables.

69 The projections change the color of the wall ...

70 ... and hence the atmosphere of the room.

71 At the *Nil*, patrons are afforded an unusual view from the gallery onto the central chandelier. The reflections in the golden sphere are reproduced on the wall lamps.

72 The old floor plan of the dining room of the *Schiffergesellschaft* illustrates the austere arrangement of the space and of the benches, which still exists today.

73 In the course of the centuries, luminaires were added again and again, most recently the upwardly directed wall washers, which make the dark paintings visible.

quently take second place. Hence, warm light sources, which produce a soft, subdued light, are usually suitable. The colors of the bar, tables and also of the walls, which should reflect warm light, play just as great a role with regard to the light effect. Non-glaring and dimmable light is considered pleasant. In restaurants, moreover, the food is supposed to look outstanding, which means that halogen incandescent lamps and ordinary incandescent lamps are frequently the right choices.

Checklist
The typical questions in the design of lighting systems for cafeterias, restaurants, or cafés are:

· What contributes to a pleasant atmosphere for dining?
· At what times is the room primarily used?
· What is the influence of daylight?
· Does it make sense to have a variety of lighting moods?
· Will the space also be used for special events (presentations, Christmas parties)?
· Are individual areas to be separated from each other?

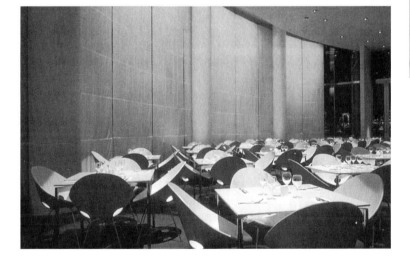

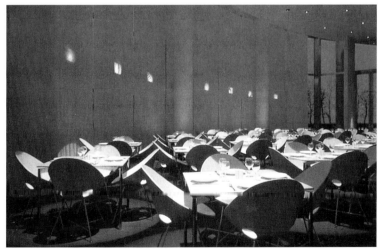

138

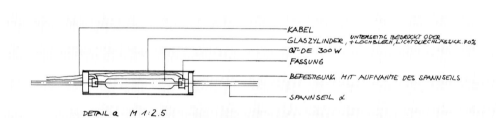

KABEL
GLASZYLINDER, UNTERSEITIG BEDRUCKT ODER + LOCHBLECH, LICHTDURCHLÄSSIG. 70%
QT-DE 300 W
FASSUNG
BEFESTIGUNG MIT AUFNAHME DES SPANNSEILS
SPANNSEIL α

DETAIL α   M 1:2.5

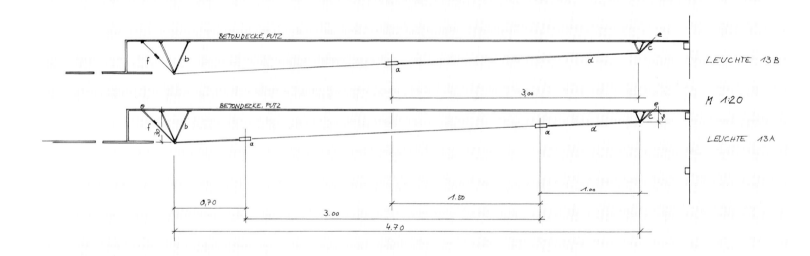

LEUCHTE 13B

M 1:20

LEUCHTE 13A

74 Wire ropes hold the halogen incandescent lamps under
the ceiling of this cafeteria.

75 They radiate downwards through perforated sheet metal,
while creating a bright ceiling in the upward direction.

76 In this dining hall, table luminaires shine their light
downward from the ceiling.

77 The flexible luminaires can be guided to new table positions or may be pushed up and out of the way, when room
for a dance floor is required.

78 In the *EXPO-Café*, free airspace was desired. All light-
sources are integrated into the ceiling and into the floor.

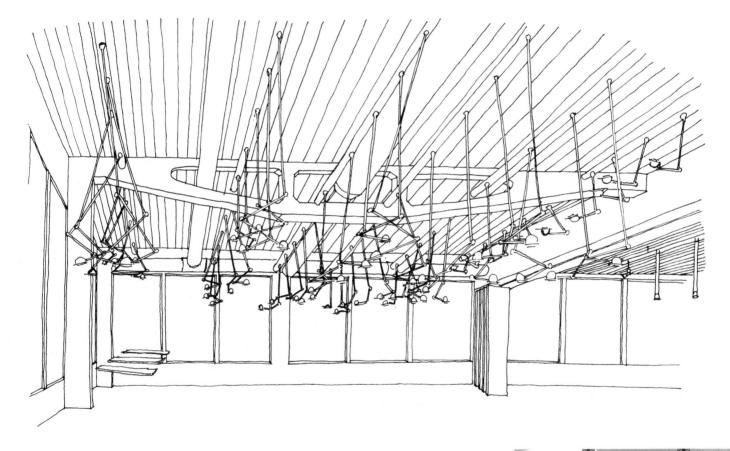

Shopping Centers

The early forerunners of today's shopping centers or shopping malls were the numerous *Passages* which emerged towards the end of the 19th century in Paris. The advances in the technology of sheet glass production in conjunction with modern steel construction made it possible to build shopping streets which were covered and yet flooded with light. People value the advantages of this hybrid space, a cross between the indoors and the outdoors. It allows them to stroll and shop, today like in the past.

Developers and operators of shopping centers understood much earlier than others that professional lighting design has immediate commercial advantages.

The inhabitants of a city or of a district will accept a shopping mall if it constitutes a convenient pedestrian passage from A to B and if it offers a pleasant atmosphere to stay a while. Two factors play a large role in this regard: light and climate. A shopping mall requires a finely tuned light management, particularly in the balance between daylight and artificial light. Even the relation between window display light and mall light presents difficulties. A daylight simulation will detect possible reflections in display windows, while the energy simulation in conjunction with lighting design will help to determine the required sun protection.

Several factors determine the light of the *Nordseepassage* in Wilhelmshaven:

· The entrances are bright, they radiate to the outside and are clearly visible from the street.
· Square built-in downlights fitted with high-pressure sodium vapor lamps.
· The high-pressure sodium vapor lamps generate the important focused brightness from the galleries. Lentiform glass luminaires tied vertically behind the façade provide additional visual stimulation. 5-meter tall pole luminaires stake out an exterior space while providing a warm white general light. The light source is recognizable and not anonymously hidden. A variant with an additional reflector was considered and rejected. The pole luminaires of the cross passage are continued in the street so that like elements exist outside as well as inside and the separation is less perceptible.
· Greater illuminances under the bridges create a rhythm; the mall appears livelier and more varied, especially when people move in a bright-dark contrast and are thus sometimes more and sometimes less illuminated.

· The illuminances on the floor decrease towards the display windows, therefore, light does not reflect too much in the window panes. The best recipe against reflection: the luminances should be significantly higher inside the store than in the mall.
· High-mounted wall luminaires illuminate the warm, red brickwork. Additional spotlights illuminate the high airspace.

Checklist
Daylight:
· Was a daylight simulation conducted? Are reflections and heat build-ups to be expected? Which solar protection measure would be sensible?

Artificial light:
· How are the illuminances and colors of light matched throughout the mall? There are also concepts that use two different colors of light (neutral white for the daytime, a warm white for the evening) in order to achieve more comfortable visual conditions.)
· How bright and intensive are the neon signs of the individual shops? (It would be desirable to have a set of rules worked out by the client, architect and lighting designer in order to avoid visual chaos).
· Is the visitor more likely to approach bright rather than dark vertical surfaces? (Commercial spaces that have not been rented should nevertheless be brightly lit.)
· Does the client require an option for additional spotlights for special promotional areas in the mall?
· Does the electrical installation accommodate for the possible connection of Christmas, Easter, or special events decorations?
· Is the mall accessible after closing time? This would require special nighttime illumination since security aspects would also play a role.
· What draws people into the less frequented upper levels? Lines of vision and good lighting concepts may help in this regard.

Alterations and renovations are especially difficult, since accurate plans of existing installations are rare. From experience, we know that over the years more and more technical installations are placed above suspended ceilings; therefore, surprises are to be expected when construction begins. Complete and accurate plans and documents are essential for proper lighting design as well as for other technical installations.

79 The 19th century arcades in Paris provide a rewarding field of study in the architectural incorporation of daylight.

80 Bright and friendly entrance areas invite pedestrians to step into the shopping arcade. A clear arrangement enhanced by light helps users to orient themselves.

81 Pole luminaires with various spotlights are found outside and inside, ...

82 ... continuing the street scene indoors.

83 Bright areas under the bridges indicate intersections, while sided light on the walls creates a warm atmosphere.

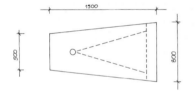

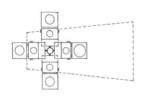

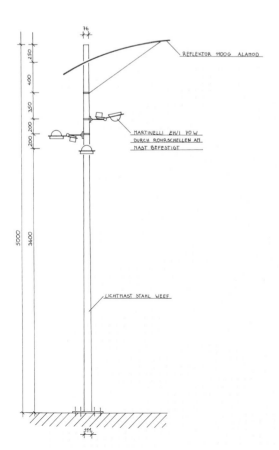

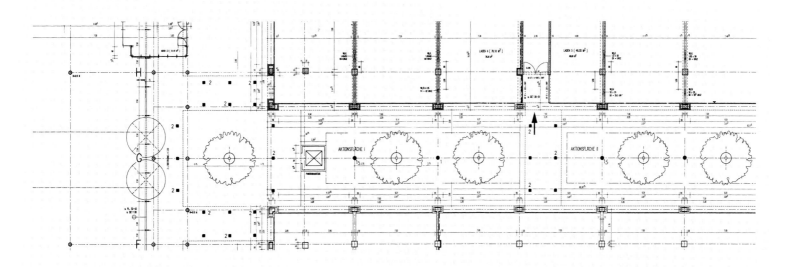

Libraries

One library towers into the sky with four "stacks" of books: the *Biblio-thèque Nationale de France* in Paris – the other burrows itself many stories deep into the ground: the *Nationalbibliothek Österreichs* in Vienna. The stacks of libraries seem endless and they grow on and on. Even if a large part of the immediate exchange and procurement of information can be managed through the Internet, libraries nevertheless offer excep-

tional work conditions with their access to the recorded knowledge of many centuries. The reading rooms of libraries are sanctuaries of peace and concentration.

A former hospital built in the 15th century today houses the *Biblioteca de Catalunya* in Barcelona. The current reading rooms are located on the upper level. The unplastered walls, the distinctive flying buttresses and the visible timber frame structure of the gable roof make this an unmis-

takable location. Also the daylight reflected from the reveals of the overhead windows almost appears filtered. During the day, low-voltage halogen spots mounted on a lighting track at a spacing of 0,5 meters create the vertical illuminance on the shelves. Due to their extensive and uniform beam, the books are clearly visible all the way to the floor. The valuable old books may only be illuminated using UV filters. The reading areas recall in an imaginative way the "good old" brass lamps with the green shades, as they were found in the *Bibliothèque Labrouste* in Paris and in many other establishments. The modern successor consists of a contoured housing with a curved frosted glass diffuser in which two fluorescent lamps, one behind the other, each illuminate a pair of facing workplaces. In the evening, the artificial light imitates the asymmetry created by daylight: small metal halide lamps beam into the reveals of the windows along one side of the room. Only on this side do upwardly di-

rected and narrowly focused halogen incandescent lamps accentuate the consoles and flying buttresses. They are mounted behind the bookshelves and hence do not disturb the clear appearance of the room.

The alternation of the various colors of light of the metal halide lamps, the fluorescent lamps and the halogen incandescent lamps is an intended feature of the design.

The *Bibliothek am Luisenbad* in Berlin is housed in a building which unites old and new walls in a sensitive and exciting manner. In preserving old remnants of walls and sections of buildings, the architects had the intention, not of glossing over or whitewashing history, but of displaying "injuries" and of integrating them respectfully into the rehabilitated building. The result is a district library of high architectural value which, particularly in terms of lighting design, features several thrilling details. Almost everywhere, the luminaires form an integral part of the architecture, permeating inside and outside, floors and ceilings. Considering the small budget which the designers had at their disposal, it was the dedication and perseverance of the architects which made the unconventional lighting solutions possible.

Skylights, a glass façade and small window sections cover the whole gamut of daylight integration options in a harmonious way.

The "table", an oversized protrusion into the reading room features a surrounding shelf with embedded work surfaces. Downlights integrated into the floor of this table and into the ceiling below provide light not only for that part of the reading room but also give off light upwards which shimmers through a round glass brick.

The radial strips of light in the ceiling of the reading room were worked with similar precision and care for particular requirements. They seem to break through the glass façade, thus negating the separation of inside and outside.

Such lamps built into the ceiling require precise planning and detailed descriptions for the tradesmen.

The *Mira Mesa Library* in California has a completely different character. Situated in rather unspectacular surroundings, the building plays on the alternation between closed and open architecture. The architects seek to enliven the solidity of traditional public libraries with new vigor and dynamism. The various functional areas in the interior are not separated by walls but by distinct furnishings. Thus, even a small staff can manage the library effectively.

Wide-beaming fluorescent lighting systems mounted closely under the ceiling create vertical brightness on the shelves. A skylight borders on the unconventionally arranged reading area, which receives much light from the courtyard. Outside and inside there is a loosely distributed group of street lamps, which due to their low mounting heights throw a personal and cozy light onto the colorful armchairs. As the architects proudly point out, the young people of the town are especially fond of this place.

86   The lighting slots of the library at the Luisenbad penetrate the façade.

87   What seems like of a complicated special luminaire ...

88   ... is actually a simple corrosion-proof luminaire, which was recessed into a ceiling slot.

89   Here is another play on the theme of indoors – outdoors. The pole luminaires, which, amazingly, are standing on the carpet of an interior space, ...

90   ... are also continued in the inner courtyard.

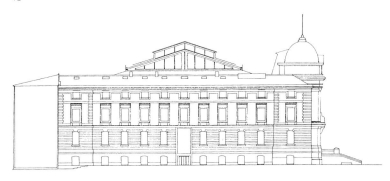

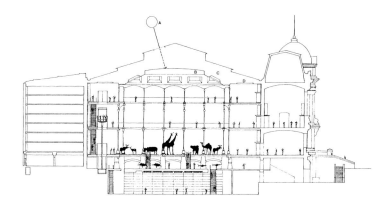

Museums

The illumination of museums is a complex and difficult task. Two requirements on light must be reconciled: the displayed objects must be highly visible, but at the same time many of them are very sensitive to light. Museums come in many varieties. Two contrary types are the staging or animating museum for objects of art, natural history, technology and human history and the museum which aims to offer no more than a neutral background, e.g. a art gallery. Both make use of different types of light management and different techniques.

The *Galerie de l'Evolution* in Paris belongs to the first group. The architects Chemetov and Huidobro won the competition for this project because they did not seek the required expansion of the museum in an annex but rather moved the space for the temporary exhibits below the building. Their idea was to explicitly display the new, modern part very clearly and to preserve the old in the historical part of the building. One of the principal questions for the lighting designer was whether, as was

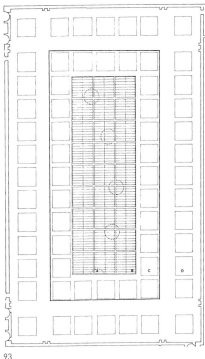

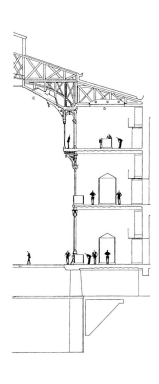

91 The animals in the hall of the *Galerie de l'Evolution* tell the story of the procession of the animals into Noah's ark.

92 Originally, the hall received daylight, ...

93 ... should it be allowed in again, even if in a reduced manner?

94 The artificial sky recalls the daylight ...

95 ... of the various continents at different times of day and in different seasons.

96 A musical composition accompanies the light atmospheres.

97 The designers were not very keen on the starry sky, but the public loves it.

98 The light from the hatches in the ceiling changes constantly. At times, it is bright with long shadows, at other times, it is softer and darker.

99 The bottom view of the ceiling and the section of the hall without the surrounding galleries. Sections offer a convenient means of verifying the directions of light.

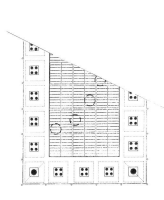 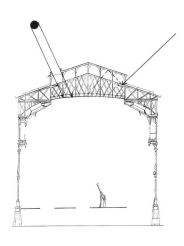 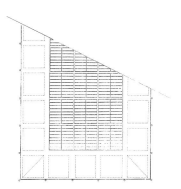 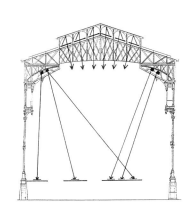

originally the case, daylight should again be let into the museum or not. The initial consideration pursued the goal of bringing daylight back in. But the first inspections revealed a gigantic interior space exuding 30 years of non-use: the dusty exhibits seemed to doze in this gloomy place. By the time one's eyes had finally adjusted to the prevailing dimness, one found oneself already among the exotic animals. The lighting design was supposed to help salvage some of this atmosphere for the new museum. The section and the drawings show some of the ideas regarding daylight. Since the exhibits are extremely sensitive to light, a reconstruction of the glass roof would have required an expensive sun protection system which, moreover, would usually be closed. Hence, an artificial sky, the *ciel actif*, seemed to offer the better solution. In the 17-meter space between the roof and the vaulted glass ceiling of the hall, spotlights could easily be installed which, directed against the white underside of the roof, would produce a soft and extensive reflection. The spotlights mix their colored light of variable intensities to create ever changing moods in the "sky". In this way, the *ciel actif* recalls the various native landscapes and continents of the exhibited animals. Associations with different times of day and seasons also influenced the design. These visual effects are combined with music, a composition for instruments and the most diverse repertory of animal sounds.

The *ciel actif* emits diffuse light. Thus it is suitable for influencing the room as a whole but not for staging the individual animal exhibits on the ground level of the hall. The surrounding hatches in the ceiling accommodate various spotlights with halogen incandescent lamps which are partly equipped with contoured lenses or gobos. The central control

also changes their light, dimming it or letting it emerge. This can create surprising effects: two spotlights illuminate an animal from two sides, and in the slow transition of the brighter light from one side to the other, the animal seems to move. The large group of animals in the central hall represents the procession of the animals into Noah's ark. Grouped around it there are small arrangements of interactive toys and learning tools, some using light effects. Upon clicking on an animal symbol, a text appears on the screen; at the same time, for example, the monkey will be illuminated high up on a branch, or the armadillo sitting between other species, and may thus be identified. The historical pendant luminaires above the galleries form a further component of the lighting concept. Originally conceived merely to complement daylight, they do not contribute substantially to the illumination of the room, even today. They are equipped with compact fluorescent lamps and form attractive pools of light – nothing more. In order to ensure that the objects are clearly visible in spite of the demand of the restorers to limit the illuminance to 50 lx, the surroundings are kept dark. The main light on the galleries was installed in the display cases themselves, partly in the form of halogen incandescent lamps and partly through the use of fiber glass technology. The entire lower level of the museum shows the animals of the sea. Here fiber glass lamps with small optics (prisms, lenses) shine light onto large and small exhibits. A blue basic light creates the underwater atmosphere. Glass walls reaching up to the ceiling form transparent backgrounds for the exhibits mounted in open space. Light is fed into the upper and lower edges and becomes visible on the frosted glass surface.

100 The variety of exhibits requires individuated light: the reserved basic light of the historical pendant luminaires ...

101 ... alternates with soft islands of light.

102 The colors of light vary as well: warm-white light shines on the land-bound animals.

103 The pale whale skeleton reflects light well, contrasting nicely with the background.

104 Using a panel with light switches, visitors are able to illuminate the animals that interest them.

105 The underwater animals in the basement are bathed in a blue light. Light fed in via the edge makes the glass walls glow.

106 A planetarium has a lot of blue: the blue light
of the sky ...

107 ... corresponds to the blue of our planet Earth as seen
from space. Here the art of the architectural lighting
designer resembles that of the stage lighting professional.

The *Museum of Natural History* at Central Park in New York received its nineteenth annex at the beginning of the year 2000: a planetarium. It is one of the *New York City Landmark Projects*. A glass hall encloses a sphere with a diameter of approx. 30 m, within which projections of the starry sky are carried out. The sphere is also suitable for projections from the outside and moreover demonstrates the proportions in the solar system: the sphere itself represents the sun, and the hovering planets are represented on the same scale. The lighting designers used powerful color filters in order to accentuate a given thematic focus by means of color. Thus, the blue color of the celestial sphere is reiterated in the entrance hall, where three light domes emerging from the coves are presented in intense blue. These illustrations show that the principle of enhancing contents of the museum by means of colored light is supplemented by two further principles of light, one illustrated by the light from display cases, floors, walls, and balustrades. Many objects and illustrated charts emit from within, often simple backlighting from fluorescent lamps.

A third principle consists of the spotlights which, recessed in lighting channels almost invisible, illuminate the exhibits from great distances. The large spiral ramp leads into the dark sphere; the balustrade, in turn, has many small backlit charts. Again, colored light falls downwards, recalling the spectral colors of sunlight. If one looks along the glass façade from top to bottom, one will recognize the individual lighting systems. Below the glass strip along the edge of the roof and above a maintenance catwalk made of grating there is the row of aligned light boxes equipped with fluorescent lamps and anti-glare louver blades which emit a blue light. These find their counterpart in the light coming from below in the area of the balustrade of the gallery on the first floor. The dim light of the blue hour at the time of the photo makes the blue color appear softer than it really is. A contrasting effect is achieved by the warm light of the halogen incandescent lamps which throw their narrowly focused light directly onto the objects.

108 The lower level shows almost exclusively backlit panels and objects, which produce the most intense effect in areas with little daylight.

109 The bottom view of the corridor that provides access to the sphere accommodates discreetly directable spotlights.

110 While the sphere always receives blue light from the arrays of floodlights, ...

111 ... the ramp can take on all the spectral colors of sunlight.

112 Soft shadows pass across the surface of the sphere. The light from above and below reveals the three-dimensionality of the sphere.

113 Captivating images arise at dusk, when the planets move in front of the illuminated windows of a New York apartment building.

158 The *Museum Inam* near Toyama in Japan accommodates the works of the region's carvers and stonemasons. The British architect Peter Salter designed a complex building with light chimneys and many closed exterior walls set in a mountainous landscape that is often covered in several feet of snow. The rooms are well suited for displaying exhibits in artificial light. Tapering and opening corridors create new views between large and small rooms. All of the light emanates from built-in floor luminaires (outside), built-in wall luminaires (corridors), and flexible spotlights on lighting tracks in the exhibition rooms. The spotlights produce shadow plays as in the two-story air spaces and in the exhibition areas.

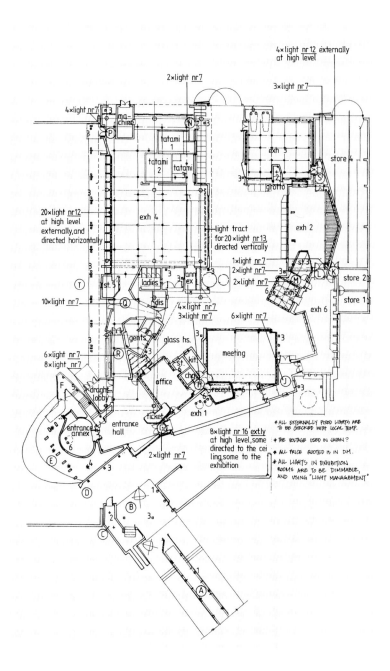

114 The *Museum Inam* is located behind a mountain range.
In summer, the peaks disappear in the clouds, while the
winter landscape is covered in waist-deep snow.

115 The craft exhibits are displayed in interlocking succession of rooms, which plays on the alternation between
large and small, high and low, bright
and dark.

116 In place of general basic lighting, the concept relies
exclusively on the light directed onto the exhibits.

The cultural center *Jean-Marie Tjibaou* in New Caledonia also belongs to the staging variety of museums. A dramatic effect is achieved through daylight management as much as through artificial light. The wooden shell act as protective shields against wind and weather. The northeastern, windward side only lets in a small amount of light; the windows are additionally shaded by the numerous trees in front of them. Soft and mild daylight enters through the wooden slats of the outer façade. The light atmosphere is unusual in its sequence from bottom to top: At the very bottom there is a bright window, in the middle of the wall there is wood of a mid-brown tone, above, there is dark wood and a dark ceiling. Individual halogen incandescent lamps on the ceiling, equipped with anti-glare shutters as in a theater, emphasize parts of the exhibited sculptures. The warm halogen incandescent light goes well with the wood and contrasts the daylight. The open connective corridor prepares the visitor for the dim light of the individual "huts", the exhibition and special event spaces.

117 Illuminated by a point source of light and set against the backdrop of a nearby wall, the filigreed carvings cast clear shadow.

118 Uniformly lit spaces ...

119 ... are succeeded by a narrow and high area with light emanating from lateral overhead windows, reflected diffusely downward by the ceiling.

120 The small amount of daylight from the lower quarter of the room creates a mystical atmosphere, in which spotlights emphasize parts of the sculptures.

121 The huts shut daylight out almost completely.

122 The *Fondation Beyeler* utilizes daylight across its entire roof area.

123 The filtering roof juts out far beyond the façade, thus protecting the windows against direct insolation.

124 The soft, uniform light in the exhibition rooms ...

125 ... creates a calm and neutral background. Spotlights with soft compact fluorescent lamps supplement the daylight when required.

The *Fondation Beyeler* near Basel, a museum by Renzo Piano, follows exactly the opposite lighting principle. The entire roof area of 4000 m² allows diffuse light to enter: the museum is bright! The exhibition spaces are aligned alongside a duct with technical installations conceived as a "backbone". The museum affords many views of the natural surroundings – the sole backdrop of the sculptures and paintings, aside from the subtle architecture of the museum itself. The light creates a neutral and functional background to the exhibited objects. Through its multi-layered structure, the roof filters the daylight. On top there are inclined sun protection elements facing south. They consist of glass and are covered on one side in white enamel. The glass plane below constitutes the building's proper shell. The girders also support electrical current duets which supply an artificial lighting system consisting of numerous floodlights with compact fluorescent lamps. Suspended metal grid elements covered with white fabric hide the lighting installations. The final level, at a distance of 1.40 m from the upper glass roof, a glass ceiling forms the lower enclosure of the roof space.

124

125

126 A square is created in the landscape by means of light. In
the twilight, it is marked by points of light secured
by long cables.

127 The sense of space is created by the façades surrounding
the *Campidogli*. The square is darker in the center than
at the periphery, where brighter areas are subtly differentiated.

Public Squares, Exterior Spaces and Master Plans

In recent years there have been more and more opportunities for supplying lighting guidelines for entire urban development designs. Light
constitutes an outstanding and economical means of creating a shared
space for a variety of buildings.

In the case of new developments for which development plans already
exist, it is easy to find a starting point for a typical lighting scheme.

The existing architectural fabric is often quite banal; therefore, the only
option is to add a further atmospheric component to the functionally determined light, by leaving the buildings in the dark, for example. The
light for pedestrian zones, streets, and squares should be designed by taking junctions, overriding axes, important views and architectural
"treats" into account. Although grown districts are more chaotic, they
have a lively charm; here the difficulty is for the lighting designer to keep
his technical possibilities in check. The motto should be "less is more!"
One of the world's most beautiful and peculiar squares is the *Campidogli*
on the Capitol in Rome with its ground curved towards the center. How
fortunate that the Italian authorities did not insist on a uniform illumination of the square! The sense of space is created solely by its enclosing
walls, the façades. No more than one row of discreet light contours are
created on the façades by a warm white, three-dimensional light from incandescent lamps. The edge of the roof is discernible because the roof
surround and the statues appear in an ingenious counter light. Twelve
street lamps, in circular formation and in groups of two, mark the entrances of the square and of the houses. A little light on the clock, the
fountain and the statue completes the harmonious picture of the public
square. It seems alive in the light of the night because the mat, dark
paving stones reveal a nice contrast to the pale shine of the marble.
Although not exactly a square, an intersection in *Lisbjerg*, Denmark, is
nevertheless a special place due to its unusually accented illumination.

The junction linking a number of traffic arteries lies in a flat landscape.
The designer marked it with a luminaire construction reminiscent of the
securing rope structure of a circus tent, making it visible from afar. Due
to the extensive network of cables it was possible to position pendant
metal halide lamps above the road with a precision impossible to achieve
by means of regular pole luminaires. The example shows how imaginative lighting design can turn even an ordinary road into a charming place.

The grounds of *Schönbrunn Palace* are a very popular place in Vienna.
The entire park is designed in a strictly axial manner and contains a very
beautiful zoo. As a look-out, the *Gloriette* offers a magnificent view over
the park and the city of Vienna. The managing body of the palace sought
a general lighting concept for the park, even though the individual sections would have to be realized over a number of years in many small
construction stages and in part still need to be completed. Thus, it all began with a master plan which ties in all the individual projects.
The lighting concept for the palace and its grounds aims at making visible the spatial relations between the individual buildings. The illuminated elements will be:

· the obelisks at the entrance
· the cour d'honneur (Ehrenhof)
· the northern façade of the palace
· the Neptune fountain
· the Gloriette
· the Rundbrunnen fountain
· the obelisk
· the Sternbrunnen fountain
· the pavilion in the zoo

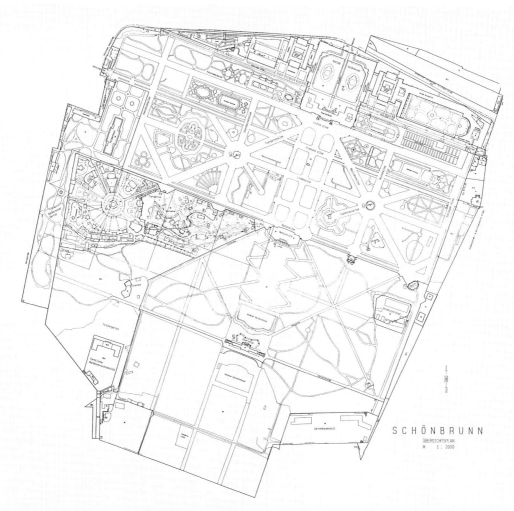

SCHÖNBRUNN
ÜBERSICHTSPLAN
M 1 : 2000

128 The *Neptunbrunnen* was one of the first newly staged
structures on the palace grounds of *Schönbrunn*. During
certain festivities colored spotlights complement the
normally white light.

129 The master plan defines the connections between the
light characteristics of the individual objects. All of the
projects realized in subsequent years abide by the stipu-
lations of the master plan. Today, the views have been
enhanced and the nocturnal park provides a tasteful setting for the illuminated objects.

130 The *Gloriette* appears in its full three-dimensionality,
since the center is brightly illuminated, while the
receding sides are kept a shade darker.

The Obelisks at the Entrance

The main axis of the palace grounds runs through the palace and the
Gloriette and extends through the Schloßallee boulevard all the way to
the Museum of Technology. If one approaches the grounds from this direction, the two eagles on the entrance obelisks frame the Gloriette. For
the long-distance effect, only the eagles receive bright, bundled light,
while the obelisks at the base remain in darkness to give the eagles the
appearance of flying.

The Cour D'Honneur (Ehrenhof)

The two fountains are important design elements; the sculptures in their
centers are illuminated by means of spotlights. The arcades to the sides
receive little light, one can still discern the park beyond.

The Northern Façade of Schönbrunn Palace

The former illumination made the façade look flat. In reality, the façade
is structured into various vertical planes. The new lighting concept emphasizes these various planes. The eastern and western wings received
more light on their fronts, the adjacent areas of the façade received light
at a medium level of brightness. The central part of the palace is illuminated in a very reserved manner. The entrance below the large staircase
appears as a bright passageway and highlights the pilasters in the area of
the first and second upper levels in their three-dimensional quality.

The Neptune Fountain

If one enters the grounds from the palace, one steps out-of-doors, yet one
has the feeling of entering an enclosed, defined interior space at the end
of which is the Neptune fountain. In the field of vision above the fountain is the Gloriette. There is also a view across the Rundbrunnen to the
obelisks and across the Sternbrunnen to the pavilion of the zoo.
The light emphasizes this relationship.
The Neptune fountain consists of a dramatic sculpture above a large and
peaceful pool of water. From here, the ensemble receives its basic illumination extending over a large area. Dramatic light accents from below
make the Neptune group come alive.

The Gloriette

At night, the Gloriette seems to hover above the palace. Formerly it was
illuminated too brightly and ostentatiously. A refined floodlight brings
out its architectural features in a more subtle way. Every pillar received
a single spotlight. The ceilings of the Gloriette were brightly illuminated.

Like the light on the northern façade of the palace, the light on the façade
of the Gloriette varies in brightness so that the various planes which
stand out very nicely in daylight appear three-dimensional also at night.
The central area is more brightly illuminated, while the side wings remain in a dim light. It was also important to ensure that the trees in front
of the Gloriette were not included in the illumination, therefore, the
building does not continue to be smothered by vegetation.

The Rundbrunnen

The Rundbrunnen is located in front of the obelisk. In this spatial context, it receives a fine and pointed light falling onto the sculpture in the
center of the fountain.

The Obelisk

As an upright element, the obelisk receives a narrow beaming, vertical
strip of light beginning at its base. The lower areas of the obelisk are
darker. Reflections of the light on the surface of the water complete this
lighting concept.

The Sternbrunnen

In the Sternbrunnen, underwater luminaires make the surface of the water appear calm and glowing. Here, in contrast to the Rundbrunnen, the
topic of a large area of illumination is broached, as it is in the case of the
pavilion.

The Pavilion in the Zoo

The pavilion forms the center of the zoo which extends in a star-shaped
arrangement around it. The pavilion with its baroque yellow façade is illuminated across its entire area. Light also emanates from within the
pavilion in order to show its vivacity.
In this project, which has not yet been completed in all its sections, the
qualitative improvement of the nighttime appearance of the grounds is not
only a delight for the visitors and the client, but also means economic savings on account of the lower energy consumption of the new luminaires.
A new and very different park, one which there are numerous features
or pavilions, is the "automobile city" *VW-Autostadt* in Wolfsburg. In recent years, the Volkswagen company acquired many makes of cars which
are now likewise presented in the new park. Situated directly in front of
the factory premises, the Autostadt is readily visible from the center of
town and from the railway station.

The lighting design in the *VW-Autostadt* in Wolfsburg takes into account the perspectives of the visitor and observer from the town and from the railway station.

The modeled park and lake landscape receives discreet and atmospheric light. In this landscape, the pavilions glow like bright crystals. There is a contrast between buildings and landscape, between brightness and darkness, between point-source and linear light which marks the transitions between landscape and water. Functional, technical and atmospheric illumination complement one another.

The park with its pavilions stands in marked contrast to the technical-functional illumination of the parking lots and access roads. Low light sources with warm white colors accentuate the paths and the topography of the park landscape and highlight certain areas, while others are left in the dark. The reserved and atmospheric style of lighting is continued in the area of the buildings and pavilions so that these structures, whether they are illuminated from the outside or from the inside, may be fully appreciated. Side emitting fiberglass units trace the curved embankments to the south in the form of a line. The paths following the embankments receive sided light from built-in ground luminaires. Bridges and planks connect the small peninsulas. Orientation luminaires on the lateral concrete ledges discreetly retrace the contours of the bridge. Built-in luminaires installed low in the banks illuminate the access roads to the elliptical, transparent customer center. In addition, diode luminaires built into the ground mark the access roads to the building. The tower basin to the north with its underwater luminaires creates a calm surface for the car towers which, like a round set of shelves, display the production of the previous day. Unfortunately, the idea of the lighting designers to integrate the headlights of the cars into the lighting concept, has not yet been pursued.

Light accentuates the building supports and the glass wall sections of the hotel driveway. Surface-mounted downlights in the canopy of the hotel entrance and sided light near the ground from built-in ground luminaires complement one another. Next to the tables of the outdoor sitting area, electrical outlet posts facilitate flexible temporary lighting.

Low pole luminaires mark the promenade south of the water basin; the luminaires are aligned with the axes along which the trees are planted. At the embankment there are only occasional pole luminaires. The edge of the bank itself was consciously left dark in order not to interfere with the splendid view of the curved promenade across the water which is traced by side-emitting fiber and built-in ground luminaires. Low pole luminaires and treetops illuminated by spotlights accentuate the southern path along the embankment of the canal.

In terms of their type of lighting, the parking lot and the park differ substantially. The parking spaces receive a neutral white light from tall (25 m) pole luminaires. The distribution of the pole luminaires is very economical, since their height allows for large spaces in between. Besides, they ensure a uniform illumination without glare.

In spite of the great diversity in the architecture of the pavilions, in the light at night they give the impression of belonging together. The aim of the overall lighting concept is to coordinate the nighttime effect of light in its intensity and colors on the façades of buildings with the effect of light emanating from inside the buildings and with the light emanating from the park landscape. For the buildings featuring large areas of glass, a nighttime reduction of light levels will allow the building to be accentuated through interior lighting.

The last ten years have seen the development of an increasing sensitivity for city lighting. At least in some cities, the days of the flat and isolated floodlighting of buildings are over. The city of *Lyon*, has received much attention in this regard, hence some other examples shall be mentioned here.

Another well-illuminated city is *Edinburgh*. The lighting designers had the task of finding "a fresh, innovative (…) interpretation of the city after dark which highlights its history and tradition by means of the new developments in lighting technology". In accordance with this task, the lighting designers focused on the skyline of the city at night, developing hierarchies of buildings and determining the relations of skylines, embankments, look-outs and distinctive topographical features in order to arrive at a common conception for the entire city. This master plan is now the model for all districts of the city in which new lighting systems are implemented step-by-step.

131 The lighting plan shows the hilly terrain between
the tributaries. Low light delicately traces the landscape
with exciting effects.

4
169

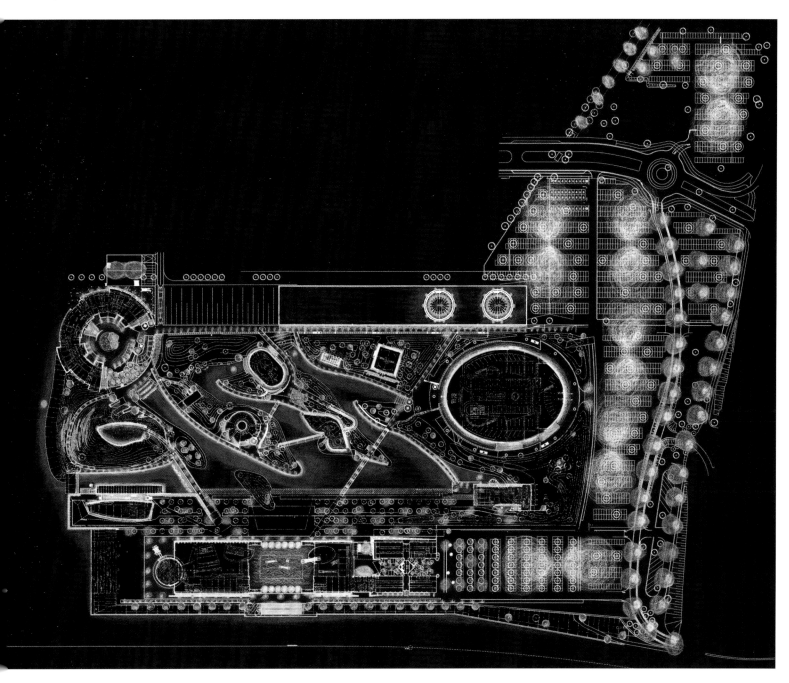

132 The relative darkness of the park allows the pavilions
to shine brightly.

133 Calm expanses of water reflect the surrounding
buildings.

134 The sided light on the ground shows the way ...

135 ... but does not prevent the view into the distance.

The projects presented here progress from a single square to parks and on to ever larger areas. One of the largest projects is the master plan for the illumination of *EXPO 2000* in Hannover.

EXPO 2000 differs from previous world fairs by taking place on a partly existing site and on a building area, the ground of the Hannover Trade Fair. A large number of the newly erected halls and pavilions will remain to be used further more in the future, as operators and investors hope. Thus, the illumination of the exterior spaces of the exposition grounds had to be planned not only for five months, the duration of the exposition, but also for the continued usage of the grounds by the Hannover Trade Fair, the city of Hannover, and the Land of Lower Saxony.

During the months of the EXPO, the sun sets at 9:30 p.m. in June and at 5:00 p.m. in October. The grounds are usually open until 10:00 p.m., frequently also until 1:00 a.m.

Different lighting conditions affect the experience of the EXPO: brightest sunshine or gray and rainy days, various cloud formations, twilight, different colors of the sky and the darkness of the night are all part of the basic atmosphere of the grounds. The lighting master plan supplements the various daylight scenes with artificial light and uses them artistically. The plan creates a unifying structure and network covering the entire exhibition grounds. The premises accommodate a great variety of elements: buildings of high architectural value but also buildings displaying less aesthetic sensitivity, and they all come in a wide assortment of sizes. Add to this a new landscape: squares (large and small), parks, boulevards, streets, and finally parking lots. In this manifold environment, light is the common denominator. As a public phenomenon, light is visible to everyone. And thus it can connect the most diverse areas, while being featured in a manifold of artistie designs. Every area receives its lighting in accordance with its function and its design. In a manner typical of world fairs, certain lighting elements correspond to those of other areas, they coalesce in new ways and refer to each other in a manner visible to everyone. The light also varies in terms of the mounting height. The height of the light source greatly affects the atmosphere. A high source of light produces a uniform but rather anonymous light (as floodlight in a stadium). A lower mounting height achieves a more intimate light, radiating a sheltering atmosphere (as good illumination does in pedestrian zones). And light from the ground appears even closer since it shines in the opposite direction as daylight.

Between these extremes, the master plan provides for an extensive repertory of light scenes which could lead to a varied and yet harmonious whole at *EXPO 2000*.

The light for the individual EXPO areas was designed in distinct ways:

The Entrances

Open roofs receive a combination of indirect light on the ground and indirect light against the roof structure. The illuminances measure 100 lx in peripheral areas and otherwise approximately 15 lx. EXPO marks embedded into the ground bear the glowing EXPO logo.

The Parking Lots

The parking lots are illuminated uniformly and sparingly. The arrangement of the luminaires follows a strict grid pattern. Orientation and structure is achieved through emphasis on the surrounding tree-lined avenues. Here, the color of the light is warm and the mounting height is low. In the parking lots the color of the light is neutral white, and, at 16 m, the mounting height is significantly higher than in the surrounding tree-lined avenues. The illuminance is approximately 12 lx.

Highlights

The "highlights" are found at the end points of large streets and avenues as well as at junctions connecting the old and the new areas. They create attractive light sculptures or continuous light shows that also facilitate orientation.

The most important junction is the flight of stairs and bridge connecting the existing fair grounds with the new pavilion grounds. The light of a high-mounted spotlight falls through a holographic-optical element and paints a rainbow onto the bright steps.

Pavilion Areas

Like the landscape design, the light in the areas of the pavilion is reserved and discreet. This provides a calm background for the varied architecture of the individual pavilions.

Pole luminaires provide direct light. They follow a strict grid pattern and a designed hierarchy. Low light accentuates the intersections, thereby forming a rhythmical pattern. The EXPO marks reappear. In these areas, the illuminances are between 15 and 20 lx, and in some cases reach up to 150 lx.

Green Spaces

The green spaces are designed along a variety of different themes, each with its own particular lighting. In certain areas, light is concentrated through an accumulation of luminaires, while other areas remain dark. The points of light are designed as though they were scattered by accident, the light is variable and lends a dramatic air to plants and objects. The illuminances in this area vary from 0 to 200 lx in order to achieve powerful contrasts.

Urban Squares

The squares in the EXPO grounds are urban in character. This includes light accents which provide orientation and make accessible space for people to move around in and to spread out.

Bridges

The bridges connect the fair grounds with the new eastern pavilion area. Illumination on rows of poles makes the bridges visible from afar. The ground surfaces of the bridges are lit from the poles. The illuminances measure 20 lx, on the steps between 100 and 150 lx.

Important Streets / Axes

As the most important connective axis between the fair's railway station and the EXPO Plaza, the Allee der Vereinigten Bäume (Avenue of United Trees) was equipped with special light. The build-in ground luminaires underscore the treetops, while accompanying pole luminaires provide a transition to the steles of the bridge leading to the Plaza. The remaining streets and paths in the fair grounds feature, as far as possible, reserved lighting through pole luminaires combined with low luminaires at the intersections. In the case of narrowly spaced buildings, it was possible to provide light by stringing tubular lamps across. Some streets are enhanced through projections against the façades. Important streets and main axes are illuminated at 15 lx, secondary streets are lit at 5 lx.

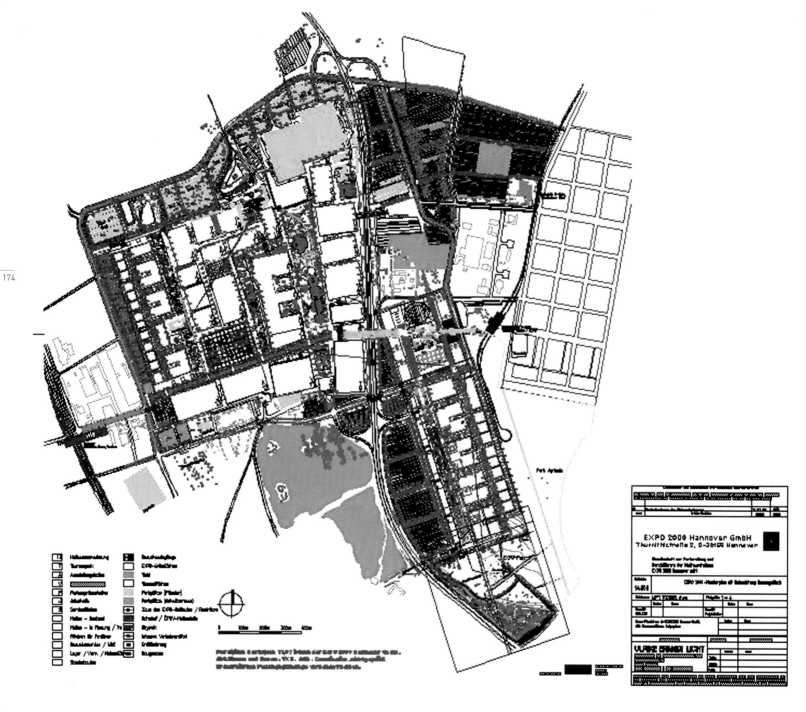

136 All of the additional detailed plans are based on the
urban master plan for *EXPO 2000*, which was constantly
amendet and updated.

137 The lighting master plan specified the nocturnal light
settings and the types of light. Connecting paths and
main axes require a different light compared to parking
lots. Gardens and plants require a different light compared to important squares and intersections. And yet,
everything belongs together.

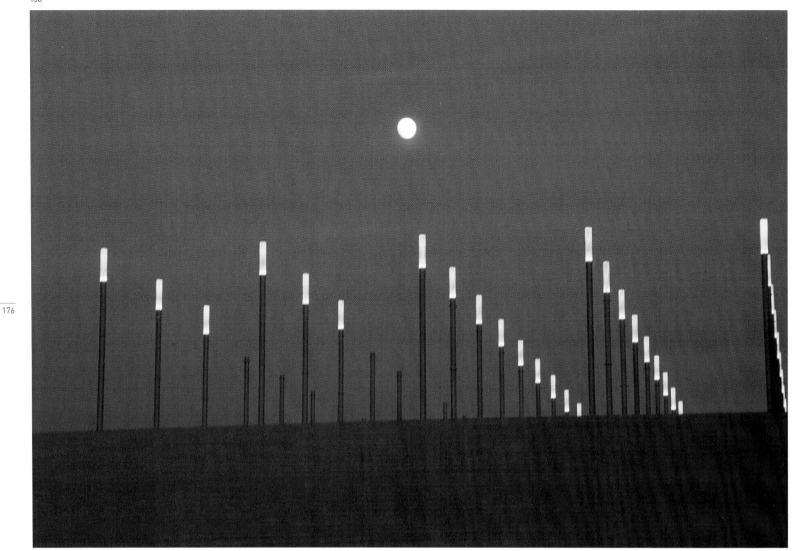

138 While the majority of the luminaires belong to the family of specifically designed EXPO luminaires, exceptions to this rule are made in special places.

139 Such places are the bridges with their dual rows of luminaires.

140 They were part of the ideas of the Hamburg based architects Gerkan, Marg and Partners presented in the competition and were then incorporated into the lighting master plan.

141 The idea stated in the master plan – that each element of a bridge receives its own luminaire and that this luminaire illuminates precisely its element of the bridge – could only be realized to a certain extent.

142 Holographic-optical elements mounted in front of the spotlights break the white light down into the colors of the rainbow.

143 The tallest luminaires of the EXPO family of luminaires are found in the parking lots.

144 Intersections are especially emphasized.

145 The lightwave in the pavilion grounds East and West: wide floodlights and narrow-beam spotlights alternate with varying illuminances on the ground.

146 The parking lot luminaires with a height of sixteen meters emit neutral-white light, while the eight meter lamps give off warm-white luminaire.

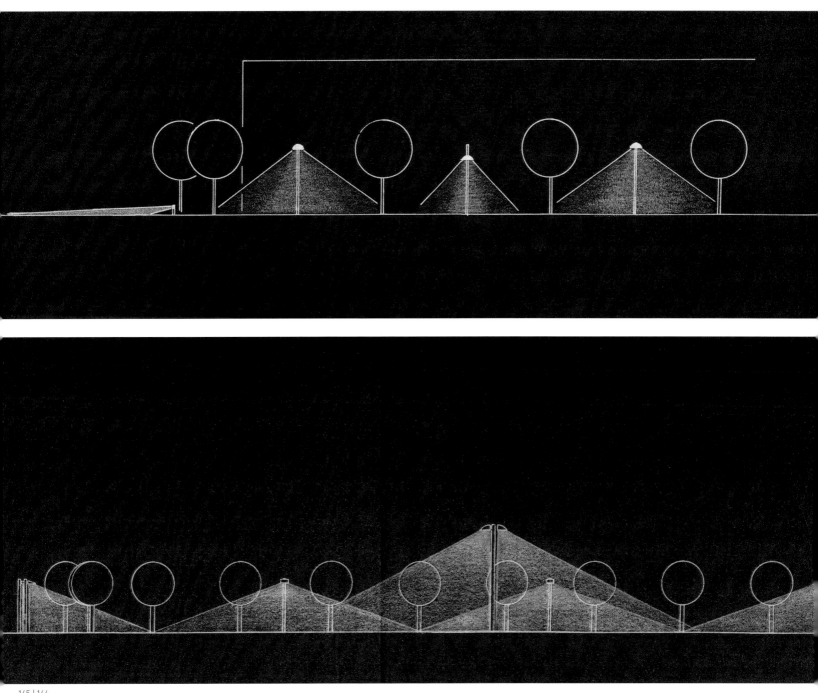

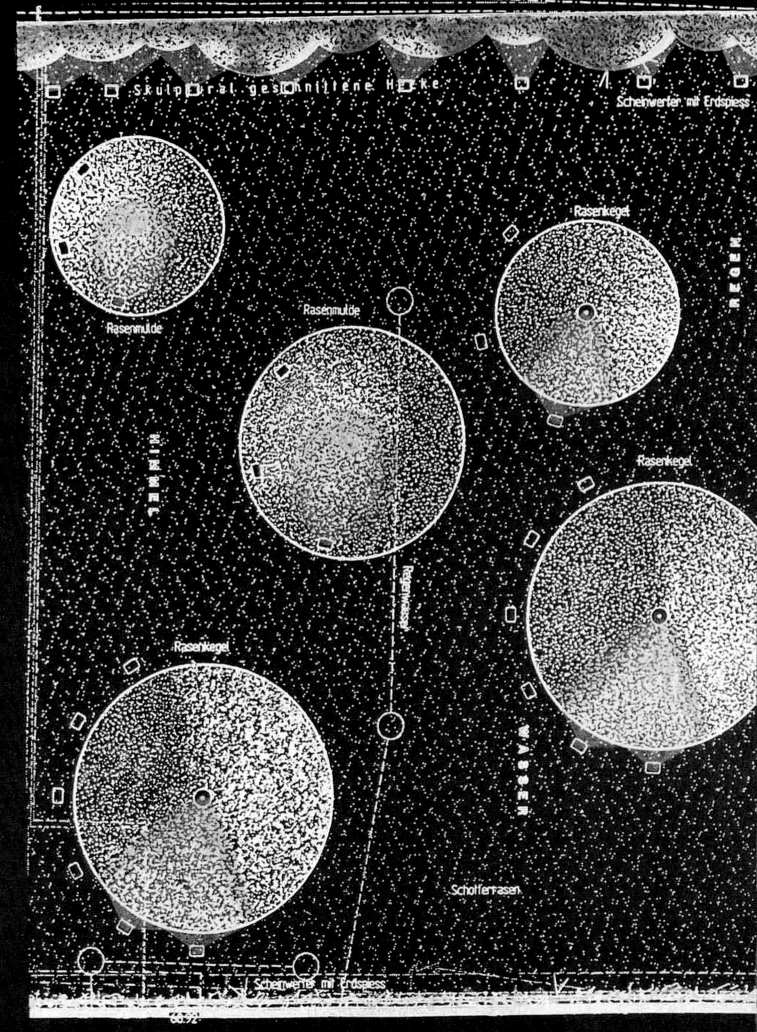

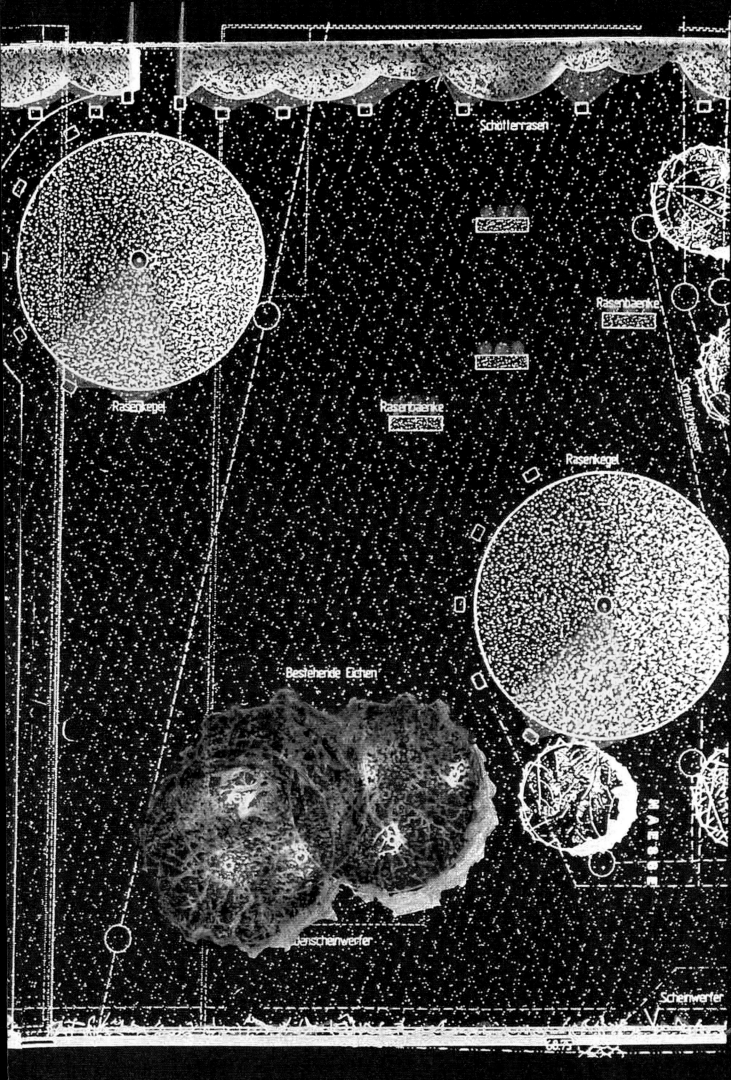

147 (Previous page:) Visitors are amazed at the sight of
    the lawn cones in the "Earth Garden".

148 Illuminated by day with sunlight ...

149 ... and from below in the evening.

150 Originally, the light was supposed to travel – like the
    light of the sun.

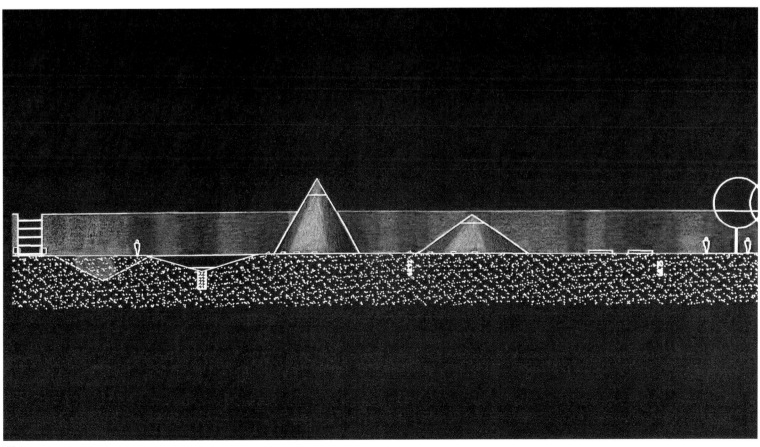

151 Next to the EXPO lake, the EXPO roof covers a large area parts of which are occupied by wooden buildings. Blue light from side-emitting fibers marks the water´s edge.

152 The indirect light reveals the beautiful structure and the soft curves of the roof.

153 This detailed view shows the narrow-beaming spotlights hidden high in the pillars.

154 White and partly green light illuminates the trees in the park wave, creating islands of light.

155 Sided light from the hedges accentuates the "waves" in the ground.

156 The *Allee der vereinigten Bäume* or "Avenue of United Trees" forms the main axis between the fair grounds train station, the EXPO lake and EXPO Plaza.

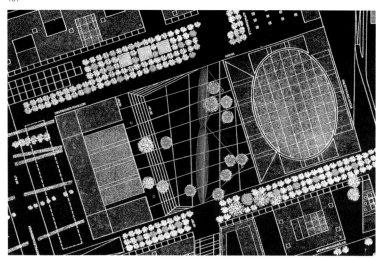

The EXPO Plaza as a large-scale, open, central space features four poles which permit very flexible and variable lighting. The basic lighting consists of an illuminated diagonal which forms the main crossing of the Plaza. The hollows around the trees receive low, warm and local light.

Summary

Designing lighting systems for exterior spaces can span several years, and the resulting installations must perform over several decades. Once a community has decided on a certain canon of luminaire types, it will not want to change it every couple of years.

During the design of the lighting master plan for *EXPO 2000* there were, as in any construction project, practical problems which affected designing: what made things difficult was the fact that two clients were involved in the project: the *EXPO 2000* GmbH and the Hannover Messe AG. In part, these two participants pursued different interests which sometimes made reaching decisions difficult.

After the lighting master plan had been commissioned by a single overall authority on the part of the *EXPO 2000* GmbH, this jurisdiction dissolved upon completion of the master plan and its approval through the committees. During the phase of preparing the construction documents of the lighting systems, there were three project managers among whom the grounds were divided. These three project managers followed the guidelines of the master plan with varying consistency. This is one of the reasons why exactness of execution is not the same in the three areas.

On one important point of the concept *EXPO 2000* did not follow the lighting designers: the idea to invite independent designers to a competition for a "family of luminaires". Instead, this competition took place among luminaire manufacturers. The result is quite different to an independent design competition, for a manufacturer must act much more pragmatically within the framework of his product line than an independent design firm would have done. Hence, the product was less avant-garde than it could and should have been at a world fair. Fortunately, the family of luminaires now used is very beautiful and matches the master plan guideline. A very different practical problem arose through the supply of luminaires on the construction site. Electricians were not, as usual, commissioned to supply and install luminaires. Rather, the luminaires were bought directly from the manufacturer and the electrician only provided the installation service. In such a case, it is very difficult to determine who is responsible for errors, the supplier or the electrician. If one party is responsible for both, supply and installation, this question is solved for the client.

157 The plaza offers space for tents for various events. Trees stand in sunken pits lined with steps. Diagonal streaks of light trace the main visitors´ path.

158 The seating steps of the tree pits and rises are lit from within.

159 At times, steam exits from the gaps in the steps, an effect which is dramatized by the light.

160 The illuminated *Erasmus Bridge* is a nocturnal symbol of Rotterdam. During the day, the bridge blends in rather modestly with the light of the sky.

161 The glass *Skywalk* in Hannover glows as a filigree dual tube.

162 Fluorescent luminaires behind rib mesh also let the *Skywalk* shine and shimmer from below.

163 The luminaires are integrated into the structure and not visible as independent objects.

Bytes

Bridges

Bridges capture the imagination. They connect people and conquer valleys, ditches, rivers, roads, channels in the sea and are civil engineering projects of sometimes gigantic proportions. No wonder that they tend to become landmarks. The *Erasmus Bridge* in Rotterdam is such a landmark. In the asymmetric construction, a pylon of a height of 139 m holds the bridge with wire cables. Architects and lighting designers were searching for light to emphasize the inner side of the pylons, while leaving the outer side in the dark. The cables and the pylon form a new space which only arises with the light. The color blue seemed to be appropriate for the floodlight. At certain times of the day, the bridge is hardly distinguishable from the color of the sky.

The *Skywalk*, which connects the trade fair train station with the EXPO grounds across an unattractive street, presents a wonderful and unusual case. The *Skywalk* is one of the first construction projects completed for the *EXPO 2000* in Hannover. It is approximately 350 m long. Transparent tubes accommodate speedwalks for the transportation of visitors and provide sheltered access to the grounds. As the characteristic element of Münchener Straße, the *Skywalk* runs along the center of the street and forms a kind of "backbone", existing independently of the surrounding developments. The transparency of the *Skywalk* and its construction provides for an interplay between inside and outside. The road surface is designed like a uniform carpet structured through a 6 meter grid which takes up the grid of the structure of the railway

station. Light is generated from two functionally independent lighting systems. The general illumination of the traffic areas by means of pole luminaires creates a static and uniform light. The lighting inside and underneath the *Skywalk* is accentuated and adjustable. The pole luminaires follow the 6 meter grid and provide the required uniform illuminance at a lengthwise distance of 30 m between poles and a pole height of 8 m. At both ends of the *Skywalk*, the distance is shortened to 24 m. In addition, luminaires are positioned in the axes of the entrances and exits, providing visual emphasis to these important areas. In the lower part of the *Skywalk*, there are fluorescent lamps installed behind transparent paneling. This illumination is supposed to enhance the visual effect of the light and transparent construction. The curved

ceiling in the interior of the *Skywalk* is backlit during the EXPO with computer-controlled colored light. The blending of the basic colors red, yellow and blue at varying intensities produces a lively, continuously changing atmosphere of light. This "movable light" will accompany visitors on the "people mover" from the train station to the western entrance of the EXPO. The luminous intensity distribution is darker at the center and brighter towards the sides, thus bringing out the arch of the ceiling even more dramatically.

Like the *Skywalk*, the *bridge* of the *Miho Museum* in Japan also represents an entrance to an enclosed site. The *bridge* of the *Miho Museum* additionally leads into a tunnel to let the visitor experience an extreme transition from brightness to darkness, from open and airy

164 The entrance tunnel of the *Miho Museum* turns into
a bridge and offers spectacular light experiences due to
the abrupt encounter of daylight and artificial light.

165 At night, the light conditions are reversed: ...

166 ... against the dark sky, the tunnel appears in a glaring
light.

167 The tunnel with its low ground light and the dark
vaulted ceiling does not smooth the transition to daylight.

surroundings to a subterranean, enclosed space. Only the sides of the road on the bridge receive light so as to draw attention to the illumination. The radially arranged wire cables of the bridge's structure themselves resemble rays of light. The front outside wall of the tunnel and the tunnel itself appear just as dazzlingly bright. Built-in floor luminaires with halogen incandescent lamps illuminate the outside wall. Precise positioning and direction of the spotlights and the over-lap with more distant light sources prevented distracting shadows of the wire cables on the outside wall. In the interior of the tunnel, special lights installed at a height of six feet, partly shaded towards the front, create fiery light and complement the continuous band of indirect light in a wonderful rhythmical pattern. During the day, the light effect is reversed: the tunnel appears bright, while the exit to the museum is dark.

168   A cross section of the railway station *Alexanderplatz* in Berlin ...

169   ... and a longitudinal section with the historical base of the viaduct and the spacious hall from the 1960s.

170   The lighting test reveals the colors of the light in the large and small fields. The yellow light was subsequently performed less yellow.

171   Not only the light on the platforms but especially the light in the trusses of the roof give the hall an interesting and friendly atmosphere.

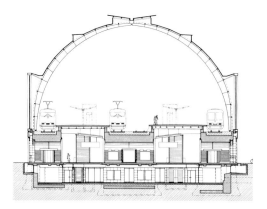

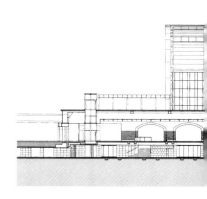

Railway Stations

Railway stations often consist of imposing, self-supporting platform halls and appurtenant structures such as ticket booths, underpasses, restaurants, kiosks. The spacious halls present an ideal field of activity for a lighting designers. The other areas of railway stations are presently taking on an increasingly uniform look in Germany – causing one to look with wistful nostalgia at the photographs of old train stations with their peculiar characteristics.

One railway station which, in spite of its renovation for new commercial uses, has not lost its history in its present appearance is *Alexanderplatz* station in Berlin. In a first step, the architects exposed what was left of the original building, constructed around 1880, following the alterations of the 1920s, 1930s and 1960s, thereby developing a concept which they called "temporal layers". On the lower levels of the viaduct, under the typical arches, shops were installed behind simple glass panels which leave the old walls visible. Recessed in the historical walls, there are rectangular luminaires illuminating all the ceilings. Some of these luminaires flood light within the arches in order to increase their height visually and to convey a light, friendly impression upon entering the train station. In the two mall areas with their high ceilings, additional luminaires shine against the level white ceiling contrasting the suspended metal ceiling. This ceiling suspended at an angle hides many necessary technical installations above and contains slots for direct lighting. The lighting slots were equipped with special slats to minimize reflections in the display windows. The way to the lower level is unusually open and attractive: it leads down a round staircase which almost gives the impression of being a small arena. The ceilings in the lower levels and underpasses are low, and often there are no suspended ceilings. Recessed downlights with shallow installation depths, surface-mounted downlights, or wall luminaires solve the problem. The new lighting of the hall is simple and effective: pendant luminaires with metal halide lamps mounted high above the ground illuminate the platforms. Since the platforms are designed in bright colors, much diffuse light is reflected into the space but also back to the ceiling, giving it a light appearance. Narrowly focused spotlights installed into the trusses accentuate the rhythm of the axes. Even though all of the luminaires used in train stations must appear on an internal list of approved luminaires for train stations of the

170

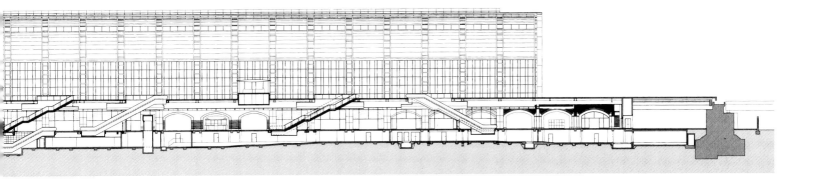

172 The round staircase connects the underground station with the shopping mall level.

173 Recessed built-in luminaires, especially developed for this project, ...

174 ... illuminate the ceilings above the staircase and above the mall.

175 The lentiform luminaires are a recurring theme of the train station's architecture. With the glass insulators of the overhead lines, these luminaires liven up the curved bottom view of the wooden trusses. Due to the northerly directed skylights, the daylight quality is exceptionally high.

176 The entrance to the train station at *Oslo Airport* already has a downward curvature in its ceiling.

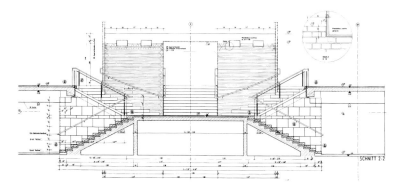

Deutsche Bahn, it was possible to use a modified luminaire (lighting slots in the metal ceiling) as well as two specially developed products (the built-in wall luminaire in the viaduct and the light-emitting diode strip at the edge of the platform). Recessed alongside the guiding strip for the visually impaired, the light-emitting diode strip signals the edge of the platform. The light strip takes on various flashing and lighting functions. Operational experience has shown that the diode strip works well and that passengers do not step too closely to the edge of the platform. In addition, it provides a discreet aesthetic attraction.

The *railway station* at *Oslo Airport* is exceptionally beautiful. It is adjoined to the airport in such a clever way that one can simultaneously watch trains and planes from a single vantage point. A low area at the edge of the hall forms the transition to the train station. At first sight, the oversized, lentiform luminaires seem astonishing. While in other areas the use of luminaires is reserved, here they present themselves as objects. Only when one turns to the platforms it becomes evident that a new lighting theme has been introduced – the train station luminaire is distinct from the airport luminaire. The designers also designed this luminaire especially for the airport. The luminaires large surface distributes the luminance well. As the luminaires also radiate upwards, the wooden trusses are illuminated at nighttime as well. During the day, the soft light from the northerly oriented shed dormers provides a warm and pleasant atmosphere.

Airports

An airport represents the "gate" to a city or an entire region and thus helps determine the first impression a visitor receives. Airports organize the simultaneous movement of so many people that light is a very significant means of orientation. The superior aesthetic quality of a lighting system must be accompanied by an efficient use of energy and simple maintenance procedures.

Brisbane Airport with its three-story building was equipped with a glass façade in order to make use of the sunny climate of Queensland. The lighting concept provides a harmonious blend of daylight and artificial light to allow plants grow on the one hand and, on the other hand, to highlight the sculptures and other works of art displayed in the building. During the daytime, a number of cloth kites below the glass roof project a beautiful play of light and shadow onto the ground, while serving as sun protection. After sundown, the spotlit kites shape the evening and nighttime atmosphere in the hall. The

gates in the departure area appear as an orange corridor of light and guide the passengers to the airplane by means of built-in floor lamps. The subtly differentiated interior lighting makes the building gleam at night.

In 1993, *Hamburg Airport* received a new terminal as well as a new pier. The new departure hall with a ceiling height of up to approximately 24 m is characterized by daylight. Almost a third of the roof's surface is taken up by neutrally colored sun protection glass, while the remaining ceiling area made from silvery sheets with trapezoidal corrugations provides a good reflector for the indirect artificial light. Thus, daylight and artificial light alternate in a lively manner. The approximately 350 metal halide spots are hidden from the travelers on the check-in counters and on the support heads. They do not disturb the view of the spacious hall. Other areas and especially the pier also receive much daylight, the "support" of artificial light is needed only in the evening hours. Through a skillful positioning of the skylight with

177 *Brisbane Airport* seems very transparent, thanks to its bright ceiling. The illuminated bottom views of the ceilings are continued on the outside.

178 The hall of Terminal 4 at *Hamburg Airport* is enlivened by the curvature of its ceiling and the abundance of daylight.

179 Hardly visible above the check-in counters are ceiling floodlights which brighten the ceiling at the onset of dusk.

180 Groups of spotlights illuminate the pillars and the roof.

181 The pier too features reserved artificial lighting and a great influence of daylight.

respect to the softly reflecting wall, the lighting designers and architects were able to achieve optimal daylight factors.

Probably up to 85 million airline passengers annually will soon visit the new *Chek Lap Kok Airport* in Hongkong. Its roof area is so large that it is visible from space. Nine barrel-shaped roofs with a span of 36 meters and centered skylights cover the two large halls which are connected by a pier. The roofs consist of 128 sections of 36 x 36 m. Only about 10% of the triangular glass surfaces of the roof are open to sunlight, which, in Hongkong, enters at a very steep angle most time of the year. Below the glass roof there is a row of light diffusers, called "bow ties" by the designers, which have a shape formally derived from the diagonal strut-braces of the roof. It prevents excessive luminance contrasts between the glass surfaces and the closed roof area. The bow ties consist of perforated metal and also accommodate the artificial light components: especially the indirect luminaires which bathe the undersides of the barrels in a soft light that diminishes towards the outside and replaces the daylight in the evening. In each half of the barrel, additional ceiling washers shine, with very asymmetric optics spaced at two meter intervals, against the ceiling and achieve a lighting effect over 18 m. The middle duct which houses the electrical wiring also accomodates the directable metal halide downlights which enhance the indirect light with a direct component. The beautiful course of the light on the undersides of the ceilings continues seamlessly on the eaves outside of the hall.

186 The section also shows the lighting concept for the lower floors: there is a visual connection towards the upper level and in addition there is much indirect light on ceilings and walls.

187 The roof is composed of long arches, which feature skylights at their highest point.

188 The reflector elements, which direct the sky's light back against the ceiling, also hide the luminaires.

189 Pairs of wooden joists support the roof of *Oslo Airport*.

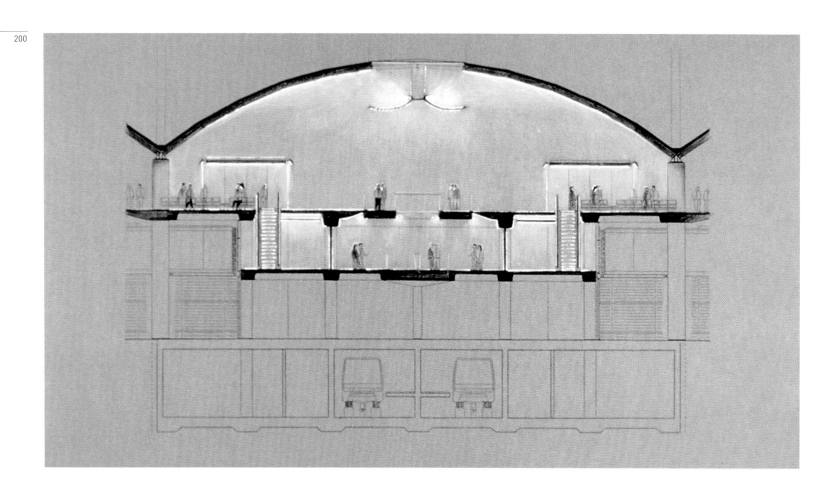

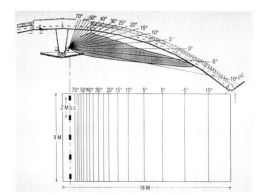

186 | 187   188

The same principle of the lighting designers, but under a completely different type of roof, makes the glass façade of *Oslo Airport* transparent and hardly noticeable: the same type of lamps are used inside and outside. The architecture of the airport lives through its remarkable clear span and the natural combination of glass, wood, concrete and stone. The large hall receives diffuse daylight through the roof. It opens towards the runway and the approach side with large glass facades which shape the character of the departures level as well as that of the arrivals level below. Here as well, the lighting designers developed special main laminaires for this airport: In the large hall, between curved wooden trusses, there are downlights which produce the basic light of the hall (therefore, they are also switched on during the day). In the evening, ceiling washers mounted in pairs on the pillars or, alternatively, arranged on separate, delicate poles in groups of four illuminate the 17 m high ceiling. On the arrivals level there is a pendant version of the ceiling washer.

The glass skylights only cover 8% of the roof area, and daylight which enters through them passes through additional filters, a perforated metal ceiling of 50% translucence below the glass and 30% translucence below the closed areas of the roof. In spite of the glass, the office structures built into the hall are elegantly shielded against too much public exposure: a second façade made of wooden slats reflects light softly and reduces the harshness of the glass. In the façade area of the offices and lounges, warm wooden strips, indirectly illuminated, determine the effect towards the hall. Even the arrivals area on the lower level, which is often neglected, receives much daylight. On both sides, large air spaces establish the connection from the bottom to the top. Only the middle area must do with low ceilings. The timbering of the ceiling, covered in white lacquer, appears higher than it is, since here, as well, ceiling washers provide extensive brightness. In this area, direct light is only found in secondary corridors. The grand, wide pier is flooded with daylight, glass façades on either side and recurring high ceiling sections with side-windows create the opening to the Scandinavian sky.

The ceiling of *Terminal 2* of *Munich Airport* covers the grand hall with its large airspace like a sky. Like the dual façade, the dual shell ceiling construction forms a volume, a moulded upper enclosure of the space. As the sky has its firmament, so the roof has an outer shell with closed glass surfaces. As the sky has its clouds, so the roof has its suspended diffusion panels. Three daylight situations determine the artificial light: When the sun is shining and the skies are blue, the glass surfaces have a bright appearance, the rays of the sun enter through the window, and the panels partly shield against light that is too intense. At the same time, they reflect the light diffusely against the undersides of the closed surfaces. When the skies are gray and cloudy, indirect light directed towards the solid ceiling creates the lacking natural brightness and brilliance. When it is dark outside, the alternation between cool light against the solid ceiling and warm light through the light elements creates a three-dimensional formation of background and clouds. The pillars supporting the roof appear as vertical lines which are illuminated by narrowly focused spotlights. The suspended ceiling elements do not touch the façades. They keep the distance necessary to offer the guest a full view of the façades all the way to the top. Near the façades, there are the only few spotlights of the hall which are aimed directly downwards: they take up the light theme of the pier. Direct light prevails in areas where, especially at night, the view outside should be disturbed as little as possible by interior reflections.

190 The pendant downlights that produce the basic light in the hall are discreetly positioned between the joists. Skylights above the ceiling panels shine their light through the perforated metal layer.

191 The arrival area receives an exceptionally large amount of daylight. And the lamps offering indirect illumination are pendant variants ...

192 ... of the large ceiling floods in the hall, which provide illumination at night.

193 Much daylight enters through the glass façade across from the runways and also supplies the offices.

5   TERMINOLOGY

LIGHTING DESIGN
FROM A TO Z

Adaptation

Adaptation refers to the process of adjustment of our organs to the environmental conditions as they change over time. In the context of lighting technology this refers to the adaptability of the eye to the surrounding light. Seeing is a very refined process consisting of several steps and involving the eye and the brain in equal measure. In the adjustment to darkness, the the eye adapts to the changed light conditions in three stages: a first, quick adaptation within 0.1 seconds; the adaptation of the retinal cone within 1–10 minutes; the adaptation of the rods within almost an hour. The adaptation from darkness to brightness is much quicker.

It is part and parcel of good lighting design to support this adaptive process by avoiding excessively strong temporal contrasts in the luminances offered to the eye. An example is the correct lighting for tunnels. Driving into a tunnel during the day, and especially in sunshine, will lead to a short-term "blindness", since the eyes cannot get used to the darkness fast enough. This is why the entries to tunnels, and even the exits, are brightly lit, while avoiding glare, so as to support the adaptation of the eyes. In the design of computer monitor workplaces, the adaptive abilities of the eyes play an important role as well. The eyes are focused on the monitor. If the surroundings of the monitor are too bright, the eyes are constantly required to adapt, causing additional strain. This occurs especially if the monitor – for purposes of diversion – is positioned in front of the window. In this condition, the eyes are forced almost continuously to adapt to the bright surroundings and then again to the comparatively dark monitor. This process quickly leads to fatigue.

Vision is based on four basic conditions:

· In order to see a minimum luminance is required from daylight or artificial light. In darkness, objects are invisible.
· Objects must also be distinguishable through a minimum contrast; this contrast is formed by various colors and luminances.
· For the naked eye, of course, visible objects must have a minimum size.
· The eye requires a minimum length of time for perception. Objects which are too "fast" are no longer visible.

Aging of Lamps and Materials

→ Useful Life

Ampere

The unit ampere (**A**) measures the electrical current, I. Multiplication with the tension U (volt) yields the power P (watt) of a system. P = U x I. The more consumers (luminaires) there are, the higher the power consumption (measured in watts) and the higher the capacity of the safety fuses and electric feeds must be.

Low-tension systems with high currents and low voltages (e.g. the cable systems for halogen incandescent lamps) show that in spite of low power, the high currents require the wires to be relatively thick, since otherwise too much resistance would cause excessive power dissipation and heat generation.

The determination of wiring diameters etc. is part of the planning service of electrical engineers.

→ Volt, Watt

Approval Marks

The luminaires of most manufacturers are classified according to European or national standards. The German approval mark is provided by the VDE (Verband Deutscher Elektrotechniker – Association of German Electrical Engineers) with its test center in Offenbach.

European Approval Marks

Country National Safety Mark	Test Center
Austria	ÖVE
Belgium	CEBEC
Denmark	DEMKO
Finland	FIMKO
France	UTE
Germany	VDE-PZI
Great Britain	BSI
Greece	ELOT
Hungary	MEEI
Ireland	NSAI
Italy	IMQ
Luxembourg	SEE
Netherlands	KEMA
Norway	NEMKO
Portugal	IPQ
Spain	AENOR
Sweden	SEMKO
Switzerland	SEV

The approval marks describe the tested properties of the luminaire according to type of protection, protection class, and other classification abbreviations. They establish how waterproof and/or dustproof a luminaire is or what kind of mechanical stresses it could withstand (protection against ball impact/vandalism) and other criteria. This may be very important for correct planning. The respective properties can be gathered from the identification plate on the luminaire.

Types of protection exist for various areas of use. Protection against dust and humidity is guaranteed accordingly by the specification IPxy (IP = Ingress Protection, x = level of protection against foreign substances, y = level of protection against humidity) on a scale of 0 to 8.

→ Protection Types

Architects

Architectural firms play an important coordinating role in the planning and implementation process. They often make a preliminary selection of specialist planners, whom they then propose to the client, and thus participate in deciding which lighting design firm to commission.

Consequently, the architects are responsible for the cooperation of the parallel working specialist planners. It is incumbent on them to prepare the working drawings (only in rare cases, separate lighting system plans are needed at a construction site). Not only the quality of the result depends on this cooperation, but also the economic success of the firm. In their daily operations, lighting design firms, which cooperate with a great number of different architectural and engineering firms, are confronted with many different ways of working.

How well thought out the architectural plans are as a basis for lighting design, and wether the client requests last-minute modifications, are decisive. If modifications are frequent, lighting designers can work economically only if the client pays according to the time spent, which does not always happen in practice. In comparison to architects or mechanical engineer, the lighting designer's remuneration of a project is too small. The architects designed the buildings for which the light is planned. Today, there is no architect who does not give light an important role in his design. The topic of light runs through the architecture of the centuries like a guideline. To grasp the architectural idea of a building and of its light is the basic precondition of successful lighting design. Lighting designers emphasizing the design are closer to the architect than to the engineer. This sometimes leads to architects modifying the lighting design to the detriment of the project. Being the first among equals gives the architect this prerogative. As (specialized) architects frequently work in lighting design firms, there is an area of conflict that often requires patience, as experience shows.

→ Clients

Avoiding Design Errors

Practical experience shows that most design errors occur when modifications are made under time pressure. Detailed records should always be kept of requests for modifications. The designer must insist on sufficient time to be able to work out his modification proposal in coordination with the other trades, and in consideration of the consequences for other parts of the building. If confronted with a delicate situation at the construction site, the designer must never rashly consent to a supposed solution, and should always insist on sufficient time for reflection at the office.

Design errors can also occur due to a lack of communication. Particularly detailed information must be exchanged if employees change in one of the participating firms. It is human to make mistakes; hence, project leaders of good firms mutually support one another. Troubleshooting among designers in detailed steps can be just as helpful as the coordination with the owner of the firm.

Ballast Units

These devices are required for the operation of discharge lamps, i.e. fluorescent or compact fluorescent lamps and metal halide lamps. The ballast unit may contain further devices for ensuring a trouble-free operation of the discharge lamps such as a starter or capacitors. The units are very important with regard to the efficiency and the life of the discharge lamps. In the case of fluorescent lamps there are four competing types:

Conventional ballasts for starter operations (= conventional type)

Low loss ballasts (= further development of the conventional type)

Electronic ballasts (= new development, most economical in consumption, most gentle on lamp)

Electronic ballasts which make it possible to dim operation of fluorescent lamps

Electronic ballasts are now most commonly used, since, in spite of their higher acquisition costs, they have many advantages such as good energy utilization, a quick and flicker-free start, quiet operation, and automatic shutdown in case of a fault in the lamp. They can also be used with direct current for emergency lighting. The use of dimmable electronic ballasts is the precondition for dimmability of discharge lamps.

If only very little space is available for installation, e.g. in concrete recess lamps or hollow ceilings, one must observe that electronic ballast units cannot handle ambient temperatures in excess of 70° C.

Billing

What counts as a "correct" invoice depends on the client and the contract. First of all, the designer should ensure that the invoices for his fees are written very shortly after the service performed, and be sure to write meaningful interim invoices, say, following the completion of a service stage, and more frequently in larger projects. If this procedure is followed, invoices can become a subtle instrument for the early detection of irregularities during the progress of construction, imminent insolvencies or refusal of the client to pay.

On the invoice, the net fee for the services performed is stated. In addition there should be a provision for the office overheads. This includes telephone, postage, photocopies and travel expenses. Incidental expenses may be settled at a flat rate and/or against proof. If the incidentals are accounted for with receipts, no sales tax is applied to these costs (sales tax is already settled and enters into the pre-tax deduction of the paying firm, while in the design firm it is an item that is passed on). Finally, sales tax must be calculated and listed. Everything added together then yields the gross invoiced amount. If the design firm does not work on the basis of the HOAI, services on a time basis will usually be agreed upon (individually or in skeleton contracts). The time spent must be documented and listed on the invoice. Sometimes there are fixed price arrangements. Some clients request "cumulative" invoices for their cost centers. These facilitate the control of the budget. To this end, the invoice states the total commissioned amount of the project, adds the amounts of the interim invoices and subtracts them from the total amount so that the share of the commissioned fee still available for the progress of services is always visible to the respective cost center.

→ Fees, HOAI

Building Location

One of the first steps of good lighting design is the establishment and evaluation of the geographical orientation of the building. In this way, the incidence of daylight and the positions of the sun can be determined. Surprisingly, many clients know very little regarding the exact location and orientation of their buildings.

→ Chapter 2: Fundamentals

Built-in Floor Luminaires

For a long time, light from ground level or near the ground was the preserve of outdoor lighting and was used primarily to illuminate objects and parks. Nowadays, luminaires recessed into the ground, which often produce a narrow beaming light, are no longer a rarity indoors as well as outdoors. The luminaires are mounted into insert casing flush with the surface of the ground, or are fitted directly into suitable recesses.

The use of built-in floor luminaires is not without problems. Frequently, people feel blinded by them, since our eyes are naturally directed more towards the ground than towards the ceiling. If one accidentally steps onto a built-in floor luminaire there is a danger of skidding. Their surface consists of clear glass; frosted and hence skid-proof materials would not permit enough light to exit the luminaire. Finally, the surface of the luminaire, depending on the model, sometimes heats up to 120° Celsius. Many people do not expect such temperatures on the ground. Thus, it is advisable to use built-in floor luminaires only in less frequented areas.

→ Concrete Insert Casings

Built-in Luminaires

This type of luminaire comprises all luminaires recessed in walls, ceilings, floors, or in the ground. One characteristic of built-in luminaires is their "immovable" position, another is the hidden luminaire body, which gives pride of place to the architecture. Built-in luminaires are more demanding, and also more expensive, in their installation than surface-mounted or pendant luminaires. But they look significantly better and approach the ideal of the lighting designer – of creating illumination without mounting visible luminaires – much more closely than financially more attractive luminaires. For reasons of cost, built-in luminaires cannot always be used for general illumination; they are usually only found in more frequented or more up-market areas.

Downlights are the most common types of built-in luminaires. They are usually round, the necessary ceiling cutout varying from 3.5 cm (halogen) to 25 cm (high-pressure discharge lamp); in addition, there is the necessary installation depth (up to 30 cm). Normally, downlights are built into suspended ceilings or with concrete insert casings into the bare ceiling.

Part of the accessories are antiglare louvers or antiglare glass covers, filters, and diffuser lenses, which are mounted into the reflector openings. Contrary to what one might expect, this frequently increases the glare of the light emanating from the lamps. Darklight reflectors have defined antiglare angles; they are largely glare-free and feature high utilization factors.

Built-in luminaires come in wide-angle (flood) and narrow-beaming (spot) varieties. Many downlights are available as swiveling and pivoting directional spotlights.

→ Downlights, Formwork Layouts, Maintenance Openings

Bus Technology

Bus technology is a relatively new but important aid in controling the technical equipment of buildings by building automation. The electronic "bus" is able to transport control and switch functions ("switching, controling, regulating, displaying, measuring, reporting, monitoring") through a network of interconnected receivers, which are often very varied and are distributed over entire properties. The information passes through low-voltage (24 V DC) wires, arranged in a series, a star or tree structure, to the receiver, which are luminaires, air conditioning units, façade elements, alarm systems etc. Transmission via radio waves is also possible. Software encodes the digital bus information for the individual receivers. This is recognized and executed by the targeted devices, each of which has its own "address". The "result" of the initiated process is sent back so that the functioning of the system is constantly controled. In this manner, individual devices and functions or whole systems (groups) can be controled in accordance with instructions (through centralized or decentralized software) or parameters of connected receivers. The bus system as a whole thus consists of the network, the software that defines requirements, a bus connector (sending and receiving unit) and storage devices for digital addresses, parameters and other information. In addition there are sensors and actuators. The sensors measure states and register differences: they respond to changes in the weather or register if someone enters or leaves a room. The actuators convert registered changes into switch signals for the connected devices.

The LON and the EIB (European Installation Bus) are established standards, for which there are already many supplies. The system is compatible and based on an EIBA guideline which follows the DIN VDE 0207 and 0815 standards.

Systems specialized for the control and regulation of light are also known as lighting control systems. By no means all luminaires on the market today are "bus compatible". Bus technology still requires a relatively high initial investment. This is why some clients initially buy "bus compatible" luminaires in order to upgrade the network with its modules only a few years later, once prices have dropped and experiences of the building have been gathered.

CAD (Computer Aided Design)

The preparation of drawings using (personal) computers, called CAD for short, has become standard for professional planning firms. Compared to traditional techniques there are two advantages in particular: drawing speed and the design options are increased substantially – provided that one has mastered the programs through practice and intuitive understanding. In addition, the program facilitates the administration of the luminaire quantities ascertained and of the plans and hence also the preparation of tender specifications.

→ Chapter 3: Processes and Procedures, Section Planning Tools for the Office

Calculation of Illuminances

In all firms, computer programs for the calculation of illuminances have replaced the formulae which only a few years ago were still used to calculate of the mean illuminance.

These formulae, however, still produce fairly good estimated values and often save the input work on the computer. The efficiency procedure, among others, is a suitable method. It calculates the number of luminaires required depending on the desired illuminance. The method calculates a mean value for a rectangular room. The number of luminaires is obviously one of the decisive criteria for planning.

$$N = \frac{p \times E \times A}{z \times \varphi \times \eta_{LB} \times \eta_R} \; .$$

· N is the number of luminaires calculated.
· p is a planning factor which takes the aging of the luminaires and the soiling of luminaire and room into account. The standard value is 1.25.
· E is the illuminance in lux (e.g. approximately 500 for monitor workstation).
· A is the floor space in length x width.
· z is the number of lamps per luminaire.
· φ is the luminous flux of the planned luminaire.
· η_{LB} is the operational efficiency of the luminaire. This must be measured by the manufacturers. If the value of η_{LB} is not listed among the technical data of the luminaire, the planner must request it. The operational efficiency states how much light of the luminaire's luminous flux actually leaves it.
· η_R is the room utilization factor. It depends on the size and shape of the room, the reflection factors of the ceiling, walls and floor, the luminous intensity distribution of the planned luminaire and its mounting location. The planner can find the respective room utilization factor in tables supplied by the luminaire industry or the LiTG (German Society of Lighting Technology).
· The product of η_{LB} and η_R is the illumination efficiency.

Candela

Candela (cd) is the unit of luminous intensity (I). I is the luminous flux (φ) emanating from a light source (lamp or luminaire) in a certain direction per solid angle (Ω):

$$I = \frac{\varphi}{\Omega}$$

The following relationship exists between the luminous intensity I and illuminance E:

$$E = \frac{I}{a^2}$$

Where a is the distance of the light source from the illuminated surface. The luminance is given in candela per square meter (cd/m^2). Luminous intensity distribution curves are a suitable means for assessing the radiation characteristics of luminaires in combination with their lamps.

The luminous intensity distribution curve also forms the basis for light calculations using software.

→ Lamp, Lumen, Luminous Flux, Luminous Intensity Distribution Curves, Lux

Candles

Not all light sources have to run on electricity…

Catalogues

→ Manufacturers

Ceiling Drawings

These drawings prepared by the architects convey a view of the ceiling on the basis of the room measurements. They show luminaires, loud-speakers, smoke alarms, air conditioning and ventilation units, maintenance openings and the outlets of the sprinkler system. In addition, the ceiling joints are visible (in analogy to the tile pattern of a floor). Ceiling drawings are necessary in order to place the luminaires correctly in the ceilings. The correct installation depth and the options for fastening the luminaires must be verified. The decisive issue then is whether the intended luminaire can indeed be positioned at the right place or whether supply channels or pipes are in the way or can be installed in a less obstructive way. Here conflicts may arise between the solutions of the engineers and the aesthetic preferences of the architects or the lighting designer.

Ceiling Luminaire

The most frequently used type of luminaire.

→ Ceiling Outlet, Ceilings

Ceiling Outlet

Ceiling outlets often form the interface between the services of the electrical engineers and the lighting designer. The lighting designer states the power requirements for the planned luminaires and determines the circuits and switching options. The electrical engineers then plan the appropriate wires and circuits including the supply to the corresponding outlet. Stating the attachment of the luminaire and planning it for the respective ceiling is the task of the lighting designer and the architect.

Ceilings

A bon mot says that one can recognize a lighting designer by the fact that upon entering a building, his gaze first wanders to the ceiling. Artificial light enters the room primarily from the ceiling, and hence its construction determines what types of luminaires may be used. There are, of course, very different types of ceiling constructions. For the use of luminaires, it is important to know whether the ceiling is suspended, how great is its load capacity, whether installation casings will be necessary, and whether the ceiling itself will be a component of the lighting concept as a reflective surface for indirect luminaires.

Suspended ceilings permit the use of built-in luminaires. The luminaire disappears almost completely behind its lighting effect. The ceiling suspensions often carry only a limited weight; hence, on larger ceilings the weight of luminaires can actually be a factor.

Just as in the case of walls and floors, in the planning of concrete ceilings one must consider early whether the luminaires require concrete built-in housings, since this would require recesses in the correct positions.

Indirect light reflected via a bright ceiling is of a high quality. The space between the luminaire and the ceiling, the reflector, the luminous flux and the reflection factors should be planned carefully and dimensioned liberally, taking into account that luminaires radiating against the ceiling have a stronger dirt buildup than other luminaires.

Luminous ceilings, i. e. ceiling elements with integrated luminaires, are a special case. Today, there are luminous ceilings which recall daylight scenes by dimming of fluorescent luminaires recessed above them.

Central Battery System

→ Emergency Lighting

CIE

The "Commission Internationale d'Eclairage" is the international association of "light scientists" with branches in many countries and a series of publications. The commission, however, does not work in a very application-oriented way.

→ The central office is located in Vienna: CIE, Kegelgasse 27, A – 1030 Vienna, Austria, Tel: +43–1- 7 143 187–0, Fax +43–1- 7 130 838–18, e-mail: ciecbb@ping.at

Clients

Lighting design firms do not normally work for private individuals, since their specialization requires a certain minimum project size. Commercial clients include investors such as institutions or firms, general planning firms and public authorities represented by the governmental construction offices. All three domains have different requirements. For contracts with governmental construction offices, the Budget Document for Construction (Haushaltsunterlage Bau or HU-Bau) forms the contractual basis. It differs in minor details from the Regulations Regarding Fees for Architects and Engineers (Honorarordnung für Architekten und Ingenieure, HOAI). The remuneration of services is relatively secure, even if it takes a very long time; recently, security retentions (up to 5%) have been coming into use (should be replaced with bank guarantees). Public construction assignments are often professionally very rewarding, since they include the whole field of museums and theaters and the outside spaces around them. Nowadays, the public construction offices work in very diverse ways; there are public authorities which only want to act traditionally, but there are also receptive and effective offices which are open to innovations. Institutions and firms commission very different tasks; sometimes new lamp developments can be agreed upon. Because in-house construction departments are often insufficiently staffed, fiduciary corporations or project managers are frequently entrusted with the contractual side and with the supervision of the progress of construction. Alternatively, large architectural firms can act as general planners. In this case, the contractual partner of the lighting designer is the architectural firm. Problems can occur if the flow of funds from the client to the general planner comes to a halt and the general planner is either unwilling or unable to remunerate services performed before his client has paid. In such a case, the commissioned lighting design firm normally has no way of getting to the true beneficiary of his services – the client – since his contract is with the architect. Investors usually have no interest in using the buildings for themselves; proper lighting design helps to sell or rent their project more favorably. Hence, issues of cost are always very prominent, for example, in the tender negotiations with contractors.

Color Rendering

It is much easier to achieve good color rendering indoors than outdoors. Luminaires for interior spaces generally have relatively good color rendering, while this is not necessarily true of outdoor luminaires. The color rendering of luminaires must not be confused with the color of their light. Whether or not a luminaire portrays a room, objects, and people well depends on the color rendering. In the end, this can only be determined by sampling and visual inspection! The determining factor of color rendering is the spectral composition of the light produced. In every situation, this light meets different colors and surfaces, the color spectrum of which always diverges. A good result can only be achieved on site and through direct comparisons. This fact is frequently underestimated, which may unintentionally lead to very poor results.

A general, comparative color rendering index according to DIN 6169 provides a rough classification. It describes the deviations from a standard light source with 2950 K or from daylight and the reference value Ra = 100. According to DIN 5035–1, these limits are divided into the gradations 1 A – 4.

Classification according to DIN 5035	Color rendering index value Ra, Rated = 100	Corresponding lamps
1A	90 and more	Fluorescent and compact fluorescent lamps, metal halide lamps, color of light "deluxe"
1B	80 to 90	Triphosphor fluorescent lamps, compact fluorescent lamps
2A	70 to 80	Fluorescent lamps, color of light universal white
2B	60 to 70	Fluorescent lamps, color of light bright white, metal halide lamps
3	40 to 60	Fluorescent lamps, color of light warm tone, high-pressure mercury vapor lamps
4	20 to 40	High-pressure sodium vapor lamps
	Below 20	Low-pressure sodium vapor lamps

→ Kelvin

Compact Fluorescent Lamps

The incandescent lamps in use for over almost one hundred years in which a filament gives off light have two economic disadvantages: their life is relatively short (approx. 1000 h) and at 10–20 lm/W their luminous efficacy is low. The various types of "energy-saving lamps" which have been available for about 20 years eliminate these disadvantages. They work like the rod-shaped fluorescent lamps, only their form and structure are different (which was not easy to achieve from a constructional point of view). Normally, the useful life of the lamps is approximately 8000 h, that is, ten times as long as the life of the incandescent lamp, while electricity consumption is 2/3 lower. Aside from the saving in electricity, it is especially the substantially longer exchange intervals of the lamps that help reduce high costs in the operation. Compact fluorescent lamps are used with inductive and electronic ballasts, the latter offering almost all the advantages of rod-shaped fluorescent lamps. The lamps are well suited for indoor and frequently also for outdoor use. The ambient temperature affects the emitted luminous flux and the lamp's ability to start: in low temperatures, the luminous flux drops sharply. Compact fluorescent devices are available for many lamps and areas of use. Most are available in the colors warm white, neutral white and daylight.

Computer Simulations (Light Technology Software)

→ Chapter 3: Processes and Procedures

Concrete Insert Casing

Concrete insert casings are required to install luminaires in concrete recesses – in ceilings and increasingly also in floors. The future position of the casing and hence of the luminaires are drawn into the formwork layouts.

Sometimes, manufacturers supply the corresponding casings for the concrete along with their built-in luminaires (usually downlights). These housings have to be delivered very early during the construction of the shell of the building and be fitted very precisely since it will be impossible to change their position later on. They are flush with the surface and are thus suitable for exposed concrete.

→ Formwork Layouts, Maintenance Openings

Contour Spotlights

Conventional spotlights and floodlights create a cone of light and a light surface with soft edges. For a sharp-edged image of light, contour spotlights make possible the sharp-edged illumination of surfaces at certain distances by means of inserted diaphragms and lenses. Adjustable diaphragms also allow for arbitrary rectangular or trapezoid light exits.

Contracts

Following submission of a tender and the subsequent commissioning, written contracts may be concluded regarding planning or consulting services. This is always to be recommended. Only this way it is possible to regulate, with some degree of certainty, the service to be performed, the liability and the modalities of remuneration.

For small, easily manageable commissions, a separate contract and the added expense is not necessary. A written contract award with reference to the tender is sufficient in such a case. Some contract awards contain general conditions of business to regulate part of the planned course of events. Performance specifications can also become part of a written contract award. In both cases, a formal contract is approached; however, it must be accepted that the client dictates conditions. In any case, the designer should read his contract award carefully and balance it with his tender. If he is unable or unwilling to accept particular points of the general conditions of business or of performance specifications, the designer must voice these concerns and negotiate before countersigning the contract award.

Some clients use standard contracts from which they do not want to deviate (often for administrative reasons). Because lighting design is complex, this can be very detrimental, since all the services, for example sampling, are not detailed sufficiently in the standard contracts. Sometimes the clause "special services", which is added to these standard contracts

and defines services not covered by the contract, may be useful. Caution is advisable with the general conditions of business in standard contracts; they are usually formulated to the advantage of the client.

The use of standard contracts, however, also offers advantages. They can be concluded quickly and do not cost the designer any money in the short term.

It is different with contracts proposed by the designer himself, and the additional costs diminish the profit from the project. The advantage of using one's own contracts lies primarily in a more subtly differentiated description of services and their delimitation vis-à-vis the services of others. Furthermore, one can attempt to limit liability (very important), to maintain as many rights in the design as possible, and to arrive at advantageous arrangements regarding incidental costs. One should leave the drafting of one's own contracts to specialized lawyers, since building law is very complicated.

Control Systems

→ Light Control Systems

Customers

→ Clients

Daylight

→ Chapter 2: Fundamentals

Daylight Factor

This is the relation between the illuminance at a defined point inside a room and the illuminance outdoors under a completely overcast sky. The daylight factor decreases continuously from the window area into the inner reaches of the room. During the day, the interior of a building is somewhat darker than the exterior space around the window, and substantially darker at greater distances from the window. If the rooms are deep, the daylight share at some distance from the window areas often drops to less than 1% of the outdoor illuminance. For permanent workplaces, the DIN 5034 standard requires a daylight factor of at least 1%.

Design

The task of design is to unite the technical, functional, and aesthetic requirements of a product. Some manufacturers employ their own designers, others leave the design to the design engineer, and some commission independent lighting designers.

Many innovations in commercially used luminaires are mostly technical. Hence, the form of a luminaire closely follows technical guidelines. Size and weight, the thermal conductivity of the material, the ease of maintenance in the replacement of lamps and of cleaning, and the mounting options are all important criteria in addition to the manufacturing process. The luminaires on the market do not always fulfill the special tasks of lighting, so the development of special luminaires is an option. The designer of such luminaires will want to fall back on existing components. In this way, special luminaires of superior lighting quality can be produced in small series at economically viable cost. Some medium-size manufacturers specialize in such orders and act flexibly. Afterwards, some manufacturers gladly incorporate luminaires from these project-oriented orders into their product line. This is why, at an early stage, the designer should ensure copyrights to the design using a licensing agreement.

Around the luminaires themselves there are also occasional design tasks to be fulfilled. For public spaces, poles and steles as mounting elements must be included in the plan. In interior spaces, display cases, cabinets and suspended lighting elements must be designed.

The design of new luminaires takes place under a separate contract, independently of planning tasks. The design of special luminaires or details is not a part of a normal (HOAI) planning contract, but should be commissioned separately. This should therefore be pointed out when agreeing a planning contract.

Design Errors

A designer is liable for planning errors. Designers are required to have professional liability insurance; proof of such insurance is part of the contract with the client. In Germany, the liability amounts for lighting designers are DM 300 000 for property damage and DM 2 000 000 for personal injury. Whether or not damages for design services are included should be settled at the conclusion of the contract. Normally these cases are excluded. Design errors may be due to technical flaws (e.g. guide values were not adhered to or incorrect measurements were stated) or may arise through gross negligence (e.g. the use of unqualified employees, failure to examine plans).

The design firm must report the claimed or actual damage to its liability insurer. The client usually grants the designer the right to rectify the fault himself (modification of the planning, supplements). If construction has already been executed in accordance with the faulty plans, costs are incurred for repair. These must be borne by the designer or his insurer. There is a differentation between additional costs due to error and costs that would have been incurred in any case. For example: if too few lamps were planned in order to achieve the illuminance required in a room, additional lamps will have to be installed. To the extent that the lamps already installed do not have to be moved, the additional installation results in costs which would have arisen in any case and hence must be borne by the client. If, however, scaffolding which had already been disassembled must be reassembled, if ceilings must be repainted and the final cleaning of the construction site repeated, then these costs must be borne by the designer.

In the very rare case of intent or of gross negligence, the liability insurer may refuse to pay for the damages and hold the owner of the firm personally liable.

Dimming, Brightness Control

The option of continuous dimming significantly increases the comfort of a lighting system and contributes substantially to efficient usage. Dimming incandescent lamps and halogen incandescent lamps is, technically speaking, a relatively simple affair. One option is to use transformers in conjunction with special dimmers. Another option is of employing electronic transformers triggered with 1–10 V or using potentiometers. Some lamp manufacturers now offer dimmers for metal halide lamps, although they do not yet guarantee the functionality of their lamps if these dimmers are used, since dimming is not yet flawless. Many dimmers for fluorescent lamps do not dim down to 0 %, but only to 10 % or 1 % luminous flux.

→ Ballast Units

Discharge Lamps

→ Fluorescent Lamp

Downlights

All lamps that emit their light directly downwards and have a round or square (reflector) shape belong to the large family of downlights. The spectrum ranges from suspended industrial floodlights of the highest protection class used to illuminate of large halls down to the miniaturized reflector with a halogen incandescent lamp for ceilings in plaster-board construction.

→ Built-in Lamps

Efficiency Procedure
→ Calculation of Illuminances

ELDA

A lobby group for lighting designers, the European Lighting Designers Association gathers independent designers for activities and to represent their interests. Compared to the LiTG, which represents lighting engineers, this organization is distinguished by cultivating a decidedly more design- and practical planning-oriented image.

→ ELDA e.V., Postfach 3201, D-33262 Gütersloh, e-mail: ELDA_Head_Office@Compuserve.com

→ LiTG

Electrical Engineers
→ Specialist Engineers

Emergency Lighting

Emergency lighting should provide orientation in buildings in case of a failure of the electricity supply, and thus ensure a safe exit from the building. Two systems are possible, separately or in combination: emergency sign illumination and emergency exit or escape route illumination.

There are national regulations for emergency lighting systems in Germany, standards, which are linked by references. These regulations refer both to electrotechnical requirements (VDE 0108) and to lighting regulations (DIN 5035,5 and 4844,1–3). Requirements of building or workplace regulations sometimes vary between the *Länder*.

At least one emergency sign must be visible from every position, and the luminaires must be installed above head height. These luminaires have the sole purpose of backlighting the emergency sign, and do not illuminate the escape routes.

According to DIN 4844 and the Union of Professional Associations (Verband der Berufsgenossenschaften) standards, emergency sign lamps must be green and white or transparent and have directing arrows; a running figure symbol may be added for emphasis. The distance from which the symbol can be recognized depends on its size.

The sizes for emergency signs recommended by the DIN 4844, T3 standard prescribe the following recognition distances:

Height of the emergency sign	as a luminaire	as an unlit sign
52 mm	11 m	5.5 m
100 mm	20 m	10.0 m
105 mm	21 m	10.5 m
148 mm	30 m	15.0 m
200 mm	40 m	20.0 m

The luminaire and the sign, with or without illumination, may be contained in a casing.

Emergency exit luminaires must illuminate escape routes, main rooms, or entire sections of buildings over a certain period and with a prescribed minimum illuminance to enable safe orientation and use. They are prescribed for all public buildings, assembly halls and their emergency escape routes.

Depending on the type of building, the nominal duration of operation is between one and three hours. As a rule, the minimum illuminance is 1 lx. In certain types of buildings, or according to special conditions imposed by the responsible building regulation authority, the minimum illuminance can also be higher (e.g. 15 lx for main escape routes). This illuminance is measured at a height of 0.2 m above the finished floor level in the least visible place. The data are laid down in VDE 0108.

Emergency lighting is provided by spare power sources in accordance with VDE 0108, T1.

These spare power sources may be battery systems (single batteries in small buildings, sets of batteries in medium-sized buildings, and central battery systems in large facilities) or emergency generators (for garages, high-rise buildings, hospitals).

With central battery systems, the potential number of luminaires and their power consumption is almost unlimited. The luminaires are supplied with alternating current during mains supply operation and with direct current during emergency operation.

Fluorescent lamps must be operated with electronic ballast units. Systems with sets of batteries are subject to a power restriction. During one hour of operation, they must not support more than 900 W, and during three hours of operation, they must not support more than 300 W.

Single battery systems have similar restrictions. The maximum number of luminaires is two per battery, although without power restriction but with a control luminaire indicating the charging state (normally LED).

Emergency Sign Lamp
→ Emergency Lighting

Energy-saving Lamps
→ Compact Fluorescent Lamp

Façade Illumination
→ Chapter 4: Examples

Fees

The market fees for services such as lighting design vary a great deal. Lighting designers work with the same equipment as architects and engineers, and with equally qualified and specialized employees. Yet they have a very small share in the construction process, normally around 3% of the total costs of the project. Lighting design firms must therefore juggle a considerably greater number of projects than the architects and engineers in order to achieve a comparable turnover. The greater number of projects entails enormous administrative and travel costs and requires very highly motivated employees. The HOAI does not take this structure into account, which is why the fees obtained and the expected profit remain far below those possible in architectural and engineering firms. Hence there are many lighting designers who additionally offer the manufacture and installation of luminaires, but who consequently do not have the market neutrality of an independent designer.
→ Chapter 3: Processes and Procedures, Section Tenders and Contracts

Fiber Glass
→ Fiber Optic Light Guide Technology

Fiber Optic Light Guide Technology

Using fibers made of glass or plastic, light can be transported from one or more feeding points. The light may then leave from the end or the sides of the fiber. This technology has three main advantages. The light which is centrally fed into the system may be transformed, say, with respect to its color. Moreover, the system does not transport heat, making it suitable for the illumination of sensitive objects. Finally, electricity is required only at the feeding point.

Due to the high costs, however, fiber optic light guide technology does not offer a solution for basic illumination, but it is often suited for artistic accentuation.

Filters

Filters allow certain wavelengths of visible light to pass through (transmitting them), while filtering out others (reflecting and absorbing them). Dichroic filters appear metallic, since they are vapor-coated with thin yet partly translucent metal layers; they allow, for example, one color to pass through, while reflecting its complementary color. These filters find application in cold-light reflectors: they reflect the visible light in one direction and transmit the infrared radiation backwards into the luminaire

housing. UV filters are useful in museums for the protection of light sensitive exhibits. Infrared reflecting coatings of the glass bulbs of modern halogen incandescent lamps redirect the infrared radiation back onto the filament, thus increasing the luminous efficacy. Color filters are available from manufacturers as standard accessories for indoor and outdoor luminaires. For the requirements of the theater, there are additional glass and film filters which, however, must not be installed on the luminaires without prior consultation with their manufacturer, since they build up heat inside the luminaire. Theater film filters are light-sensitive and have a limited life.

Finish Schedule

The room is normally the smallest unit for the equipment of a building. The finish schedule lists and helps manage all the movable objects of a room, permanently installed devices such as electrical outlets or luminaires, and features such as paint coatings and flooring.

Advanced CAD programs are able to generate finish schedules automatically and also calculate the corresponding floor spaces.
→ Room Usage

Floors

Floors reflect or absorb incident light according to their color. Hence, the design of the floor can affect the luminances achieved or the brightness perceived in a room.

Floor Space
→ Room Usage

Fluorescent lamps

The fluorescent lamp developed in 1925 is a type of discharge lamp, which remains the most frequently used lamp in the commercial sector. It is popularly known also under the (misleading) name "neon light". Today, the fluorescent lamp is available to everyone, a rare success for an industrially implemented innovation. Accordingly, the worldwide production and supply of fluorescent lamps is today extremely varied.

The long tubular shape is still typical of this lamp, even though, as the further developments (e.g. circular and U-shaped lamps) and the compact fluorescent lamps show, many other shapes are possible. Such technical conditions often determine the shape of the luminaires. The fluorescent lamp works at low pressure, primarily through the discharge of small amounts of mercury vapor in which the energy absorbed transforms into UV radiation (to facilitate ignition and in order to achieve a better adjustment to the ambient temperature, other elements or compounds are added in very small quantities). Through the UV radiation generated, the mercury vapor (or another compound), excited between two heated electrodes at either end, causes materials deposited on the interior surface of the glass tube to fluoresce in the desired colors of light. Luminous efficacies of up to 100 lumens/watt often mean a saving of more than two thirds of the expended energy compared to conventional incandescent lamps. The rod-shaped fluorescent lamps are very standardized in terms of their lengths and diameters – a further reason for their success.

Formwork Layouts

For luminaires which are to be built into concrete, recesses must be provided which are attached as blocks of wood or polystyrene to the formwork. Sometimes the manufacturer provides concrete insert casings. Hence, the luminaire positions and luminaire sizes (via the insert size) are determined at a very early stage and almost unalterably in the formwork layouts. The structural engineer must verify that the recesses do not interfere with the concrete reinforcements and do not weaken the static equilibrium.

→ Concrete Insert Casings, Planning Processes, Chapter 2: Fundamentals

Fresnel Lens

The Fresnel lens is a rotationally symmetric lens split into prism segments (invented in 1820 by Augustin Jean Fresnel), and was originally constructed for use only in lighthouses. It's technological advantage over conventional lenses lies in the significantly lower material requirement and a corresponding lower weight. Fresnel lenses are manufactured from pressed glass or may be cut, and are used in spotlights and floodlights with variable radiation angles.

Furniture

According to the type of room usage, the furnishings also determine the position of the luminaires in rooms. New European standards allow the illumination to be zoned. The required illuminance is then only necessary near the workplace as such, while significantly lower values are permitted in peripheral areas.

Gaslight

Light generated from gas developed "the light" of the industrial revolution around 1800. At first, the installation of the new luminaires was confined to factories. The great step forward resulted from the installation of general (street) lighting with a central gas supply and the related construction of a distribution network, at first in cities.

Glare

Glaring light should be avoided or minimized through good lighting design. Glare can emanate from a luminaire or arise through reflections on shiny materials.

Glare caused by reflections can be reduced through mat and flat surfaces or through a favorable positioning of luminaires. The luminaires should be placed so that the reflections, which normally exit at the same angle as the angle of incidence, do not strike the field of vision in working areas and common areas. Antiglare rings, antiglare flaps, shutters, slats and mirror screens on luminaires prevent people from looking directly into the lamps, and minimize the angles from which glare can occur. The glare reduction of luminaires is stated in degrees in the directions of the x and y axes.

→ Monitor Workstations

Glass

→ Chapter 2: Fundamentals, Section Transmission

Gobos

Gobos are templates used mainly in theaters as accessories to spotlights in order to project patterns, lettering or logos. They are etched from thin pieces of sheet metal according to individual designs. They only work on projection spots, i.e. luminaires fitted with lenses, the optical system of which permits focusing on various distances, like a slide projector. Additional motors turn the gobos in front of the spots in order to produce effects such as splashing water surfaces or a rotating starry sky. Another technique uses mirrors to move the image.

Group Battery Supply

→ Emergency Lighting

Hallway Lighting
→ Chapter 4: Examples

Heating/Ventilation/Air Conditioning Engineers
→ Specialist Planners

High-pressure Mercury Vapor Lamp
High-pressure mercury vapor lamps belong to the family of discharge lamps. They usually have an ellipsoid shape with an E27 or E40 socket. They produce a bluish light, which was very widespread in the 1980s in street lighting and the illumination of industrial halls due to its efficiency. Nowadays, this lamp is frequently replaced by the high-pressure sodium vapor lamp.

High-pressure Sodium Lamp
This newer high-pressure lamp offers a much better, warmer and more pleasant color of light with a wider spectral range than the low-pressure lamp, and is now gaining widespread acceptance. It primarily replaces the mercury vapor lamp with its cool bluish light.

HOAI (Honorarordnung für Architekten und Ingenieure – Fee Schedule for Architects and Engineers)
The Fee Schedule for Architects and Engineers is, from a legal point of view, a still powerful relict of professional law, which regulates the remuneration of planning services on the basis of estimated or arising costs. Currently, every planning service performed in Germany in the construction sector must be settled via the HOAI; every individually concluded contact can be appealed if one of the disputing parties cites the law-like regulations of the HOAI. As a rule, this security for the designer is accompanied by reduced fees, since only the respectively stipulated minimum rates can be claimed with certainty.
Modified and edited over and over again, this sometimes very complex fee regulation is, as far as its structure is concerned, a practical instrument for the calculation and preparation of tenders. Its characteristic and legally anchored experiential knowledge reflected in the fee tables often agrees with the results of completed construction projects. Nevertheless, the general applicability of the HOAI continues to decline, because the regulations offer little leeway for individual agreements regarding the extent and type of service, and because the rigid linking of the fee to the construction costs frequently does not reflect the actual expenses.
The service of lighting design is not yet properly anchored in the HOAI. It is practical to assess the services of the lighting designer according to §§ 73–75, Technical Equipment, and to offer them accordingly following a

cost estimate. It is advisable to agree upon the remuneration of "special services", at least for the design of luminaires and for samplings. Presumably the provisions of the national HOAI will be further weakened and replaced in the future by a European law of service contracts.
→ Fees

Holograms
→ Light Guiding Systems

Identification Plates
→ Types of Protection

Illuminance
The DIN 5035 standard stipulates illuminances for many room uses. These vary a great deal. The following table lists only the most important values:

Office spaces	500 lx
Offices with monitor workstations	500 lx
Open-plan offices	750–1000 lx
Technical drawing	750 lx
Traffic zones	50–100 lx
Stairwells	100 lx
Classrooms	300–500 lx
Sports facilities	200–1500 lx
Sales rooms	300–1000 lx
Workshops	300–500 lx
Emergency lighting	more than 1 lx

→ Calculation of Illuminances, Lux

Incandescent Lamps
In these lamps, a filament is heated by means of an electric current and thus made to glow. The classical "light bulb" as well as its variants and the family of the halogen lamps are all constructed in this manner.

Individual Battery Supply
→ Emergency Lighting

Induction Lamps
The development of discharge lamps without electrodes and a very long life is still at a very early stage. Currently, only few manufacturers have various lamp systems on the market. The most promising of these are the QL lamp by Philips, the sulfur lamps by Fusion Lighting (currently on hold), as well as a "fluorescent lamp" Endura by Osram.

The QL and the Endura systems could be regarded as an extension of the series of (compact) fluorescent lamps, since they are available as 55 W/ 85 W or 150 W lamps. The sulfur lamp with a nominal power of 1400 W targets the area of application of the high-pressure discharge lamps.

In contrast to the traditional discharge lamps, the electrodeless lamp system is based on an inductively excited discharge, i.e. the voltage is produced (induced) through the change in magnetic flux density. An inductive lighting system consists of the discharge tube, an inductive energy coupling link, and a high frequency generator. The operational frequency varies greatly in the individual systems. Thus, in the Endura, it is very high at 250 KHz, and in the QL lamp relatively low at 2.65 MHz, compared to the sulfur lamp at 2.45 GHz, which already lies in the area of a microwave discharge. This system consists of a magnetron, a waveguide and a microwave cavity.

The discharge itself is very similar to the discharge in a conventional fluorescent lamp. The excited metal vapor filling emits UV radiation in the discharge. This radiation is transformed into visible light through the fluorescent layer on the inner glass wall of the discharge tube .

Since there are no electrodes in the discharge tube, the life of the system is determined primarily by its electronic components. This results in a very long life for the induction lamp, which makes this lamp, if it can be mass-produced, the absolutely most efficient source of illumination. The productive life of the QL and Endura lamps, for example, is 60 000 h.

Most induction lamps have a very compact form (similar to the all-purpose incandescent lamp). Although induction lamps are electronically operated devices, they produce electromagnetic waves. This real advantage can become a disadvantage if it leads to electromagnetic interference, i.e. if these waves jam other signals. This means that, especially with higher outputs of the lamp, expensive luminaires must be used in order to meet the requirements for radio-shielding.

None of the electrodeless luminaires currently available is dimmable. Yet since they all have electronic ballasts, this is possible in principle and merely a question of further development.

The new generation of induction systems combines the advantages of the fluorescent luminaires with new approaches in the field of illumination to produce an even more efficient source of light.

Institutes

→ Links

|K | L |

Kelvin (K)

The color temperatures of the lamps are stated in the unit Kelvin (K) as indications of the colors of light.

· Warm white (ww) corresponds to a color temperature up to 3300 K
· Neutral white (nw) comprises the range from 3300–5300 K
· Daylight (dl) has a color temperature measuring higher than 5300 K

Although the color of light chosen also determines the impression of the room, it does not describe the color rendering characteristics of a lamp. The color quality of the illumination results only from the combination of the color of light and color rendering.

Lamps

Lamps are used in two ways: to create luminescent objects (e.g. as a signal light) and for illumination (e.g. in order to illuminate a room). The variety of the lamps available today is very large and growing constantly. Luminaires are constructed around this technology and its capabilities. The use of the appropriate lamp is an essential aesthetic, technical and economic criterion of good illumination. Electrical light sources may be classified, according to their manner of light production, into thermal radiators and discharge lamps. Incandescent lamps, halogen incandescent lamps, and low-voltage halogen incandescent lamps are all thermal radiators. Discharge lamps are divided into low-pressure lamps (fluorescent lamps, compact fluorescent lamps sodium low-pressure lamps) and high-pressure lamps (mercury vapor lamps, metal halide lamps, sodium high-pressure lamps). The table lists the most common types:

→ The most complete and readily available list can be found on the final pages of the catalogues of the German firm ERCO.

Type	Life in h	Abbreviations according to the regulations of the ZVEI
Low-voltage tungsten halogen reflector lamps	2 000–4 000	QR…
Low-voltage tungsten halogen lamps	2 000–3 000	QT…
Tungsten halogen parabolic reflector lamps	2 000–6 000	QPAR…
Tungsten halogen incandescent lamps	1 500–2 000	QT…
Incandescent lamps	1000	A…, D…, IT…,CO…
Parabolic reflector lamps	2000	PAR…
Mercury vapor lamps	8000	HME…
Metal halide lamps	5 000–9 000	HIE
High-pressure sodium discharge lamps	8 000–10 000	HSE…, HST…
Fluorescent lamps	8 000–15 000	T…
Compact fluorescent lamps	8 000–12 000	TC…
Induction lamps	up to 60 000	
Sulfur lamps	60 000	

→ Compact Fluorescent Lamps, Fluorescent Lamps, High-pressure Mercury Vapor Lamp, High-pressure Sodium Lamps, Incandescent Lamps, Induction Lamps

Laser

Lasers (light amplification by stimulated emission of radiation) produce a very narrowly focused and monochromatic light of high intensity. Lasers are not used for general illumination, but their specific characteristics open up a multitude of other possible uses; for measurement, for the transmission of information, for surgery, material processing and decorative lighting. Energy-intensive "laser light" can easily injure people. The devices must therefore be certified by security classes. Even relatively weak laser pointers may be hazardous, if they do not meet the standards of the security class; their beams should never be directed at the eyes. The European standard is EN 60825–1. It has been adopted into the regulations for the prevention of accidents "Laser Radiation" (VBG 93).

LED

LEDs or light emitting diodes are lamps of a special character. The small "light points", at first only green or red, were initially used as signal luminaires. Their luminous flux is very high in relation to their size, and hence they are easily recognized. The technological development of the last few years has produced more and more colors for light emitting diodes, among them "white", and has further increased their luminous power (although this still varies greatly according to color). Several grades of power exist. Light emitting diodes will soon no longer be limited to signaling functions but will be able to fulfil lighting functions as well. The advantages of the LEDs consist mainly in their robustness as semiconductors: they consume very little electricity and currently have a theoretical life of 200000 hours, or about 20 years. The diodes are operated with transformers at 12 V and 24 V AC or DC, and also at a mains voltage of 230 V. They may be used outdoors as well as indoors.

Lenses

In addition to reflectors, the optical system of many luminaires (spotlights) includes lenses.

→ Reflectors

Licenses

Licensing agreements with manufacturers allow the lighting designer to share in the expected success of "his" product. Experience shows that it is not easy to convince manufacturers to conclude licensing agreements. The designer's share should be between 3% and 5% of the net sales price, and it should be determined when licensing fees are due.

Life of a Lamp

→ Useful Life

Light Control (Brightness Control)

It is often not enough to be able to switch lighting systems or parts of them on or off. In order to adjust the light to various room uses and surrounding conditions, control of the brightness is necessary and advantageous, since energy is saved by the nearly loss-free phase-angle control. According to the type of light source used, the preconditions and options may be manifold.

Dimming is most easily achieved with incandescent lamps and halogen incandescent lamps. Simple phase-angle controls regulate the brightness. The dimming of incandescent lamps may cover the complete range from full light output to complete darkness. A minimal decrease of current changes the characteristics of the lamp dramatically: a disproportionate decrease of the luminous flux, significant extension of the life of the lamp, and a change of color. Since this resembles natural phenomena (sunset, extinguishing flames), it is experienced as something pleasant.

When dimmed, low-voltage halogen lamps respond in a similar way to incandescent lamps. Interactions between dimmer and transformer, however, make higher demands on these devices. Aside from special dimmers for low-voltage systems, the transformers approved for dimming must be protected against the high initial currents. Fundamentally, only primary dimming is possible. Conventional dimmers may be used with some electronic transformers, depending on the make.

Electronic transformers may also be dimmed by means of a separate potentiometer (potential divider, adjustable resistor for tapping partial resistors). The cable from the potentiometer to the transformer must not be longer than 0.5 m. The use of a potentiometer represents the inexpensive version of brightness control. Electronic transformers may also be operated with phase-segment dimmers. The advantages of phase-segment dimmers are numerous:

· Their range is extensive (per device 60 to 750 W), and this initial power may be multiplied by connecting several devices.
· The prescribed minimum load of the transformers must be reached or surpassed, since otherwise flicker effects may occur. The following allocations are recommended:

20 VA transformers, a minimum load of the phase-segment dimmers	of 20 W
50 VA transformers, a minimum load of the phase-segment dimmers	of 35 W
60 VA transformers, a minimum load of the phase-segment dimmers	of 35 W
105 VA transformers, a minimum load of the phase-segment dimmers	of 75 W
210 VA transformers, a minimum load of the phase-segment dimmers	of 150 W

Fluorescent lamps may also be dimmed, yet they behave completely differently than incandescent lamps. This is primarily due to the fact that luminous flux and the lamp's current correspond almost linearly. A reduction of the lamp current to an incandescent bulb by 10% reduces the luminous flux to 50%, but for a fluorescent lamp, the current must be reduced by 50% in order to achieve the same level of dimming. The color of light does not change when are dimmed, which may appear unnatural at low illuminances.

Special dimmers are required for fluorescent lamps. Low illuminances cannot be achieved with every type of brightness control. This may be an important issue if very low dim levels are required, for example, for slide or video projections. In the use of fluorescent lamps on lighting tracks with only three leads, dimming is not possible, since a fourth lamp feed is needed for the heating of the electrodes.

An important factor in achieving the correct layout of wiring and power units is the significant idle currents accompanying dimming, which can only be compensated outside of the dimmed circuit.

Lamp types, ballast units and dimmers determine brightness control in very different ways. With the use of electronic ballast units, the irritating flicker effects which occur when dimming with mains frequency are eliminated.

Fluorescent lamps connected to inductive ballast units require dimmable electronic ballasts with 1–10 V control output. The triggering normally occurs via the two-pole interface for a control direct current of 1–10 V conforming to the European standard EN 60 929 regarding "electronic ballast units supplied by alternating current". The control interface of 1–10 V allows for the simultaneous operation of several electronic ballast units. The maximum number of electronic ballast units to be operated in parallel on one dimmer is determined by the input current and the maximum admissible current. For example, with a maximum admissible current of 50 mA on one dimmer and a maximum input current of 1 mA per electronic ballast unit, 50 electronic ballast units may be simultaneously controlled via one dimmer. The T 16 fluorescent lamps which came on the market only recently are now also available from certain manufacturers with dimmable electronic ballast units so that standardization is expected here in the near future as well.

Compact Fluorescent Lamps

Fluorescent lamps with a two-pole socket (integrated starter) cannot be dimmed. Lamp types with four-pole sockets are dimmed in the same way as conventional fluorescent lamps.

High-pressure Discharge Lamps

The options for dimming high-pressure discharge lamps are very limited and are currently offered only by a few specialized power unit manufacturers.

Problems associated with the dimming of high-pressure discharge lamps are irregular burning and a deterioration of all lamp characteristics (change of the color of the light, flickering and similar phenomena). Planners must discuss these issues in particular cases with the manufacturers.

Light Control, Types of

Remote control systems offer the option of controlling individual luminaires or load circuits by means of a remote switch. For this purpose, receiver components are built into luminaires, units of interconnected luminaires, or distribution boxes. These receivers switch or dim the connected luminaires in response to an infrared signal. Through the appropriate signal coding, several luminaires or load circuits in a room can be addressed separately. Remote control systems may be used to control the lighting by means of a handheld transmitter from anywhere in the room. More significant, however, is the possibility of dividing a single circuit into several, separately controllable load circuits. For operation on lighting tracks, special receiver components control all the load circuits of the track. In this way it is possible to provide flexible room illumination without costly installation work, especially in older buildings with only one available electrical circuit per room.

Furthermore, a keyboard control from a central location might be useful. Via a switchboard, the lighting system is set by keystroke to the desired brightness level. The available brightness levels may be adjusted in advance as desired.

Light Control Systems

A lighting system should create the best conditions possible for seeing in any situation. In so doing, however, it must not disregard aesthetic and psychological effects, i.e. it must provide orientation, underscore architectural structures and emphasize their message.

A single lighting concept cannot satisfy these requirements, even in simple tasks. A change in the surroundings demands different conceptions (nighttime illumination – supplementary illumination during the day). Apart from the various surrounding conditions, different uses of a room also require a flexible lighting system (multi-purpose halls – from sports events to gatherings; museums – the most various kinds of exhibitions; office spaces – from secretarial work to employee meeting).

A lighting system that satisfies these manifold demands must be able to produce light scenes or settings. A light setting is the optimum illumination of a room or of an open space for a certain use, with regard to light quality and illuminance. The precondition for this is that parts of the system or individual luminaires can be switched separately. For complex lighting systems with frequently changing uses, the ability to save the various light settings electronically and retrieve them via a switchboard or computer is a great advantage.

Aside from simply switching between light settings, such a light control system can also define this switch from a complete and sudden change to a slow and hardly noticeable transformation. It is also possible to vary the brightness of the light settings as a whole without new programming. In addition to the manual control, light control systems also feature automatic controls which may, for example, respond to the changes in daylight conditions.

Light Guiding Systems

Transporting light over long distances in order to use it far away from the source is one of the most interesting tasks of lighting technology. The options for the guiding of daylight and of artificial light are very different. Daylight varies from one building to another and from location to location and depends on numerous parameters in the planning of a building.

It is easier to guide or transport artificial light, since here the light sources present largely constant factors. Reflectors, mirror techniques, fiber optic cables and holograms can be arranged so that they transport artificial light effectively.

Lighthouses

The Pharaoh – more than 100 meters tall – at the entrance to the delta of the Nile was built around 300 B.C. and was one of the Seven Wonders of the World. It was the oldest lighthouse in the world and fulfilled its function for 1600 years until it was destroyed by an earthquake.

Early beacons were open fires fed by coal, wood, fish oil, or rapeseed oil. In 1784, Argand improved these beacons by means of the kerosene lamp with a circular wick and a glass cylinder. These lamps provided an almost perfect point source of light, which could be easily directed and which increased the efficiency of the system, parabolic mirrors directing it to the sea and Fresnel lenses directing it to the horizon. Today, liquid gas is still used for lighthouses and beacon buoys, allowing the light to burn from several months to several years without servicing. Metal halide lamps with up to 2000 W output beacon from large lighthouses and are visible in normal weather from distances of up to 50 km. Since gas discharge lamps are difficult to switch, the characteristic is achieved by means of rotating lens systems.

Light Pollution

In the modern world, the concept of light pollution has established itself in analogy to the concept of air pollution. It describes the phenomenon of uncontrolled light, especially in outdoor lighting. Satellite

images impressively reveal the industrialized and densely populated areas of the Earth; the artificial brightness of the cities appears as bright spots, the burned-off remnants from oil production appear as yellow spots, and the places of the Japanese fishermen who lure fish by means of high-pressure lamps appear as green spots. Everyone is familiar with the bright pall of haze covering cities at night. The rays reflecting diffusely in dust and moisture particles disperse in all directions and are visible from all directions. They outshine the starry sky to such a degree that in large cities up to a hundred times fewer stars are visible than from dark points of observation. This is an aesthetic loss. For astronomers, this light pollution has developed into a problem that interferes with their sensitive telescopes all the way into distant mountain regions. Lighting designers may keep light pollution to a minimum by means of precisely directed light in outdoor and façade illumination. The frosted spherical luminaire popular in the 1960s that radiates upwards should be history.

Light Protection in Museum Lighting

The sensitivity of exhibits plays an important role in the illumination of museums. Because materials can fade, maximum illuminances were set for paper, textiles and leather. As a rule of thumb, restorers still require a maximum of 50 lux for this type of exhibit, even though the problem should be treated more subtly.

The spectrum of the radiation determines its destructive power on certain materials: the particularly aggressive UV radiation is today kept away from exhibits by means of UV filters for halogen incandescent lamps and fluorescent lamps. Cool beam reflectors and fiber glass technology avoid infrared radiation, which also destroys wood through the temperature fluctuations caused by switching lights on and off in the day-and-night rhythm of the museum.

Light-emitting Diodes

→ LED

Lighting Tracks

Lighting tracks have increased the flexibility of ceiling lighting in buildings. These tracks were first conceived to accommodate spotlights so as to offer the option of rearranging and redirecting them in flexible ways. Yet in practice this option is exercised much less than was originally expected. Lighting tracks are still frequently planned. In old buildings they allow for an electrical installation without wires having to be laid over long distances in walls and ceilings. The common three-phase lighting track allows for three independent circuits, while the one-phase track accordingly provides one circuit, and both supply mains voltage. The (one-phase) low-voltage lighting track delivers 12 V or 24 V, hence, sufficient transformers must be planned as well. Pendant lighting tracks must be suspended in sufficiently short spacings.

Linear Fluorescent Luminaires

This luminaire type represents a common standard in the commercial sector. Conceived for the rod-shaped fluorescent lamp, linear fluorescent luminaires are characterized by their rectangular, narrow, or oblong form; mounted in a continuous row, linear fluorescent luminaires can grow into lighting strips. Grid patterns are also possible. There are countless variations of these arrangements with T26 and TC-L lamps. Through the usually high degree of standardization in the manufacture and in operation, linear fluorescent luminaires are comparatively attractive with respect to total cost.

Links

Below is a collection of links to lighting websites of major German manufactures (further addresses can be found on the website of the Society for the Promotion of Good Light (Fördergemeinschaft Gutes Licht) at www.licht.de), to download areas of software developers and to institutes.

Manufacturers (Selection)

Artemide	http://www.artemide.com
AEG	http://www.aeglichttechnik.com
BEGA	http://www.bega.de
ERCO	http://www.erco.com
Hess	http://www.hess-form-licht.de
Hoffmeister	http://www.hoffmeister.de/deutsch
Iguzzini	http://www.iguzzini.de
Kreon	http://www.kreon.com
Lampas	http://www.lampas.de
LEC	http://www.lec.fr
Louis Poulsen	http://www.louis-poulsen.de
Martini	http://www.martini.it
Modular	http://www.supermodular.com
Norka	http://www.norka.de
Osram	http://www.osram.de
Philips	http://www.philips.de
Regent	http://www.regent.ch
RSL	http://www.rsl.de
RZB	http://www.rzb-leuchten.com
SILL	http://www.sill-lighting.com
Siteco	http://www.siteco.de
Staff	http://www.zumtobelstaff.co.at
Targetti	http://www.targetti.com
Trilux	http://www.trilux.de
Wila	http://www.wila.de
Waldmann	http://www.waldmann.de
Zumtobel	http://www.zumtobelstaff.co.at
further manufacturers	http://www.licht.de

Software Developers and Download Areas

Adeline	http://www.ibp.fhg.de/wt/adeline
Accurender	http://www.accurender.com
Autodesk	http://www.autodesk.de
AutoPlot	http://www.autoplotvw.com
Blue Moon Rendering Tools	http://www.bmrt.org
Cophos	http://www.cophos.co.at/download
Cosmo	http://cosmosoftware.com/download
Design-Drafting Software	http://www.design-drafting.com
Dial	http://www.dial.de
Elaplan	http://www.elaplan.com
Electronic Theatre CS	http://www.etcconnect.com
GE-Lighting-Software tools	http://www.ge.com
Georg Mischler - Radview	http://www.schorsch.com/download
Integra Software Programme	http://www.integra.co.jp/eng
IRC Screen Survey	http://www.cisti.nrc.ca
Ledalite Software Tools	http://www.ledalite.com
L.E.O.S.	http://www.hewcontract.de
	http://www.ulrike-brandi.de
Lenneper	http://www.lenneper.de
Lightscape	http://www.lightscape.com/main
Lighting Analysts	http://www.lightinganalysts.com
Lighting Produkt	http://www.lighting-technologies.com
Lightworks Software	http://www.lightwork.com

Ludwig Leuchten - Software	http://www.ludwig-gebr.de
Martini LUX 6.0 Download	ftp://bbs.stardust.it/martini
Microsoft Download	http://www.microsoft.com/downloads
MiniCAD	http://www.diehlgraphsoft.com
Osram ECOS 99	http://www.osram.de
Pit	http://www.pit.de
PRC-Krochmann (Easyplan)	http://www.ingenieur.de/prc
Prima Lighting Download	http://www.primalighting.com
ProSTEP e.V.	http://www.prostep.de
Radiance	http://radsite.lbl.gov/radiance/papers/sg94.1
Reggiani Quick Illum	http://www.reggiani.net
RELUX	http://www.relux.ch
RIDI LUXvision	http://www.ridi.de/LUXvision
Schuch Download	http://www.schuch.de
Soft++	http://www.softplusplus.com
Stardraw-Software	http://www.stardraw.com
Systempartner HH (Magic)	http://www.systempartnergmbh.de
Targetti Luxus Win	http://www.targetti.it
Trilux Software Download	http://www.trilux.de
wired4motion	http://www.wired4motion.de
WysiCAD	http://www.castlighting.com

Universities, Institutes and Organizations

Ag Solar	http://www.ag-solar.de
Bartlett School of Architecture	http://www.bartlett.ucl.ac.uk
ETH Zürich	http://caad.arch.ethz.ch/research
FGL	http://www.licht.de
Fh-Hildesheim	http://www.fh-hildesheim.de
Fh-Ulm	http://www.fh-ulm.de/vrml/studienarbeit/linkverz.htm
Frauenhofer Institut	http://www.ise.fhg.de
Lichtprojekt	http://www.on-light.de/on-light.htm
Light-Link	http://www.light-link.com
Parsons School of Design	http://www.cyburbia.org
TU-Berlin Fb Elektrotechnik	http://www.ee.tu-berlin.de
TU B Elektronik/Lichttechnik	http://www.ntife.ee.tu-berlin.de
TU Ilmenau	http://www.tu-ilmenau.de
TU Ilmenau Fb Lichttechnik	http://www.spektrum.maschinenbau.tu-ilmenau.de
TU-Darmstadt	http://www.tu-darmstadt.de/fb/arch
Uni-Bochum	http://sabix.etdv.ruhr-uni-bochum.de/seminar/ray02/ray02.htm
Uni-Erlangen	http://www9.informatik.uni-erlangen.de/ger/teaching/fakad97
Uni-Karlsruhe	http://www-lti.etec.uni-karlsruhe.de

LiTG

This is the abbreviation for Deutsche Lichttechnische Gesellschaft e.V. (German Society for Lighting Technology), a union of manufacturers, institutes and associations with offices all over Germany. The Society maintains contacts with similar lobby groups worldwide. Aside from organizing events, its committees deal with questions of standardization and certification.

→ The address of the head office is: LiTG, Burggrafenstr. 6, D-10787 Berlin, Tel. 030-2601-2439, Fax 030-2601-1255.

Local Lighting

→ Illuminance, Light Control, Workplace Guidelines

Low-pressure Sodium Lamp

This lamp is very economical and is characterized by its monochrome light; it has the highest luminous efficacy. Nowadays, however, it is only used in outdoor lighting.

Lumen

Lumen (lm) is the unit of luminous flux (light power).

→ Luminous Flux

Luminaire

A luminaire consists of
· lamp, socket, power unit
· optical components such as a reflector, lens, filter etc.
· housing
· fixture

The luminaire is the tool of illumination for lighting designer and engineers. A further characteristic feature is the installation location and the installation type of the luminaire.

→ Luminaire Types, Luminaires, Fixed and Movable

Luminaire Types

Every type of luminaire has its characteristic places of use and specific lighting properties. This glossary describes the characteristics of:

Luminaires, Fixed and Movable

The costs for permanently installed luminaires, i.e. for luminaires which are part of the building, necessarily belong to the budget of the lighting designer and engineer. They are wired and hence also a quantifiable part of electrical planning and facility management.

Movable luminaires such as desk luminaires, standard luminaires, or night table luminaires in the project planning for hotels may be omitted from the chargeable costs and attributed to the furnishing budget. Thus it may be better to arrange the planning services of movable luminaires separately.

Luminance

Luminance (unit: cd/m^2) is a measure for the luminosity or apparent brightness of a light source or an illuminated surface. Since luminance quantifies the visibility of the light, it is easy to grasp this measure. Thus, for example, a point of light forming an accent on a surface has a noticeably "higher" luminance than its darker surroundings of a "lower" luminance. An extensively illuminated ceiling in turn has a higher luminance than the walls of the surrounding room. Luminance is especially important for computer monitor workstations. The luminance of the screen should not diverge too much from that of the background. The mean luminance of luminaires reflected in the monitor should not measure more than 200 cd/m^2, and the luminance of walls or other objects in the room should in general not exceed 400 cd/m^2. For monitors of superior quality, the limit lies at 1000 cd/m^2.

The brightness of a self-luminous surface is described in the same way: the luminance on the surface of a fluorescent lamp, for example, is higher than the luminance of an opal glass surface backlit by the fluorescent lamp, since in opal glass the luminous flux is distributed over a larger area.

→ Adaptation, Candela, Monitor Workstations, Reflection

Luminous Efficacy

The relation between the luminous flux (φ) (measured in lumen) and power consumption (measured in watts) is described by the formula:

$$\eta = \frac{\varphi \; (\text{lm})}{\rho \; (\text{W})} \; .$$

A lamp should produce a large amount of light energy (= luminous flux) using as little electric power (W) as possible.

Examples of luminous efficacies:

All-purpose lamps (A)	15 lm/W
Tungsten halogen incandescent lamps (QT)	20 lm/W
Low-voltage tungsten halogen incandescent lamps (QT NV)	25 lm/W
Compact fluorescent lamps (TC)	50–70 lm/W
Fluorescent lamps (T)	up to 100 lm/W
Metal halide lamps (HIT)	up to 100 lm/W

→ Luminous Flux

Luminous Flux

Luminous flux (φ) measured in lumen (lm) is a basic quantity of lighting technology. It quantifies the light power generally emanating from a lamp in all directions. Luminous efficacy and light power together are a good measure for comparing the efficiency of lamps. Their economic efficiency is evaluated in conjunction with their life, their mounting options and service intervals.

→ Luminous Efficacy

Luminous Intensity Distribution Curves

Luminous intensity distribution curves indicate the lighting effect of a luminaire. In addition to the choice of a lamp, the corresponding color of light and the chosen shape, the luminous intensity distribution curve describes the distribution characteristics of the light planned for the particular architecture. It is dependent on the luminous flux, on the arrangement of the lamps inside the housing, on the reflector and on the light exit. The light distribution is represented as a three-dimensional graph extending the light exit point. A section of this graph shows the curve in a polar system of coordinates.

For a direct comparison of the luminous intensity distribution curves of different luminaires, a luminous flux of 1000 lm is assumed. Luminaires with a rotationally symmetric luminous flux (e.g. all incandescent lamps) can be sufficiently characterized by means of one luminous intensity distribution curve. Axially symmetric luminaires (e.g. the linear fluorescent luminaires) require one luminous intensity distribution curve for each of the two axes.

Due to the inexactness in the polar system of coordinates, very narrow-beaming light sources are better described in a Cartesian system of coordinates.

The luminous intensity distribution curves of luminaires are evaluated using software for light calculation (currently Eulumdat formats in Europe and IEA formats in America).

Luminous Intensity
→ Candela

Lux

Lux (lx) is the unit of illuminance. It is is measured by means of an illuminance-measuring instrument (luxmeter) pointed in the direction of the light source. For traffic zones, the measuring point is 20 cm above the ground, while for work spaces it is 85 cm above the ground (corresponding to table height, with the European Union standard of 70 cm soon to be implemented).

The illuminances achieved through artificial light constitute key values of lighting design. Although they do not describe the quality of the planned light, they count as one of the objective standards at least for quantitatively good lighting. Values are often prescribed; these use the corresponding standards as their guide, CIE internationally, and DIN and ASR (workplace guideline) in Germany. Too low or too high values may be regarded as errors in planning.

→ Calculations, CIE, Illuminance, Lumen, Design Errors, Standards

Maintenance
→ Useful Life

Maintenance Openings

These are openings for the maintenance of luminaires and installations primarily on plaster board ceilings. They are unpopular because they often disturb the appearance of the surface, but are nevertheless necessary. Sometimes they are planned exactly where the lighting designer would like to position luminaires, and sometimes they cannot be moved, because otherwise the technical installations to be maintained would no longer be within reach. In metal grid ceilings, maintenance openings are not necessary.

Manufacturers

Luminaire manufacturers are usually medium-sized firms in fierce competition with each other. Lamps are almost exclusively produced and distributed by large industrial companies or their subsidiaries.

The manufacturers foster their relationships to designers with to varying degrees. The tasks of the field service include fostering contacts to lighting designers and architects as well as to the wholesale and retail distribution channels.

This includes, of course, the distribution of catalogues and price lists, which a lighting design firm should stock (it takes a long time to build up a comprehensive archive of catalogues). All technical information concerning a luminaire should, of course, also be obtainable from the manufacturer. Most manufacturers offer additional services such as the calculation of illuminances, and the supply of sample luminaires. The readiness of manufacturers to provide sample luminaires free of charge varies, depending on the size of the construction project.

An effective cooperation with manufacturers (and their field service) is a precondition for successful planning. There are many questions of detail, which only the manufacturer, who knows his products well, can answer.

→ Links

Marker Lights

These lamps serve as points of orientation and have a signal-like character. They do not produce light for the purposes of illumination, but are used as "points of light". Marker lights are usually small, are often inserted in the ground or in walls just above the ground, and should have special optical properties that make their light perceptible even during the day.

Monitor Workstations

The recurring discussion regarding the "correct" illumination of computer monitor workstations illustrates the difficulties of imaginative lighting design. From the perspective of lighting technology, much has been done for work spaces at the computer monitor. The industry has developed new luminaire types to serve a rapidly growing market. The new luminaires of the 1980s were manufactured to corresponding high quality. The relevant DIN standard (5035, Part 7) had already been formulated. Its standard requirements are an illuminance of 500 lx on the horizontal work surface and a general absence of glare.

Computer monitors are relatively small and provide little contrast or light. Since they have a glass or film surface, they reflect incident light easily, which may blind users. This reflective glare can be reduced through the appropriate positioning of the monitor. Daylight is one of the sources of reflections on monitors. Normally these reflections can be prevented by positioning the monitor such that the line of vision is parallel to the windows of the room.

The viewing angle within which the screen is visible is very small. If the surrounding brightness varies substantially from that of the (dim) monitor, creating jumps in brightness and adaptation, the eyes will tire quickly. This occurs particularly if the computer screen is placed directly in front of a bright window. This position might promise diversion to the computer user as the eyes wander from the screen to the outside, but the light from the window also forces the eyes into permanent adaptation. The direct glare from luminaires or from ceilings with an excessive luminance also causes interference.

Light conditions in relation to the monitor are an important factor. But also the keyboard and the documents should be clearly visible and not give off reflections during office work. To prevent reflections, no luminaires should be positioned directly above or in front of the monitor workstation.

Vision at the monitor workstation is also influenced by the materials used in the room. It would be easiest to read the screen if the space surrounding it were completely black and matt, but visual comfort would be extremely low. Conversely, light or reflective materials reduce the readability of the computer screen, since they can cause reflections on the monitor. The direction of the incidence of daylight generally determines the position of the workstations.

In order to reduce reflective glare, daylight should enter the workstation from the side; the work tables are hence positioned perpendicular to the windows ("window oriented workstation arrangement"). Mirror screen or prism luminaires (the glare reduction grade should be "1") should be planned parallel to the windows at a distance of about 0.5–0.7 m. If the room is deeper, a second row of luminaires should be planned at a distance of 2–3 m from the window.

An alternative to these classic office luminaires with pure direct illumination is the use of luminaires which, suspended from the ceiling, shine directly onto the workstation and indirectly against the ceiling, producing a combination of direct and indirect light. Using such luminaires, it is frequently possible to bring glare-free light onto the table and brighten the general work environment via illumination of the ceiling while reducing contrast. This principle is also achieved through standard floor luminaires and or sometimes wall luminaires. Table luminaires supplement this arrangement and allow individually adjusted light situations at the workplace.

→ Glare, Luminance

Moonlight

As a pale phantom with a lamp
Ascends some ruin's haunted stair,
So glides the moon along the damp
Mysterious chamber of the air.

Now hidden in a cloud, and now revealed,
As if this phantom, full of pain,
Were by the crumbling walls concealed,
And at the windows seen again.

Until at last serene and proud
In all the splendor of her light,
She walks the terraces of cloud,
Supreme as Empress of the Night.

I look but recognize no more
Objects familiar to my view;
The very pathway to my door
Is an enchanted avenue.

All things are changed, one mass of shade
The elm-trees drop their curtains down;
By palace, park, and colonnade
I walk as in a foreign town.

The very ground beneath my feet
Is clothed with a diviner air;
White marble paves the silent street
And glimmers in the empty square.

Illusion! Underneath there lies
The common life of every day;
Only the spirit glorifies
With its own tints the sober gray.

In vain we look, in vain uplift
Our eyes to heaven, if we are blind;
We see but what we have the gift
Of seeing; what we bring we find.

Henry Wadsworth Longfellow

Nominal Illuminance

This term from the DIN 5035 standard, often found in calculation programs, fixes the desired illuminance independently of the age of the installed luminaires and lamps in a room for a particular usage. The nominal illuminance required will be higher than calculated following the installation of the system, i.e. up to 125% in accordance with the planning factor. Towards the end of a maintenance period, this value may lie at 60% of the standard due to dirt build-up and aging of the lamps.

→ Standards

Notice of Impediment

Planning firms and contractors use this to give notice that they are being impeded by other parties in the fulfillment of their contractually stipulated task. This can lead to serious consequences, which in the extreme case may entail the loss of the contract as well as rights of recourse. Whoever writes a notice of impediment should have previously attempted to persuade the impeded party of a better solution. If this is not successful, the notice of impediment presents a means of pointing formally and "officially" to a problem, and not allowing the responsibility for the impediment reflect on one's own performance.

Office Lighting

The technical requirements of office lighting, which can no longer be distinguished from monitor workstation lighting, are described by DIN 5035, Part 2 and Part 7. The corresponding EU standards are being discussed. The DIN is geared primarily towards nominal illuminances. In a normal office work space, this value should be 500 lux. Requirements for higher illuminances exist for special work spaces.

The most widely accepted lighting systems are those that combine direct and indirect light and leave the individual a certain amount of leeway for switching the lighting.

Much energy is consumed in the illumination of offices, if the hours of usage are long and the illuminance relatively high. Office work conducted in exclusively artificial light is hard on the eyes.

Therefore, there is a trend towards increased use of the natural illumination of work places by daylight. The daylight content can be optimized through intelligent façade technology, well-considered room shapes and maximized daylight usage. Control options for lighting systems offer greater comfort and energy-saving potential. These controls turn the light off if rooms or zones are not being used, or they adjust the illuminance in the room to the daylight conditions.

The high proportion of office lighting in total energy consumption creates a large market for efficient redevelopments. Older installations for

office lighting are often oversized in terms of energy. Old and inefficient lighting systems may be the cause of this as well as generous planning of the 1960s, when energy was cheap. Normally, the use of efficient luminaires alone leads to a much smaller number of luminaires required. In addition, modern lamps have a high luminous efficacy, and an electronic ballast devices for fluorescent lamps a reduced power consumption. If a control system is added, the redevelopments can reduce energy consumption by up to 50%. Even lower savings can still lead to the amortization of the invested capital within a few years.

→ Monitor Workstations, Workplace Guidelines

Outdoor Luminaires

All existing types of luminaires may be divided into two groups: indoor and outdoor. Outdoor luminaires must be constructed in a higher protection class than indoor luminaires, usually IP 44, IP 54 or IP 65. Due to the required waterproofing of the luminaire housing, as well as for temperature reasons, the housing of outdoor luminaires is usually larger than that of indoor luminaires.

For this reason, the planning of outdoor luminaires requires a particularly sure sense of dimension. The luminaires seem large on the discussion table but are perceived as much smaller at a distance or in relation to the building. Thus, the decision regarding the size of the luminaire requires a well-developed spatial imagination.

Outdoor luminaires are available for the same product groups as those for interior spaces: ceiling and wall luminaires, downlights, built-in floor luminaires, spotlight or floodlights. In addition there are bollards and especially the pole luminaires in heights from 2 to about 20 m for the illumination of large areas. In stadiums, luminaires are mounted at even higher elevations on scaffolding and towers. Street luminaires represent a particular species of pole luminaires.

→ Street and Outdoor Luminaires

Pendant Luminaire

Pendant luminaires exist for indoors and outdoors. For a long time, pendant luminaires dominated street lighting in the form of tubular luminaires. It was less expensive to suspend these luminaires between houses than to erect special poles. In interior spaces, the pendant luminaire underwent a renaissance with the increasing popularity of indirect lighting, as manufacturers began to allow light to shine upwards to illuminate the ceiling.

In renovations, pendant luminaires can be used with great flexibility, since they are not dependent on the type of ceiling structure and can be installed quickly.

Performance Specifications

An instrument of project managers used especially in larger projects in which paths of exchange, e. g. of data, are specified in a formal and binding way for all participants. Material standards (say, with regard to environmental compatibility), design specifications, deadlines, or software to be used may also be described in the performance specifications.

Photographs of Light

It is not an easy task to take photographs of light, especially when combining artificial light and daylight. There are various ways of procuring documentation and archival photos. Perhaps the photographer commissioned by the architect can be told of some special artificial light situations in the building which would also be of interest for the documentation of the architects. In this way, the high daily fees for the photographer could be avoided, since the lighting designer would only pay for the individual photo (his own fee does not allow for more). Information about the lamps used (incandescent lamps, fluorescent lamps, warm white or daylight) make work much easier for the photographer. Since the colors of light are difficult to filter, one should rely on professionals; some are not only specialized in architectural photography but also in "light photography". If one nevertheless prefers to take the photographs oneself, the following should be observed:

· Good black and white photographs are better than poor color photographs.
· The decision between using natural (outdoor) or artificial light (indoor) film must given due consideration. Daylight film renders daylight "accurately" during the day. The "blue" hour of twilight may produce a strong blue cast in photographs. Although this can be a beautiful effect, it will show something other than what a visitor of the building sees. Artificial light from incandescent lamps has a more yellowish, warm effect, while the light from fluorescent lamps has a greenish tone, as does the light of metal halide lamps. Most of the photographs in this book were taken using daylight films.

Artificial light film is adjusted to the wavelength of the yellow-red spectrum of the incandescent lamp and the halogen incandescent lamp. This is why daylight appears as cool blue on artificial light films; in an extreme case, wood may look like metal. Frequently, one must be satisfied with a compromise, or one can decide on a type of light to focus on, if natural and artificial light shine simultaneously.

For the light from fluorescent and discharge lamps there are filters (made of glass or film) which reduce the green cast especially for daylight, neutral, or warm white colors of light. A a photographer must experiment and learn from experience.

· When a room is illuminated by reflection from the ceiling, photos may show light-dark contrasts as bright spots, which the eye does not notice in the actual setting. Professionals know clever tricks even for the irradiation of translucent materials. The light in a photo may appear more natural through a double exposure of a subject, once with and once without the artificial light.
· Some architectural photographers also work with additional artificial illumination – yet these photos are not suitable for a light documentation.

Planning Processes

In general it can be said that the earlier lighting designers are involved in the planning process, the better the result will be. This is especially true with regard to daylight planning, since the location of the building and the openings for daylight can have decisive effects even before designers discuss possible façades. The more the artificial light is integrated into the other building technology, the more efficient the function of the system as a whole will be. Therefore, it makes sense to involve lighting designers at the competition stage for a building or an area; this is a growing trend, which promotes a holistic approach.

Plans of Existing Buildings

Plans of existing buildings are used for planning modifications. These may be the original plans (if the building has never been modified, these plans should give a fairly accurate description of the building). They may also be revisions, supplements, or new plans documenting modifications of the building. Alternatively, they are survey prepared especially for the current project which are developed from site measurings. The client may commission such plans in various degrees of detail and thoroughness. Lighting design is primarily based on the state of the ceilings, and in particular of the space above suspended ceilings. The client should be advised to have this area examined thoroughly and not just by way of samples. There can be all sorts of surprises with regard to the existing structure, which may be expensive and time-consuming.

→ Chapter 3: Processes and Procedures

Project Managers

Project management firms act as representatives of the clients, especially in large projects. On behalf of the client, the project manager is supposed to organize the course of events, prepare performance specifications, keep minutes and supervise formalities, deadlines and costs. The project manager does not have a fiduciary or brokering function like the architect, but just represents of the interests of the client. The cooperation with these firms, which often employ architects, engineers and business and management graduates, goes beyond the task of planning. The instructions of the project managers are often perceived as restrictive. They often create financial and time pressure.

Protection Types

1st number: Protection against foreign-object-damage (FOD)

Reference number	Brief description
IP 2X	Protection against foreign-object-damage > 12 mm
IP 3X	Protection against foreign-object-damage > 2.5 mm
IP 4X	Protection against foreign-object-damage > 1 mm
IP 5X	Protection against dust (entry of dust is not fully prevented)
IP 6X	Dustproof (no entry of dust)

2nd number: Protection against water (waterproofing)

Reference number	Brief description
IP X0	Unprotected
IP X1	Protection against dripping water
IP X2	Protection against dripping water below 15° incline
IP X3	Protection against water spray
IP X4	Protection against splashed water
IP X5	Protection against water jets
IP X6	Protection against heavy seas
IP X7	Protection against immersion (with indication of pressure and time period)
IP X8	Protection against submersion (with references from the manufacturer)

Luminaires can become a fire hazard through their internal heat generation. Luminaires with an F symbol have a limited temperature on their mounting surface but not on their exposed surface. Rooms in which something (for example, dust) could ignite on the hot surface of a luminaire require luminaires with a temperature limit all around and are marked with two FF symbols.

During normal operation, the temperatures do not exceed 95° C in the horizontal plane and 220° C in the vertical plane (maximum values are 115 and 260° C respectively). The identification plates of the manufacturers found on most lamps provide further information.

Example of an Identification Plate:
Identification plates state the admissible ambient temperature of the luminaire, if it may be higher than 25° C. If a ballast unit is necessary for operation or is already integrated, this is indicated using an abbreviation (KVG = conventional, VVG = low-loss, EVG = electronic). All luminaires must be radio-shielded. Such shielding is certified if luminaires are labeled with the VDE symbol or the CE symbol or with the remark, "radio-

shielded in accordance with guideline 82/500/EWG". For spaces with an explosion hazard due to the presence of vapors, gases or explosive materials explosion-proof luminaires are used. Their safety is tied to the indication of the zone in which they may be used. Explosion hazard zones:

Explosion Hazard due to Gases and Vapors	
Zone 0	Hazardous or explosive atmosphere is present constantly or over long periods (e.g. in containers and pipe systems)
Zone 1	Hazardous or explosive atmosphere occurs from time to time
Zone 2	Hazardous or explosive atmosphere occurs seldom and for short periods
	Explosive hazard due to combustible dusts
Zone 10	Hazardous or explosive atmosphere due to combustible dusts is present over long periods or frequently
Zone 11	Hazardous or explosive atmosphere may occasionally occur due to the raising of dust deposits

The classification plays a role in a number of areas. Approval marks also represent a political tool to keep competing manufacturers or innovative products away from the home market. Some EU manufacturers wait for years before being granted a German approval mark, some are unable to demonstrate standards certificates which are demanded across the board in the calls for tenders, as nonsensical as these may be in some cases (the new ISO 9000 standard is a good example of this). The individual costs for the tests would be too high or would not be feasible for small, flexibly manufactured quantities.

Protective Classes

Class 0 (no symbol), Class I, Class II, Class III describe the insulation of the luminaires against electric shock. The noninsulated luminaire of Class 0 is not permitted in Germany. Luminaires of Class I have an additional protective lead (ground) which connects the conductive parts of the luminaire with the grounded conductor of the mains (familiar in the home as the yellow/green wire). Class II has no second protective ground but features an enhanced or special insulation. The luminaires of Class III protect against electric shock by means of a protective voltage which is less than or equal to 50 V. Higher voltages than this protective voltage may not occur in the luminaire.

→ Ballast Unit, Standards, Protection Types

Radio-Interference Suppression

→ Types of Protection and Protection Classes

Reflectance Factors and their Estimation

Materials reflect light from their surface to varying degrees. Bright surfaces and colors reflect more incident light back into the surroundings than dark ones. The luminance of the brighter surfaces is also higher. To calculate of illuminances, the reflectance factor must be determined. It is common to use standard values between 0.7 for white, bright surfaces and 0.2 for dark surfaces. More exact values can be obtained for comparison from color tables. The color table of the Schweizerische Lichttechnische Gesellschaft (Swiss Society for Light Technology – SLG) in Basel is useful for this. For the correct calculation of the illuminance, the establishment of the average reflectance factor in the room is important. If dark floors and wall units exist alongside white walls, the reflectance factors must be calculated proportionately according to surface in the mean and inserted into the formula or into the calculation program.

Reflectors

Technical luminaires are usually equipped with reflectors that "steer" the emanating light onto surfaces and have a decisive influence on the luminous intensity distribution curve. Good reflectors optimize the efficiency of the luminaire and have an antiglare effect, since they limit or prevent scattered light. Reflectors usually consist of metals or vapor-coated glass. Cold-light reflectors transmit much of the heat energy of the light back towards the luminaire housing, and reflect only the visible light. The designer must check the possible heat buildup in the back of the luminaire very carefully, if the luminaire is to be installed into combustible materials. There are various types of reflectors:

Type	Characteristic
Spherical reflectors	Reflect the light back into the focal point
Parabolic reflectors	Align the light from a point source in parallel
Channel reflectors	Direct the light of rod-shaped lamps
Ellipsoid reflectors	Gather the light in a second focal point

Room Usage

For the rooms of a new building there are often different budgets according to the type of use, and different associated consumption values are sometimes also specified. The simplest distinction separates a building into usable floor space (such as offices) and traffic areas (such as entrances). A third category, less significant for lighting design, is made up of functional or service areas (e.g. furnace room).

DIN 277, Part 1 classifies these areas and additional rooms. Part 2 catalogues the usage types for rooms in buildings. Although currently inadequate, a standard naming system for rooms is becoming desirable in order to facilitate references within computer programs for the planning and management of buildings.

Sample Luminaires

The sampling of luminaires is one of the labor-intensive and little appreciated tasks of the planning process. Sampling normally becomes necessary when planning is very difficult and has to be tested. Frequently, however, clients are simply unsure, and would like to "visualize" the lighting before giving their consent or making a decision. The sampling of the luminaire itself can be distinguished from the inspection of the lighting effect following installation of the sample luminaires in sample rooms or even in some of the intended eventual installation locations. Individual luminaires are often sampled in order to clarify technical details or discuss changes to the design. They are then moved to the office to be stored and sent back at the appropriate time. The manufacturers or their representatives ship the luminaire in its original packaging and enclose an invoice, which is credited upon return of the undamaged luminaire in its original packaging. Non-established firms sometimes have difficulties in obtaining sample luminaires, since the whole process is very expensive for the manufacturer as well (storage, bookkeeping and shipment of individual luminaires) and is by no means always followed by a sale. The necessary lamps are seldom included. Transformers or ballast units are sometimes not included either, since, they cannot be resold if "used".

The Lighting Test:

The installation of sample luminaires on the construction site is even more expensive, since additional labor and logistics are required. Such samplings are conducted only for very large and prestigious projects and depend on the contracts concluded and the distribution channels of the manufacturers. Sometimes the luminaires are delivered, and a firm already working on the construction site, such as a general contractor, takes care of the installation. Some manufacturers are able to do installations through their local subsidiarias. In other cases, wholesalers may mount various products so as to obtain a delivery order. These proceedings must be coordinated individually with the other planners and with the client. Generally, designers are advised to restrict their activity to merely determining the sample luminaires, or at most to ordering them, but not to managing them. This should be left to the client, who is also the addressee of the shipment and who, in any case, provides the billing address. On poorly organized construction sites, sample luminaires often get "lost", and then these frequently expensive luminaires must be paid for. Sometimes it is possible to include samplings of individual luminaires under "additional services" in the contracts and to invoice them according to time spent.

→ HOAI

Sampling

→ Sample lamps

Scale of Drawings

Lighting designers use various scales. The most common scales are listed below. Some firms, however, still deviate from them.

Scale	Plan	Light Planning
1:10000	Regional planning, town planning	Seldom
1:5000	Urban framework planning	Seldom
1:2500		Seldom
1:2000		Seldom
1:1000	Urban planning, consideration of immediate surroundings, planning of wider surroundings, master planning	illumination of outdoor areas
1:500	Site layout, preliminary design	Seldom
1:200	Design	Larger and smaller buildings, gardens
1:100	Design	Common for buildings
1:20		Wall elevation developments, completion of interior
1:10		Details
1:5		Details
1:2.5		Details
1:1		Details

Drawings generated using CAD programs can easily be displayed at any arbitrary scale. This is immensely helpful for presentation drawings, which can all be given a uniform size. The enlargement or reduction factor for the CAD or copier is calculated from the length of the pre-set scale divided by the length of the existing scale.

Sculpture Lens

A prismatic flat lens, the lengthwise prisms of which fan the circular light exit into an oval one. It permits an even illumination of sculptures.

→ Kelvin

Simulations Using Artificial Suns and Models

For a long time, the spatial miniaturization of a planned building or room in the form of a model in conjunction with an artificial sun (swiveling mirrors that produce parallel light) was the only way to study the influence of daylight and sunlight in the interior of the building. Artificial light sources can now be effectively imitated using fiber optics. The building of models still provides a beautiful and sensuous representation and impressively conveys to both the designer and the layperson the feeling of a space, but it is very time-consuming and expensive. For this reason, the traditional method now often competes with computer simulations, where input time has been greatly reduced in recent years. Programs have also been improved in terms of presentation. Computer simulations are suitable for calculating values and can hence give sound advice. They are less suitable for visualizing the light atmosphere, since they have a sterile appearance, due to the simplified representation of the surface. If skillfully edited by hand, they can, however, provide impressive images for presentations.

→ Chapter 1: Images of Light

Software Developers

→ Links

Special Luminaires

Despite thousands of luminaires being on the market, the desired luminaire is still not available for some situations. In such a case – following consultation with the client – new luminaires must be developed and adapted to a special situation. New development is sometimes necessary for technical reasons, in other cases, it is elevated artistic requirements or projects which require a unique appearance.

It is sufficient to modify existing luminaires in consultation with the manufacturer. Sometimes these modified luminaires then make their way into the product line of a manufacturer. Some medium-sized luminaire manufacturers specialize in the making small quantities of a type of luminaire, and even large manufacturers now offer such a service more frequently. Both types of manufacturers have the facilities to test the technical specifications of the new luminaire in their workshops and to prepare test certificates.

The development of special luminaires is not a planning task for the lighting designer but rather a design service. As a task of design and technical development, creation of a special luminaire does not fall under the planning contract, although this is often what the client expects. If the client requests special luminaires, their design must be remunerated as a separate service; this should be explained at the start. Aside from the separate remuneration there is the (seldom practiced) option of concluding a licensing agreement with the manufacturer. It is possible to agree on a profit of approximately 5% of the net sales price.

Special Services

→ Design, HOAI, Sample Lamps

Specialist Engineers/Specialist Planners/Appraising Firms

Lighting designers belong to the category of specialist engineering firms in the area of mechanical sevices. Mechanical sevices include electrical installations, heating, air-conditioning, ventilation and sanitation. Mechanical sevices are sometimes planned by an engineering firm, sometimes by several specialized firms. The most extensive works are normally planned by the electrical engineers and the heating, air-conditioning and ventilation engineers. Further specialists in the technical equipment of buildings include façade technicians, floor technicians, elevator builders and acoustics engineers. Lighting designers naturally have the most points of contact with the electrical engineers. Traditionally, it has properly been the task of the electrical engineers to plan the artificial lighting technology in buildings. It was not until the further development of lighting technology, along with the growth in the number of luminaire types and models, that a specialization such as lighting design became possible, even from a technical perspective. Conservatively disposed engineers still do not want to accept this development. Other firms seek to regain the market share they lose to lighting designers, by setting up their own lighting design departments. In commercial building construction, tasks are sometimes distributed in accordance with sections of the building. While the mechanical services engineers, with their high total share of building costs (often up to 50% and more), acquire the areas that are easy to plan and therefore profitable, the lighting designers are left with the "representative" and much more involved areas such as the illumination of façades, lobbies, elevator foyers, hallways, conference rooms, auditoriums and other halls. Ideally there is a division of labor between electrical engineers and lighting designers, in which the lighting designer is a subcontractor of the electrical engineer. In such an arrangement, the engineers profit from the innovative capabilities of the specialized lighting designer.

A wire outlet in the ceiling, in the wall, or in the floor has been established as the point of handing over the job between electrical engineers and lighting designer. The electrical engineers plan wires, switches, and circuits, while the lighting designers plan the luminaires and their accessories such as lighting tracks, filters including installation, i.e. details which, from the perspective of design, must be precisely coordinated with the architects. Possible installation parts which are not part of the stan-

dard equipment of luminaires may be planned as luminaire accessories by the lighting designer or, as is more often the case, by the architect as part of the façade or steel structure. For the purpose of dimensioning their circuits and bus systems, the engineers require at least an estimate of the power consumption of the planned luminaire at an early stage of planning. At a later stage, users and lighting designers determine the switching options of the light – the light settings – and this information is passed on to the electrical engineers for the planning of their circuits. Cooperation with the planners of heating, ventilation, and air-conditioning systems is also important. Their systems take up a lot of space in suspended ceilings or underneath bare ceilings – the most important installation area for luminaires – and like luminaires, they require outlets. Frequently, built-in luminaires and installation duets get in each others way, and the required installation depths can also pose serious problems. Lighting design firms should insist that there be early coordination and that the lighting designer have sufficient influence on the layout of the ceiling installations. At an early stage, it is still possible to make adjustments such as moving a ventilation duct off to the side of a centered row of downlights.

Spotlights

Spotlights are very versatile light sources. There are many varieties of fixed spotlights and those that can be moved along lighting tracks. They all share the feature of "transporting" light. The two extremes in the luminous intensity distribution curve are wide beaming floodlights and narrow beaming spotlights proper. Spotlights are used to create lighting accents.

Standards

Lighting qualities and quantities are set by DIN 5034 (daylight in interior spaces) and DIN 5035 (artificial light in interior spaces). Frequently, these standards are regarded as obstructive and obsolete in terms of the technical possibilities. But standards also have their positive sides. From a historical perspective, it is because of these standards that the lighting systems in commercially used spaces have improved in recent decades. The application of these standards is usually still national. In a few years, however, unified standards for light will apply in Europe (CEN standards).

The artificial lighting prescribed in Germany in private commercial buildings or public buildings still follows primarily DIN 5035 with regard to "illumination with artificial light", while in the last 15 years Part 7, dealing with computer monitor workstations, has gained special prominence. The demands formulated there, 500 lx for the monitor workstation achieved with reduced luminances and louvers of superior quality, are minimum requirements. The disregard or nonfulfillment of standards is treated as an error in planning, unless the client expressly insists on the non-observance (this should be confirmed in writing).

From an aesthetic point of view in particular, standards regarding illuminances, luminances and glare limits appear as obstructive restrictions. Frequently, minimum illuminances are recommended while demanding maximum current consumption values of a system, requiring the planner to optimize his system in two directions and leaving him with little choice regarding the type and arrangement of the luminaires.

One must not ignore the fact that standards are recommendations and not laws. On the other hand, these recommendations are in turn prescribed by the professional associations, i.e. workers' accident insurance is only valid if the workplace corresponds to the ergonomic requirements of the professional association. Similarly, municipal administrations follow the DIN standards in order to ensure a defined level of security. Human perception of light and dark is subjective: what appears too bright to one person may be too dark for another. It is known that with advancing age, greater illuminances are required in order to see well. A pleasant atmosphere is therefore provided by rooms in which the user can individually adjust some of the light. Another phenomenon is important here. A space in which I measure the same illuminance at the level of the table and at ground level may seem of different brightness: only a slightly brightened ceiling makes the room light and friendly; a dark ceiling and dark walls create a gloomy cave-like atmosphere even if work surfaces are bright.

→ The German, Austrian and Swiss standards can be consulted in public libraries and using on-line services (e.g. www.Baunetz.de) and can be ordered through Beuth Verlag, 10772 Berlin.

Street and Outdoor Luminaires

At the beginning of the 19th century, the first large-scale lighting systems were established in exterior public spaces. "Technical" street lighting thus has a long and significant tradition. Street luminaires must be inexpensive to maintain and operate. After the "gas lanterns" came "incandescent bulbs". Then, for a long time, fluorescent lamps were the first choice. These were followed by low-pressure sodium lamps, and now high-pressure sodium lamps (with their improved color of light) are frequently replacing the widespread mercury vapor lamp (cold bluish light). Outdoor luminaires primarily illuminate work areas (1), while street luminaires illuminate various traffic routes (streets, parking lots, pedestrian zones, parks) (2), and other outdoor luminaires illuminate objects (3). The various requirements are regulated by corresponding standards.

(1) Under workplace guideline 41/3, open-air work areas must feature the same nominal illuminance (according to DIN 5035–2) as the corresponding workplaces in the interior of building. If, for example, machines (such as circular saws) are operated in various places, on a construction site the light must correspond to the illuminance in the workshop (E = 500 lx). The values for the illumination of open areas (transshipment centers, storage areas etc.) vary between 3–5 lx (sidewalks) and 100 lx (service stations).

(2) Traffic routes are evaluated according to their various uses. Lower values of ground illuminance and luminosity apply to pedestrian zones than to motor vehicle routes. In addition to these values, on streets and roads, the uniformity of illumination is an important criterion to determine the spaces between luminaires. With today's state of technology, the rule of thumb holds that the distance between luminaires equals four times the mounting height of the luminaires. For the proper illumination of pedestrian zones it is important to convey a feeling of security and comfort to the passer-by. Other persons and their behavior should be recognizable and assessable from a sufficient distance. This can be achieved by relatively low mounting heights of 2 – 4 m.

(3) The correct illumination of outdoor objects or buildings depends solely on the task in hand. In the exterior illumination of buildings, shadows can be problematic or helpful. Shadows occur when the light cannot be directed onto the building at the perpendicular (e.g. because spotlights mounted in the ground are to be used). If the light cannot be directed in parallel from opposite buildings or poles (suitable for extensive and uniform floodlighting), it can be installed directly in the façade, for example, using fibre optics or very narrow beaming spotlights. This is

more involved and expensive than the installation of a few wide beaming luminaires at a distance, but it also delivers a much more subtly differentiated and appropriate light.

Sunlight

The Sun Rising

Busy old fool, unruly Sun,
Why dost thou thus,
Through windows, and through curtains, call on us?
Must to thy motions lovers' seasons run?
Saucy pedantic wretch, go chide
Late schoolboys, and sour prentices,
Go tell court-huntsmen that the king will ride,
Call country ants to harvest offices,
Love, all alike, no season knows, nor clime,
Nor hours, days, months, which are the rags of time.
Thy beams, so reverend and strong
Why shouldst thou think?
I could eclipse and cloud them with a wink,
But that I would not lose her sight so long:
If her eyes have not blinded thine,
Look, and tomorrow late, tell me
Whether both the Indias of spice and mine
Be where thou leftst them, or lie here with me.
Ask for those kings whom thou saw'st yesterday,
And thou shalt hear: "All here in one bed lay."
She's all states, and all princes I,
Nothing else is.
Princes do but play us; compar'd to this,
All honour's mimic, all wealth alchemy.
Thou, sun, art half as happy'as we,
In that the world's contracted thus;
Thine age asks ease, and since thy duties be
To warm the world, that's done in warming us.
Shine here to us, and thou art everywhere;
This bed thy centre is, these walls, thy sphere.

John Donne

Sun Position Graphs

These graphs help the designer to visualize the daylight conditions in buildings and to construct corresponding room surface characteristics in terms of shadow formation. The use of computer programs, which

quickly calculate the shadow formation, is increasingly replacing this intuitive method. The chapter on daylight gives a sun position graph that relates time and geographical orientation. A sun position graph applies to all locations on a certain latitude and for the true time of day at a particular place. The x-axis shows the points of the compass, south being at the center, east and west to the left and right respectively. A sun position diagram for the north pole area would be set up all the way to the north, since the sun never sets in summer and hence is also visible in the north. The y-axis shows the elevation angles in the sky: a maximum 90° would mean that sunlight comes in vertically, which, of course, does occur between the tropic of Cancer and the tropic of Capricorn. The three curves within this area of the sky show the paths of the sun in summer, spring, fall and winter, with indications of the times of day in the daily course of the sun. Every further daily path lies, with small deviations, between the three paths represented, i.e. between June 21 and March 21 there are approximately 90 additional lines. Our example shows that in the city of Halle the sun rises on December 12 at approximately 8.20 a.m. almost precisely in the south-east (47° from the south). On June 21 at 8.20 a.m. it is already at an angle of almost 36° to the east-east-south (76° from the south).

Surroundings of Building

There can be no successful lighting design without considering a building's surroundings, since light also shines out of the building onto the space around it. Surrounding buildings must also be considered, since they may reduce the incidence of light. This can be readily simulated.
→ Chapter 2: Fundamentals, Section Daylight

Techniques of Representation

It is difficult to convey an idea of the planned light for buildings or exterior spaces to clients, architects and users. Light is too universal for it to be described precisely in all states, or imagined visually.
Nevertheless, especially for lighting designers, the masterly representation of their achieved design is important. Electrical engineers, air-conditioning technicians and other specialist engineers of equal importance in the planning process scarcely have an opportunity to visualize their ability in such a profound way. But this is expected of architects, interior architects, designers and lighting designers.
A good representation of light limits itself to an abstraction. The design concept is especially clearly expressed if a drawing shows where light is coming from and where it becomes visible. This can be demonstrated simply by means of arrows. The planned luminaire positions, easily discernible on drawings or plots, at least for the other planning participants,

can be combined with the desired effect of the light on walls or various surfaces. In the imagination of the client and the planner, light is thus given a direction and a place.

Another well-tried option offers the viewer illustrations of already realized examples. These may be hand drawings, photographs, or computer-generated images of the light distribution to be expected. In direct combination with plans containing the lamp positions, selected examples offer an impressive demonstration of the design concept, since they are graspable "at a glance". It is helpful to use the suggestive power of photographs of prominent buildings and squares while remaining focused in the presentation and discussion on the situation of the building to be planned.

Usually, people expect a representation of artificial light. Hence, the examples shown always derive from interior spaces, and evening or night situations, for otherwise artificial light would not be visible. It remains important, however, to adjust the presentation of the design as dynamically as possible to the various light situations to be expected throughout the day. Only this can produce a balance of all advantages, disadvantages and costs of a proposal, which can lead to a contract.

Tender Negotiations

Especially with larger construction projects, it is customary to discuss the obtained tenders with the tenderers. The client asks the tenderers individually about their calculations in order to negotiate a price. The client may call the respective specialist planners to these meetings for consultation. The designers explain technical issues, talk about their experiences with the respective firms and comment on alternative products which the tenderer might propose. However, it is not the task of the specialist planner to conduct price negotiations.

Tender Specifications

The planner prepares tender specifications in order to make it possible for construction contractors to submit comparable bids. In comparison to other trades, tender specificationss for lighting installations are difficult to prepare.

Fundamentally, the specifications, into which the tenderer enters his prices, contains a service item (e.g., supply of a type of luminaire), the unit price, quantities and the resulting prices per service item as well as the corresponding labor time required (for the installation, in the case of the luminaire), together with the cost of labor. The planner must give very precise details in this regard.

Through Wiring

Through wiring connects luminaires in such a way that they form a ring, i.e. that the wire leads from one luminaire to another rather than connecting each luminaire with its own individual wire in a star-shaped arrangement. This leads to a significant reduction in installation costs.

Transformers

In the interior of buildings, these devices are required primarily for the operation of low-voltage halogen lamps (12 V or 24 V). In the commercial sector, electronic transformers are now used almost exclusively for this purpose. They are usually dimmable; dimming may extend the potential life of lamps and installations substantially. Transformers can be operated with direct current and thus allow for (integrated) emergency lighting operation. Electronic transformers are compact, quiet and open-circuit safe (= they are not destroyed by an absence of load, say, through a defective lamp) on the transformed (= secondary) side. With due consideration of the required spacings and ambient temperatures, transformers can easily be recessed into the wall, floor, or ceiling. The transformers used should additionally be equipped with integrated overload and short-circuit protection. The distance between transformer and luminaire is limited to a few meters.

Transmittance Factors

Transparent, clear and translucent materials react to incident light in three ways: they absorb, reflect and transmit this light. With smaller angles of incidence of light, the transmittance decreases. Likewise, the transmittance can vary greatly for different wavelengths of light. A red filter, for example, transmits most of the red wavelengths, yet does not transmit the green wavelengths. The transmittance factor is thus provided for the incidence of white light at an angle of $90°$, unless stated otherwise.

Flat material sample	Absorption in %	Reflectance in %	Transmittance in %
Clear glass, 2–4 mm	2–4	6–8	90–92
Frosted glass, 2–3 mm	(incidence of light 4–17 on the smooth side)	7–20	63–87
Frosted glass, 2–3 mm	(incidence of light 3–11 on the frosted side)	6–16	77–89
Opal glass, Class 1, 2–3 mm	3–10	31–45	47–66
Opal glass, Class 2, approx. 3 mm	8–11	54–67	27–35
Wire glass, 6–8 mm	approx.12	approx.8	approx.80
Parchment, white, thin	10–15	40–50	35–55
Silk, white	5	60	35

Tunnel Lighting, Tunnel Luminaires

The proper illumination of (road) tunnels is not a matter of artistic design. The purpose is to provide the appropriate light for an even and safe flow of traffic from the approach to the tunnel, through the entrance, the interior, and the exit. For this purpose, the illumination must be adjusted to the adaptive capacities of the eyes and to the field of vision.

The corresponding experiences and criteria are contained in DIN 61 524, Part 1 as well as in the guidelines for the equipment and operation of road tunnels (Richtlinien für die Ausstattung und den Betrieb von Straßentunneln – RABT 1994).

→ http://www.beuth.de

→ Adaptation

Underwater Luminaires

Their environment places special demands on these luminaires. Their design must always correspond to the type of protection IP X8. Many luminaires can be used only down to certain depths (they can withstand only limited pressure), while most are not suitable for seawater or saltwater baths. Changing this lamps can be very expensive, since it is not possible under water. For this reason, luminaires just below the surface of the water often feature watertight housings with integrated cables and hoses of a certain length such that the luminaires can be lifted from the water and serviced in the dry. Many underwater luminaires could not be operated at the maximum wattage, out of water for they would get too hot. If the luminaires require transformers, these must be operated outside of the water.

Universities

→ Links

Useful Life

The economic efficiency of a lighting system depends on various factors: costs of luminaires and lamps, installation costs, recycling costs, electricity costs and quantities over which the designer has no control, such as capital costs. In this mesh, the life of the lamp is a decisive factor as well as its luminous efficacy (lm/W). The reasonable possible useful life of a lamp is derived from its life considered under the aspect of maintenance costs. Labor costs for the exchange of lamps are high. Hence, it is desirable to determine as precisely as possible the time for the exchange of entire series of lamps, if possible, prior to the expected failure. Long experience has shown how difficult this is. If the actual useful life of a lighting system is known, the theoretically possible maintenance period can be determined quite precisely. It is often several years. High-quality

luminaires and power units have very low failure rates. They may not fail for decades, but only become antiquated in terms of their technology and design.

The examples of the incandescent lamp and the fluorescent lamp illustrate how many different types of factors affect the useful life of lamps. The first distinction is between fluorescent lamps and the other common lamps (incandescent lamps, "energy saving lamps", or halogen incandescent lamps). For the common lamps, an average life gives the possible exchange interval (50% lamp failure in the case of incandescent lamps, 80% luminous flux reduction in the case of discharge lamps). A normal incandescent lamp ("all-purpose lamp") of good quality has an average life of 1000 h. However, this will only be reached if the mains voltage remains constant at 230 V. The utility companies, however, may make use of tolerances: currently, the mains supply may have up to 6% more and 10% less voltage. The rule is rather a higher voltage (the measured consumption is increased). An increase of the voltage by 5% already lowers the life of the incandescent lamp by 50%. The lamp gets too hot, the tungsten filament burns up, and the higher luminous flux costs dearly. A decrease of the voltage by 5% increases the life by 100%, that is, to 2000 h, but also lowers the luminous flux (= more lamps have to be in operation to produce the desired brightness). The incandescent lamps work optimally at a voltage of 230 V. In order to achieve this constant voltage, it is becoming increasingly popular to buffer large systems by means of transformers.

Fluorescent lamps have a comparatively long life. Their life depends on the ballast unit used and the tolerated reduction of their luminious flux. Generally, 80% of the original luminous flux is regarded as the life limit of the system. The life of the fluorescent lamp is further dependent on its power consumption and the chosen color of light. Fluorescent lamps operated in older installations reach a useful life of approx. 8000 h. Modern triphosphor fluorescent lamps connected to electronic ballast units may reach a useful life of up 15 000 h.

The following table lists guide values for the life of the common lamps. The precise values differ depending on the manufacturer and must be requested from the manufacturer.

Type	Life in h
Comments	
Low-voltage halogen reflector lamps	2000–4000
Operation in a dimmed state extends life	
Low-voltage tungsten halogen lamps	2000–3000
Operation in a dimmed state extends life	
Tungsten halogen parabolic reflector lamps	2000–6000
Operation in a dimmed state extends life	

| V |

High-voltage tungsten halogen incandescent lamps	1500–2000
Operation in a dimmed state extends life	
Incandescent lamps	1000
Operation in a dimmed state extends life significantly	
Parabolic reflector lamps	2000
Operation in a dimmed state extends life significantly	
Mercury vapor lamps	10000
Dimming possible starting at 70 W power consumption, does not extend life	
Metal halide lamps	5000–9000
Dimming possible starting at 70 W power consumption, does not extend life	
High-pressure sodium lamps	8000–10000
Dimming possible starting at 70 W power consumption, does not extend life	
Fluorescent lamps	8000–15000
Operation with electronic ballast units extends life significantly, dimming is possible, does not extend life	
Compact fluorescent lamps	8000–12000
Operation with electronic ballast units extends life significantly, dimming is possible, does not extend life	
Induction lamps	up to 60000
Sulfur lamps	60000
Life of Power unit 15000 h	

VOB (Verdingungssordnung für Bauleistungen – German regulations regarding construction services)

This extensive set of regulations (which in case of a dispute is also of fundamental importance) is binding in commissions for the execution of public construction in Germany. Many private construction projects are also carried out under contracts in accordance with the VOB. It primarily concerns the various trade contractors carrying out the construction, and is not specific to "lighting installations".

The planned luminaires must be installed in the correct locations and with the prescribed orientation, information which must be gathered from the construction plans. Furthermore, they must be equipped with the correct lamps (a frequent mistake) and properly mounted. The VOB only states in a very general way how this is to be done. Disputes sometimes arise over invitations to bid which are subject to the VOB. If it is not mentioned, for example, that the firms executing the installation must provide ladders or scaffolding where lamps are to be installed in high places, the firms can charge for these costs separately. Similarly for the wiring of luminaires or lighting tracks: it must be described in the invitation to bid in terms of the power required by the individual luminaires or in terms of the total power to be provided for the respective section of the installation (including possible transformers, dimmers etc.).

→ In book form: Beuth Verlag, 10772 Berlin
Online: http://www.vob-online.de

| W |

Volt

Volt (V), is the unit of measure of electrical tension. The voltage of 1 V exists at a resistance of 1 Ohm (Ω), when a current of 1 Ampere (A) flows or a power of 1 Watt (W) is produced.

Voltage is standardized. In Europe, it was 220 V for a long time, but 110 V in some regions . There are still countries in which 110 V machines and lamps are the norm. A few years ago, power companies started switching the mains voltage to 230 V (with a tolerance of +6% or –10%). All new luminaires and power units are already designed for this higher voltage. Low-voltage systems (normally 12/24 V), however, have also gained acceptance, especially for tungsten halogen incandescent lamps. For such systems, transformers must reduce the mains voltage.

→ Ampere, Volt, Watt

Wall Luminaires

Wall luminaires exist in various forms and are similar only in that they are attached to walls or pillars. One may differentiate between decorative luminaires and luminaires that contribute to the general lighting from the wall. The light from decorative wall luminaires surrounds the luminaires locally and does not have to be directed. Wall luminaires for general illumination either shine onto the ground in front of them or illuminate the ceiling, thus reflecting indirect light.

Wall Washers

A type of lamp used primarily for illuminating walls in a particular, relatively extensive area, in an extremely uniform way. Moreover, the asymmetric angle of beam and the equipment options are dimensioned in such a way that the lamps can be positioned at a sufficient distance from the wall so as to minimize direct reflections. Wall washers were originally developed for museums in order to illuminate display surfaces in a uniform manner.

Walls

Walls have quite a different meaning for lighting designers than for architects, who plan walls as exterior, interior, or dividing walls in various materials and thicknesses. The attention of the lighting designer is at first focused only on the quality of the surface of the wall. Color, structure and surface determine its properties with regard to light. Walls are not always closed and not necessarily straight. They have windows and doors through which light enters or which lead into darkness. Every wall, every window, every door has its specific characteristics with regard to artificial light or daylight. These have a decisive influence on the light in every room. The determining quantities for the purposes of calculations are the luminance on the wall, which gives it a bright appearance, and the reflectance factor of the wall. The orientation of the building and the degree of shading through façade elements or surrounding buildings and landscape, as well as the weather, determine how much daylight reaches the walls (the floor, the ceiling) in proportion to the size of the window. All this can be calculated in advance or anticipated from experience.

A wall has very different characteristics for each specialist planner, something that is often not reflected in CAD drawings. The drawing itself cannot present a wall acoustically, structurally, or from a lighting perspective. The multitude of characteristic features of walls is one of decisive obstacles to the integration of the various kinds of software used for the planning of buildings. The CAD standard exchange formats dxf and dwg, in which most plans are drafted, ignore too many crucial qualities. Software to calculate illuminances, daylight incidence, or heat loads is unable to generate these formats. Although there are standards of new internationally valid exchange formats (such as .ifc), they have not (yet) been generally accepted.

Watt

Watt (W) is the unit of measure of electrical power.

Electrical power is a central quantity for lighting design. It represents the power consumption of the planned system and is thus important for the plans of the electrical engineers. It is required for dimensioning cables and transformer stations. Air-conditioning engineers also take electrical power into account, for they will want to know how much heat the lighting system is removed by a possible air-conditioning system. In this manner, the expended specific watt/m^2 becomes a measure of efficiency.

Windows

The shape and position of a window affect the possibilities of lighting design, through the daylight and solar radiation that enter. A high proportion of daylight is of course desirable in daily illumination, but the large correspondingly windows also increase the thermal load produced in the building through large-scale insolation. The proportion of daylight and the thermal loads may be simulated, but unfortunately not yet both together. Good solutions are mainly a question of the size of the budget and of the design of the façade. Very good results may be obtained with movable shading systems for temporary usage, which are installed in front of the façade.

Workplace Guidelines

These guidelines are part of the "package of standards" used to define the "quantitatively correct" light for the workplace. They refer to the DIN standards, which are being replaced by the European CEN, professional association regulations for safety at the workplace (ZH 1/190) as well as by the workplace guideline ASR 7/30 and the workplace regulation of the federal department of labor (ArbStättV).

The "package of standards" provides recommendations covering nominal illuminances, colors of light, color rendering properties, and the limitation of glare for the various divisions of activity, function and industry, indoors as well as outdoors.

→ The technical information provided by TRILUX LENZE GmbH (ISBN 3–89053–064–8) contains a useful summary.

BIOGRAPHIES
BIBLIOGRAPHY
INDEX

Ulrike Brandi | Born in 1957

A lighting planner with a diploma in design, Mrs. Brandi is the managing director of ULRIKE BRANDI LICHT GmbH in Hamburg, Germany, providing lighting designs for architecture and landscape.

1976–1983 **study of Romance languages and literature** at Hamburg University.

1984–1988 **study of industrial design** at the *Hochschule für bildende Künste* (Institute of Visual Arts) in Hamburg.

1986 **Established the firm ULRIKE BRANDI LICHT** Light Planning and Lamp Design in Hamburg, where she is the sole managing director since 1996. The firm offers planning and consulting services for artificial light and daylight for buildings and exterior spaces.
More than 250 projects in Europe and Asia.

1995–1996 **Teaching assignment** at the Technical University Düsseldorf in the Department of Architecture – Interior Design

1998–1999 **Guest professorship** at the Hochschule für bildende Künste (Institute of Visual Arts) Braunschweig in the Department of Industrial Design.

Seminars and workshops conducted on behalf of: Deutsches Institut für angewandte Lichttechnik (German Institute of Applied Lighting Technology); Hochschule für Gestaltung (Institute of Design), Linz; Architektenkammer (Chamber of Architects) Hamburg; Akademie der Architektenkammer (Academy of the Chamber of Architects) Hessen; Deutscher Werkbund; Siemens; Siteco; Philips.

Lectures for:
AEG; Deutsches Institut für angewandte Lichttechnik; Architektenkammer Schleswig Holstein; Hochschule für Gestaltung, Offenbach; Bayerische Architektenkammer; Hochschule für Gestaltung, Linz; Fachhochschule Heiligendamm; Handwerkskammer (Chamber of Crafts) Hamburg; Fachhochschule Düsseldorf; Architektenkammer Hamburg; Fachhochschule Hildesheim/Holzminden; Technikzentrum für Frauen (Technology Center for Women), Hamburg; Hochschule für bildende Künste Hamburg; HEW; Siemens; Siteco; Philips.

Numerous publications in professional journals.

2001 **Guest curator** at the Deutsche Architektur Museum in Frankfurt/Main for the exhibition "Light and Shadow".

Christoph Geissmar-Brandi: | Born in 1958

As an independent curator and an art historian (Dr. phil., M.A.), Christoph Geissmar-Brandi organizes exhibitions and conferences primarily on Western drawing and graphic arts of the 15th, 16th and 20th centuries. He is also active as an author and editor of books, catalogues and software. Dr. Geissmar-Brandi lives and works in Hamburg.

Geissmar-Brandi studied art history, literature and psychology at Hamburg University (1978–1990), where he received the degree of Dr. phil.

1989–1992 **Curator of the Albertina** collection of graphic art in Vienna.

1992–1995 **Independent curator** (Albertina and Kunsthalle, Vienna).

1996–1999 **Independent curator** (Albertina and National Museum of Western Art, Tokyo) with Ilsebil Barta-Fliedl.

Projects:

1992 **Exhibition**: "Die Beredsamkeit des Leibes" ("The Eloquence of the Body") for the Albertina Collection of Graphic Art in Vienna.

1995–1996 **Exhibition**: "Glaube Hoffnung Liebe Tod" ("Faith Hope Love Death") for the Albertina Collection of Graphic Art and the Kunsthalle in Vienna in cooperation with Eleonora Louis.

1996 **Conference**: "Image of the Earth" on behalf of the Internationale Forschungszentrum Kulturwissenschaften (International Research Center for Cultural Sciences) at the Academy of Sciences in Vienna in cooperation with Eleonora Louis and Gerhard Wolf.

since 1997 Administrative work for ULRIKE BRANDI LICHT GmbH.

1998–2000 **Software development**: "L.E.O.S." (Light, Energy Optimization and Service) for HEWContract in cooperation with Christof Fielstette.

1999 **Exhibition**: "Rhetorik der Leidenschaft" ("The Rhetoric of Passion") of the Albertina Collection of Graphic Art and the Austrian National Library for the National Museum of Western Art, Tokyo in cooperation with Naoki Sato.

1999 **Conference**: "The Faces of Skin" on behalf of the National Museum of Western Art, Tokyo and the German Institute for Japanese Studies in cooperation with Naoki Sato and Gerhard Wolf.

1999 Adoption of "Rhetorik der Leidenschaft" by the Hamburg Museum für Kunst und Gewerbe (Museum of Arts and Crafts).

2001 **Guest curator** at the Deutsche Architektur Museum in Frankfurt/Main for the exhibition "Light and Shadow".

Selected Publications:

Die Beredsamkeit des Leibes in cooperation with Ilsebill Barta Ed., Residenz Verlag, Salzburg – Vienna 1992.

Das Auge Gottes. Bilder zu Jakob Böhme, Wolfenbütteler Studien zur Barockforschung, commissioned by Harrassowitz, Wiesbaden 1993.

A Geometrical Order of the World: Otto van Veens..., in: Journal of the Warburg and Courtauld Institute, London 1995.

Glaube Hoffnung Liebe Tod in cooperation with Eleonora Louis Ed., Ritter Verlag, Klagenfurt 1995/1996.

Die Rhetorik der Leidenschaft – Zur Bildsprache der Kunst im Abendland in cooperation with Ilsebill Barta-Fliedl and Naoki Sato Eds., German: Dölling und Galitz Verlag, Hamburg 1999; Japanese: Inshosha, Tokyo 1999.

The Faces of Skin in cooperation with Irmela Hijiya-Kirschnereit and Naoki Sato Eds. (forthcoming), German: Stroemfeld Verlag Basel/Frankfurt/Main 2001, Japanese: Inshosha, Tokyo 2000.

Ian Ritchie | Born in 1947
CBE RA Dipl Arch (dist) PCL RIBA MCSD FRSA in Hove, Sussex. Studied architecture in Liverpool and London.

1981   Registered architect in the UK, France & Germany.
Established Ian Ritchie Architects, London (1981), and Leipzig, (1993–96); Co-founded Rice Francis Ritchie, design engineers Paris (1981). Director 1981–87. Principal Ian Ritchie Architects.
International Awards include:

1983   AD Silver Medal (UK)

1986|1988   Plus Beaux Ouvrages de Construction Metallique (France 1986 and 1988)

1992   The Iritecna Prize for Europe (Italy 1992)

1992   The Eric Lyons Memorial Award for Housing in Europe (UK 1992)

1994   The Commonwealth Association of Architects Robert Matthew Award for innovation & advancement of architecture (1994)

1997-1998   Benedictus Special Merit Award (USA) (1997); AIA Award (1997); Civic Trust Award 1998; RFAC Trust Arts Building of the Year (1998)

1998-2000   RIBA Award (1998 Twice) Stephen Lawrence Award (1998) Millennium Product Company (1999 twice) Académie d'Architecture VII Medaille 2000

2000   RIBA Award (2000); RFAC Trust Sports Building of the Year (2000)
Books published:
(well) Connected Architecture, London 1994 and Berlin 1994.

The Biggest Glass Palace in the World, London 1997 and Mailand 1998.

Technoecology, New York 1999.
Regular contributor to journals, radio & TV, and speaker at international conferences on art, technology, engineering, architecture & urbanism.

Bibliography

**Publications About the Work of the
ULRIKE BRANDI LICHT**

AIT-Spezial 2000 Software für Lichtplanung und Contracting, in: AIT-Spezial. Intelligente Architektur 20 (Sonderheft der AIT), No. 1 2000, p. 79.

A.K. Berlin 1995 Aedes West (Eds.): Dresden West. Intra et extra muros. Internationaler Architekten-Workshop, Kaditz-Mickten, Berlin 1995.

A.K. Hamburg 1996 Bund Deutscher Architekten BDA (Eds.): Renaissance der Bahnhöfe. Die Stadt im 21. Jahrhundert, Braunschweig/ Wiesbaden 1996.

A.K. Stuttgart 1989 Landesgewerbeamt Baden-Württemberg/ Design Center Stuttgart (Eds.): Frauen im Design. Berufsbilder und Lebenswege seit 1900, Design Center, Stuttgart 1989.

A.K. Vienna 1994 Gargerle, Christian: Sprachen des Lichts, Vienna 1994.

Architekten- und Ingenieurverein 1999 Architekten- und Ingenieurverein: Hamburg und seine Bauten, Hamburg 1999.

von Berkholz 1999 von Berkholz, Elke: Und es werde Licht …, in: Allegra, 6, 1999, p. 146.

Brandi 1992 Brandi, Ulrike: Ein Gespräch zwischen Lichtplanerin und Architekten, in: Maisch, Inge (Eds.): Lichtfest – Festival of Light, Licht und Architektur, Light and Architecture, Ingolstadt 1992.

Brandi 1993 Brandi, Ulrike: Beleuchtungskonzept, in: Licht, 11/12, 1993.

Brandi 1994 Brandi, Ulrike: Leuchtstofflampen, in: Zweck und Form 910, 1994, p. 12–21.

Brandi 1994 Brandi, Ulrike: Chambre des Metiers-Salle Polyvante, in: Licht 3/4, 1994.

Brandi 1994 Brandi, Ulrike: Beleuchtungskonzept, in: Visuelles- und Ausstattungskonzept für Patientenbereiche in den Krankenhäusern des LBK, Hamburg 1994, p. 25–29.

von Braunmühl 2000 von Braunmühl, Wilhelm: Handbuch Contracting, Düsseldorf 2000.

ElektroWirtschaft 1999 Gestaltung mit Licht im Bahnhof Alexanderplatz, in: ElektroWirtschaft, No. 4 (1999), p. 60–61.

Entwistle 1999 Jill Entwistle: Designing with Light Bars and Restaurants, Roto Vision, Hove (East Sussex) 1999.

Flagge 1994 Flagge, Ingeborg (Eds.): Jahrbuch für Licht und Architektur 1993, Ernst & Sohn, Berlin 1994, p. 57–58.

Flagge 2000 Flagge, Ingeborg: Jahrbuch Licht und Architektur 2000, Cologne 2000.

Flagge 2000 Flagge, Ingeborg: Licht-Architektur-Preis, in: VfA Profil, No. 1 (2000), p. 14–19.

Geissmar 1994 Geissmar, Christoph: Tages- und Kunstlichtbeleuchtungssystem, in: Licht 7/8, 1994, p. 630–637.

Geissmar 1995 Geissmar, Christoph: Ulrike Brandi Licht, in: Flagge, Ingeborg (Eds.): Jahrbuch für Licht und Architektur 1994, Ernst & Sohn, Berlin 1995.

Glasforum 1995 Boardinghaus am Schaarmarkt, Hamburg, in: Glasforum 4, 1995, p. 3–6.

Hamburg und Design 1999 Hamburg und Design (Eds.): Netz das Hamburger Designerverzeichnis, Hamburg 1999.

High Light 1999 Klassisches Erlebnis. Das Freizeit und Erlebniscenter II (FEC) in Stuttgart, in: High Light, März/April 1999.

Horvatitsch 1995 Horvatitsch, Thilo: Natürliches Licht ist immer in Bewegung, das will ich zitieren, in: FAZ-Beilage Immo Real 3, 1995.

International Lighting Review 1999 Skywalk. A pedestrian walkway with a difference, in: International Lighting Review, 992 (1999), p. 2.

Koester 1993 Koester, Susanne: Rückkehr in die Zukunft, in: Design & Licht, No. 2, 1993, p. 26–27.

Knoke 1998 Knoke, Mareike: Lichtspiel an der Bahnsteigkante. Wie eine Hamburgerin zwei Berliner Bahnhöfe zum Leuchten bringt, in: Berliner Morgenpost, 5.10.1998.

Krämer 1999 Krämer, Felix: Skywalk, in: Licht & Architektur, April 1999, p. 36f.

Krausnecker 1998 Krausnecker, Wolfgang: Schönbrunner Lichtachsen, in: MA-null, No. 2, 1998, p. 21–22.

Kremer 1993 Kremer, Pierre: Nouvel Immeuble de la Chambre des Metiers à Luxembourg-Kirchberg, in: Promotion & Bâtiment, No. 6, 1993, p. 10–11.

Licht und Architektur 1994 Sonnensystem. Restaurant "Nil", in: Licht & Architektur, No. 6, 1994, p. 70–71.

Licht und Architektur 1995 Barocke Lichterpracht. Neptunbrunnen. Schloß Schönbrunn in Vienna, in: Licht Architektur, No. 10, 1995, p. 40–41.

Licht und Architektur 1999 Entscheidung, in: Licht und Architektur, No. 2, 1999, p. IV.

Maisch 1996 Maisch, Inge: Dresden. Tank- und Raststätte mit viel Schwung und Licht, in: Häuser, No. 2, 1996, p. 8.

Martens 1996 Martens, Tanja: Mehr Schatten als Licht. Beleuchtungsgewerbe kämpft mit Konsumflaute, in: Hamburger Wirtschaft, No. 2, 1996, p. 6–10.

Meyhöfer 1993 Meyhöfer, Dirk: Licht im Büro, in: Intercity, No. 1, 1993, p. 24.

Müller 1998 Müller, Franziska: Lichtplanerin Ulrike Brandi inszeniert Licht in Bewegung, in: Ideales Heim, Sonderpublikation Licht, No. 10, 1998, p. 103–105.

Professional Lighting Design 1998 Lichtplanerin: Ulrike Brandi steht auf Alu, in: Professional Lighting Design, No. 1, 1998, p. 8.

Rumi/Wischerhoff 1999 Rumi, Will and Wischerhoff, Andreas: Planung per Computer, in: Highlight, November/Dezember 1999, p. 38–43.

Sayah 1988 Sayah, Amber: Eingreifend, in: Bauwelt, No. 18, 1988, p. 733–748.

Schulitz 1999 Schulitz, Helmut C.: Durch die Röhre. Skywalk für die Expo in Hannover, in: Bauwelt, No. 8, 1999, p. 378–381.

Zuber 1999 Zuber, Anne: Trautes Heim, Glück allein, in: Amica, No. 4, 1999, p. 217–218.

Wenz-Gahler 1999 Wenz-Gahler: Café, Bar, Bistro 2, Frankfurt/M. 1999.

Selected Literature on the Topic of Light

A.K. Basel 1988 Eder Matt, Katharina and Wunderlin, Dominik (Eds.): Weil noch das Lämpchen glüht. Lampen, Laternen und Licht, Schweizerisches Museum für Volkskunde, Basel 1988.

A.K. Basel 1990/91 Götz, Matthias and Haldner, Bruno: Licht, Museum für Gestaltung, Basel 1990/91.

A.K. Bozen 1990 Ultra Lux, Museum für Moderne Kunst, Bozen 1990.

A.K. Bremen 1993 Christiansen, Jörn (Eds.): Bremen wird hell. 100 Jahre Leben und Arbeiten mit Elektrizität, Focke-Museum, Bremen 1993.

A.K. Brüssel 1984 Neon. Flour et Cie, Parc d' Egmont, Brüssel 1984.

A.K. Hamburg 1985 Lipp, Achim and Zec, Peter (Eds.): Mehr Licht, Hamburger Kunsthalle, Hamburg 1985.

A.K. Hannover 1990 Elger, Dietmar: NEONstücke, Sprengelmuseum, Hannover 1990.

A.K. Ingolstadt 1992 Maisch, Inge (Eds.): Lichtfest. Festival of Light. Licht und Architektur. Light and Architecture, Ingolstadt 1992.

A.K. Cologne/Frankfurt/M. 1991 Halogen – 20 Jahre neues Licht, Museum für Angewandte Kunst, Cologne and Museum für Kunsthandwerk, Frankfurt/M. 1991.

A.K. New York 1995 Light Construction, Museum of Modern Art, New York 1995.

A.K. Olten 1968 Tschudin, W.F.: Sammlung Feuer und Licht. Kurzgefaßte Geschichte der Feuererzeugung und künstlichen Beleuchtung, Historisches Museum, Olten 1968.

A.K. Utrecht 1991 Nachtregels/Night Lines, Centraal Museum, Utrecht 1991.

A.K. Vienna 1986 Lichtjahre. 100 Jahre Strom in Österreich, Künstlerhaus Vienna, Kremayr & Scheriau, Vienna 1986.

A.K. Vienna 1991 Drechsler, Wolfgang and Weibel, Peter: Bildlicht. Malerei zwischen Material und Immaterialität, Europaverlag, Vienna 1991.

Architectural Design 1997 Light in Architecture, Architectural Design 67, 1997.

Auer 1990 Auer, Gerhard: Light and Order – Lichtkonzepte von F.L. Wright bis Louis Kahn, in: Der Architekt, No. 9, 1990.

Auer 1996 Auer, Gerhard: Die Verlichtung der Stadt – Über Lichtplanung als Nachtplanung, in: Topos, No. 20, 1997.

Baatz 1989 Baatz, Ulrike: Licht, Seele, Augen. Zur Wahrnehmungspsychologie im 19. Jahrhundert, in: Wiener Festwochen (Eds.): Wunderblock. Eine Geschichte der modernen Seele, Vienna 1989.

Baatz 1994 Baatz, Willfried (Eds.): Gestaltung mit Licht, Ravensburger Buchverlag, Ravensburg 1994.

Bachelard 1988 Bachelard, Gaston: Die Flamme einer Kerze, Carl Hanser, Munich 1988.

Baxandall 1995 Baxandall, Michael: Shadows and Enlightenment, Yale, New Haven and London 1995.

von Benesch 1905 von Benesch, Ladislaus: Das Beleuchtungswesen vom Mittelalter bis zur Mitte des 19. Jahrhunderts, Vienna 1905.

Birren 1988 Birren, Faber: Light, Color and Environment, Van Nostrand Reinhold, New York 1988.

Blumenberg 1957 Blumenberg, Hans: Licht als Metapher der Wahrheit, in: Studium Generale 10, 1957.

Böhme 1993 Böhme, Hartmut: Das philosophische Licht und das Licht der Kunst, in: Parkett 37, 1993.

Boyce 1981 Boyce, P.R.: Human Factors in Lighting, Applied Science Publishers, London 1981.

Brown 1985 Brown, G.C.: Sun, Wind, and Light, John Wiley & Sons, New York 1985.

Büttiker 1994 Büttiker, Urs: Louis I. Kahn: Light and Space, Whitney Library of Design, New York 1994.

Butterfield 1993 Butterfield, Jan: The Art of Light and Space, New York 1993.

Carey/Gross 1993 Carey, John and Gross, Neil: The Light Fantastic, in: Business Week, 10. May 1993, p. 44–50.

Coaton 1992 Coaton, J.R.: Lamps and Lighting, John Wiley & Sons, New York 1992.

DaCosta Kaufmann 1979 DaCosta Kaufmann, T.: The Perspective of Shadows: The History of the Theory Shadow Projection, in: Journal of the Warburg and Courtauld Institutes, XXXVIII, 1979, p. 258–287.

Daidalos 1988 Lichtarchitektur, Daidalos 27, 1988.

Daugherty/Hebert 1987 Daugherty, Andrea and Hebert, Paulette: Studying light and color, in: Lighting Design & Application 4, 1987, p. 12–15.

Dawid 1975 Dawid, Maria: Lampen, Leuchter, Laternen seit der Antike, Pinguin, Innsbruck 1975.

Delaunay 1912 Delaunay, Robert: Über das Licht, in: Der Sturm, 1912.

Drechsel Drechsel, Stefan: Über das Licht in der deutschen Sakralarchitektur zwischen 1350 und 1600.

Dubois 1998 Dubois, Marc: Licht/Light & Design (Interieur Foundation), Kortrijk, Belgien.

Eco 1991 Eco, Umberto: Kunst und Schönheit im Mittelalter, Carl Hanser, Munich 1991.

Erco 1990 Erco Leuchten (Eds.): Lichtfabrik, Ernst & Sohn, Berlin 1990.

Faraday 1979 Faraday, Michael: Naturgeschichte einer Kerze, Barbara Franzbecker, Bad Salzdetfurth 1979.

Feynman 1994 Feynman, Richard P.: QED – Die seltsame Theorie des Lichts und der Materie, Munich 1994.

Flagge 1991 Flagge, Ingeborg (Eds.): Architektur – Licht-Architektur, Karl Krämer, Stuttgart 1991.

Flagge 1993 Flagge, Ingeborg (Eds.): Jahrbuch für Licht und Architektur 1992, Ernst & Sohn, Berlin 1993.

Flagge 1994 Flagge, Ingeborg (Eds.): Jahrbuch für Licht und Architektur 1993, Ernst & Sohn, Berlin 1994.

Flagge 1995 Flagge, Ingeborg (Eds.):Jahrbuch für Licht und Architektur 1994, Ernst & Sohn, Berlin 1995.

Flagge 1998 Flagge, Ingeborg (Eds.): Jahrbuch Licht und Architektur 1998, Darmstadt 1998.

Friedel/Israel 1986 Friedel, Robert and Israel, Paul: Edison's Electric Light, New Brunswick (New York) 1986.

Gabriel 1974 Gabriel, Hans: Das künstliche Licht in der Architektur. Analysen, Begriffe, Definitionen, Deutsche Verlagsanstalt, Stuttgart 1974.

Gage 1994 Gage, John: Kulturgeschichte der Farbe. Von der Antike bis zur Gegenwart, Maier, Ravensburg 1994.

Garten und Landschaft 1993 Nightscape. Gestalten mit Licht, Garten und Landschaft 4, 1993.

Gfeller-Corthésy 1998 Gfeller-Corthésy, Roland: Bartenbach Lichtlabor. Bauen mit Tageslicht, Vieweg & Sohn, Braunschweig and Wiesbaden 1998.

Gibbs 1993 Gibbs, W. Wayt: Light Motif, in: Scientific American, April 1993, p. 116–117.

Gombrich 1976 Gombrich, Ernst H.: The Heritage of Apelles. Studies in the Art of the Renaissance, Phaidon Press, Oxford 1976.

Gombrich 1995 Gombrich, Ernst H.: Shadows. The Depiction of Cast Shadows in Western Art, National Gallery Publications, London 1995.

Grättner 1987 Grättner, Jörg: Ästhetik der Architektur, W. Kohlhammer, Cologne 1987.

Hamburgische Electricitäts Werke 1997
Hamburgische Electricitäts Werke (Eds.): Architektur auf der Sonnenspur, Hamburg 1997.

Heimendahl 1961 Heimendahl, Eckart: Licht und Farbe, Walter de Gruyter & Co., Berlin 1961.

Hofmann 1989 Hofmann, Werner: Wahnsinn und Vernunft. Über die allgemeine Sonne und das Lampenlicht des Privaten, in: Hofmann, Werner (Eds.): Europa 1789. Aufklärung, Verklärung, Verfall (A.K.), DuMont, Cologne 1989.

Home/Gribbin 1991 Home, Dipanker and Gribbin, John: What is Light, in: New Scientist, November 1991, p. 30–33.

Hoppe 1967 Hoppe, Edmund: Geschichte der Optik, Wiesbaden 1967.

Hyman 1993 Hyman, Jane Wegscheider: Licht und Gesundheit. Wie natürliches und künstliches Licht den Menschen beeinflussen, Rowohlt, Reinbek 1993.

Ishii 1991 Ishii, Motoko: Light to infinity. Design works by Motoko Ishii, Libroport, Tokyo 1991.

Jaffe 1960 Jaffe, Bernard: Michelson and the Speed of Light, New York 1960.

**Jun`ichiro 1996** Jun`ichiro, Tanizaki: Lob des Schattens. Entwurf einer japanischen Ästhetik (1933), Zürich 1996.

Kahsnitz 1981 Kahsnitz, Rainer: Das Licht aus dem Dunkeln und der Glanz der neuen Zeit. Ein Glasfenster aus der Nürnberger Gasanstalt, in: Buddensieg, Tilmann and Rogge, Henning (Eds.): Die Nützlichen Künste (A.K.), Messegelände am Funkturm, Quadriga, Berlin (West) 1981.

Keller 1988 Keller, Max: DuMont`s Handbuch Bühnenbeleuchtung, DuMont, Cologne 1988.

Keller 1999 Keller, Max: Faszination Licht, Prestel, Munich 1999.

Knupp 1980 Knupp, Karl-Heinz: Die Architekturphantasien Paul Scheerbarts. Ein Beitrag zum Verhältnis von literarischer Fiktion und Architektur, Diss., Hamburg 1980.

Köhler/Luckhardt 1956 Köhler, Walter und Luckhardt, Wassili: Lichtarchitektur, Bauwelt Verlag, Berlin 1956.

Lakeman 1992 Lakeman, Sandra Davis: Natural Light and the Italian Plaza, Natural Light Books, Obispo (USA) 1992.

Lennox-Moyer 1993 Lennox-Moyer, Janet: The Landscape Lighting Book, John Wiley & Sons, New York 1993.

Licht special 1999 Gestaltung mit Licht. Verkaufsräume, Repräsentativräume, Messestände, Außenwerbung (Sonderheft Licht: Licht special 1) Munich 1999.

Liess 1994 Liess, Reinhard: Die Fassade des Straßburger Münsters im Licht. Eine vergessene Wirklichkeit mittelalterlicher Bau- und Bildhauerkunst, in: Bothmer, Hans-Caspar Graf von (Eds.): Festschrift "Lorenz Dittmann", Peter Lang, Frankfurt/M. 1994.

Lindberg 1987 Lindberg, David C.: Auge und Licht im Mittelalter, Suhrkamp, Frankfurt/M. 1987.

Loudon 1981 Loudon, Rodney: The Quantum Theory of Light, Oxford 1981.

Meiss 1945 Meiss, Millard: Light as form and symbol in some fifteenth-century paintings, in: Art. Bull. 27, 1945.

Mensching 1957 Mensching, Gustav: Die Lichtsymbolik in der Religionsgeschichte, in: Studium Generale 10, 1957.

Narboni 1996 Narboni, Roger: La lumière urbaine éclairer les espaces publics, Paris 1996.

Padgham/Sanders 1975 Padgham, C.A. and Sanders J.E.: The Perception of Light and Color, Academic Press, New York 1975.

Perkowitz 1998 Perkowitz, Sidney: Eine kurze Geschichte des Lichts. Die Erforschung eines Mysteriums, Munich 1998.

Planck 1920 Planck, Max: Das Wesen des Lichts, Julius Springer, Berlin 1920.

Plummer 1987 Plummer, Henry: Poetics of Light, a+u Publishing, Tokyo 1987.

Prater 1992 Prater, Andreas: Licht und Farbe bei Caravaggio. Studien zur Ästhetik und Ikonologie des Helldunkels, Franz Steiner, Stuttgart 1992.

Rebske 1962 Rebske, Ernst: Lampen. Leuchten und Laternen, Stuttgart 1962.

Rice/Dutton 1995 Rice, Peter and Dutton, Hugh: Transparente Architektur. Glasfassaden mit Structural Glazing, Birkhäuser, Basel, Berlin and Boston 1995.

Römhild 1992 Römhild, Thomas: Kunstlicht – Lichtkunst. Über die Symbolik künstlicher Beleuchtung (Europäische Hochschulschriften/37), Peter Lang, Frankfurt/M. 1992.

Ronchi 1970 Ronchi, Vasco: The Nature of Light, Cambridge, Mass. 1970.

Scheel 1993 Scheel, Heike: Die erlösende Kraft des Lichts. Philipp Otto Runges Botschaft in den vier Blättern der "Zeiten", Peter Lang, Frankfurt/M. 1993.

Scheerbart 1914 Scheerbart, Paul: Glasarchitektur, Berlin 1914.

Schild 1964 Schild, Erich: Zwischen Glaspalast und Palais des Illusions. Form und Konstruktion im 19. Jahrhundert, Berlin 1967.

Schivelbusch 1981 Schivelbusch, Wolfgang: Straßenlaternen und Polizei, in: Buddensieg, Tilmann and Rogge, Henning (Eds.): Die Nützlichen Künste (A.K.), Messegelände am Funkturm, Quadriga, Berlin (West) 1981.

Schivelbusch 1983 Schivelbusch, Wolfgang: Lichtblicke. Zur Geschichte der künstlichen Helligkeit im 19. Jahrhundert, Carl Hanser, Munich 1983.

Schivelbusch 1992 Schivelbusch, Wolfgang: Licht Schein und Wahn, Ernst & Sohn, Berlin 1992.

Schlegel 1995 Schlegel, Kristian: Vom Regenbogen zum Polarlicht. Leuchterscheinungen in der Atmosphäre, Heidelberg, Berlin, Oxford 1995.

Schnell 1978 Schnell, Hugo: Christliche Lichtsymbolik in den einzelnen Kunstepochen, in: Das Münster 31, 1978, p. 21–46.

Schöne 1954 Schöne, Wolfgang: Über das Licht in der Malerei, Gebrüder Mann, Berlin 1954.

Schulze 1929 Schulze, Conrad Werner: Glas in der Architektur der Gegenwart, Stuttgart 1929.

Schwarz 1997 Schwarz, Michael (Eds.): Licht, Farbe, Raum. Ein künstlerisch-wissenschaftliches Symposium, Braunschweig 1997.

Sedlmayr 1979 Sedlmayr, Ernst: Das Licht in seinen künstlerischen Manifestationen, Mäander Kunstverlag, Mittenwald 1979.

von Simson 1972 von Simson, Otto: Die Gotische Kathedrale, Wissenschaftliche Buchgesellschaft, Darmstadt 1972.

Stanjek 1989 Stanjek, Klaus (Eds.): Die Ökologie der künstlichen Helligkeit, Raben, Munich 1989.

Stoichita 1997 Stoichita, Victor I.: A Short History of the Shadow, London 1997.

Svilar 1983 Svilar, Maja: Und es ward Licht. Zur Kulturgeschichte des Lichts, Frankfurt/M. 1983.

Swirnoff 1988 Swirnoff, Lois: Dimensional Color, Birkhäuser, Boston 1988.

Twarowski 1962 Twarowski, Mieczyslaw: Sonne und Architektur, Callwey, Munich 1962.

Weinmann 1980 Weinmann, Karl Friedrich: Die Natur des Lichts, Darmstadt 1980.

Wilhide 1999 Wilhide, Elizabeth: Licht. Die Kunst der richtigen Beleuchtung, Nicolai, Berlin 1999.

Zajonc, Arthur 1994 Zajonc, Arthur: Die gemeinsame Geschichte von Licht und Bewußtsein, Rowohlt, Reinbek 1994.

Selected Bibliography on Technical Issues of Light

Ander 1995 Ander, Gregg D.: Daylighting Performance and Design, Van Nostrand Reinhold, New York 1995.

Baer 1993 Baer, Roland (Eds.): Beleuchtungstechnik. Anwendungen, Verlag Technik, Berlin and Munich 1993.

Baierlein 1992 Baierlein, Ralph: Newton to Einstein. The Trail of Light. An Excursion to the Wave-Particle Duality and the Special Theory of Relativity, Cambridge University Press, Cambridge 1992.

Baker/Fanchiotti/Steemers 1993 Baker, N., Fanchiotti, A. and Steemers, K. (Eds.): Daylighting in Architecture, James & James, London 1993.

Becker/Lemanski 1982 Becker, Georg and Lemanski, Harald: Modelle des Lichts (Reihe: Kolleg-Text), Metzlersche Verlagsbuchhandlung, Stuttgart 1982.

Bennett 1978 Bennett, Robert: Sun Angles for Design, Bala Cynwyd (USA), 1978.

Bianchi/Pulcini 1995 Bianchi, Francesco and Pulcini, Giorgio: Manuale di Illuminotecnica, NIS La Nuova Italia Scientifica, Rom 1995.

Bücker 1981 Bücker, Werner: Künstliche Beleutung. Ergonomisch und erergiesparend, Campus, Frankfurt/M. 1981.

Bundesanstalt für Arbeitsschutz 1991 Bundesanstalt für Arbeitsschutz (Eds.): Einflüsse der Beleuchtung mit Leuchtstoffampen am Arbeitsplatz, Wirtschaftsverlag NW, Bremerhaven 1991.

Bundesarchitektenkammer 1996 Bundesarchitektenkammer (Eds.): Energiegerechtes Bauen und Modernisieren. Wuppertal Institut für Klima, Umwelt, Energie, Planungsbüro Schmitz, Aachen, Birkhäuser, Basel, Berlin and Boston 1996.

Buser/Hartmann 1991 Buser, A. and Hartmann, E.: Einflüsse der Beleuchtung mit Leuchtstofflampen am Arbeitsplatz, Verlag für neue Wissenschaft, Bremerhaven 1991.

Cakir 1994 Cakir, Ahmet and Cakir, Gisela: Licht und Gesundheit. Eine Untersuchung zum Stand der Beleuchtungstechnik in deutschen Büros, Ergonomic Institut, Berlin 1994

Compagno 1999 Compagno Andrea: Intelligente Glasfassaden. Material, Anwendung, Gestaltung, 2. erw. Auflage, Birkhäuser, Basel, Boston, Berlin 1999.

Cove 1994 Cove, Glen: Lighting: Exteriors & Landscapes, PBC International, 1994.

Dupont/Giraud 1993 Dupont, Jean-Marc and Giraud, Marc: L´Urbanisme lumière, Edition Sorman, Paris 1993.

Eckert 1996 Eckert, Martin: Außenbeleuchtung. Sicherheit und Effektivität (Die Bibliothek der Technik, Band 123), Verlag Moderne Industrie, Landsberg/Lech 1996.

Egan 1983 Egan, David M.: Concepts in Architectural Lighting, McGraw-Hill, New York 1983.

Epsten 1986 Epsten, Dagmar Becker: Tageslicht & Architektur. Möglichkeiten zur Energieeinsparung und Bereicherung der Lebensumwelt, C.F. Müller, Karlsruhe 1986.

Evans 1981 Evans, Benjamin H.: Daylight in Architecture, Mc Graw-Hill, New York 1981.

Fischer 1982 Fischer, Udo: Tageslichttechnik, R. Müller, Cologne-Braunsfeld 1982.

Freymuth 1973 Freymuth, Hanns: Über Grundlagen und Grenzen der Tageslichttechnik, in: Bauwelt 26, 1973.

Freymuth 1974 Freymuth, Hanns: Lichttechnik. Leuchtdichteverteilung und Beleuchtungsstärken in Räumen, in: Technik am Bau 5, 1974.

Ganslandt/Hofmann 1992 Ganslandt, Rüdiger and Hofmann, Harald: Handbuch der Lichtplanung, Vieweg & Sohn, Wiesbaden and Braunschweig 1992.

Gardner/Hannaford 1993 Gardner, Carl and Hannaford, Barry: Lighting Design, Design Council, London 1993.

Glaser/Koch/Pirweck/Weiß 1996 Glaser, Bernd, Koch, Kathrin, Piweck, Kai-Uwe, Weiß, Alexander (Eds.): Lichtideen mit Faseroptik, Pflaum Verlag, Munich 1996.

Gordon/Nuckolls 1995 Gordon, Gary and Nuckolls, James L.: Interior Lighting for Designers, John Wiley & Sons, New York 1995.

Gorman 1995 Gorman, Jean: Detailing Light. Integrated Lighting Solutions for Residential and Contract Design, Whitney Library of Design, New York 1995.

Hentschel 1987 Hentschel, Hans-Jürgen: Licht und Beleuchtung. Theorie und Praxis der Lichttechnik, Hüthig, Heidelberg 1987.

Hopkinson 1963 Hopkinson, R.G.: Architectural Physics: Lighting, Her Majesty´s Stationery Office, London 1963.

Hopkinson 1966 Hopkinson, R.G.: Daylighting, University College, London 1966.

Hopkinson/Kay 1969 Hopkinson, R.G. and Kay, J.D.: The Lighting of Buildings, Frederick A. Praeger, New York 1969.

Horden 1995 Horden, Richard: Light Tech. Ausblicke auf eine leichte Architektur, Birkhäuser, Basel, Berlin and Boston, 1995.

Illuminating Engineering Society of North America 1979 Illuminating Engineering Society of North America (Eds.): Recommended Practice of Daylighting, New York 1979.

Illuminating Engineering Society of North America 1993 Illuminating Engineering Society of North America (Eds.): Lighting Handbook, New York 1993.

IRB 1995 IRB-Literaturdokumentation: Innenraumgestaltung mit Licht (Ringhefter), 1995.

Jansen 1954 Jansen, Johann: Ein Handbuch zum Entwerfen von Beleuchtungsanlagen (3 Bde.), Philips' Technische Bibliothek, Berlin 1954.

Kalff 1943 Kalff, Ir.: Kunstlicht und Architektur, Philips' Technische Bibliothek, Eindhoven 1943.

Kay 1997 Kay, G.N.: Architectural Lighting with Fiber-Optics, New York 1997.

Köhler 1952 Köhler, Walter: Lichttechnik, Helios, Berlin 1952.

Lam 1977 Lam, William M.C.: Perception and Lighting as Formgivers for Architecture, McGraw-Hill, New York 1977.

Lam 1986 Lam, William M.C.: Sunlighting as Formgiver for Architecture, Van Nostrand Reinhold, New York 1986.

Leslie 1993 Leslie, Russell P.: The Lighting Pattern Book for Homes, Mc Graw-Hill.

Leslie/Rodgers 1997 Leslie, Russell P. and Rodgers, Paula A.: The Outdoor Lighting Pattern Book, Mc Graw-Hill, New York 1997.

Lighting Research Center 1995 Lighting Research Center (Eds.): Builders Guide to Home Lighting, Lighting Research Center, New York 1995.

Lighting Research Center 1995 Lighting Research Center (Eds.): Lighting Listings. A Worldwide Guide, Lighting Research Center, New York 1995.

LiTG 1991 LiTG: Handbuch für Beleuchtung, Landsberg 1991.

Lynes 1968 Lynes, J.A.: Principles of Natural Lighting, Applied Science Publishers, London 1968.

Lynes 1978 Lynes, J.A.(Eds.): Developments in lighting-1, Applied Science Publishers, London 1978.

Mahnke/Mahnke 1987 Mahnke, Frank H. and Mahnke Rudolf H.: Color and Light in Man-Made Environments, Van Nostrand Reinhold, New York 1987.

McCluney/Zdepski 1986 McCluney, Ross and Zdepski, M. Stephen: Proceedings I, 1986 International Daylighting Conference, Atlanta 1986.

Michel 1996 Michel, Lou: Light. The Shape of Space. Designing with Space and Light, Van Nostrand Reinhold, New York 1996.

Millet 1996 Millet, Marietta: Light Revealing Architecture, New York 1996.

Moncada Lo Giudice/de Lieto Vollaro 1993 Moncada Lo Giudice, G. and de Lieto, Vollaro: Illuminotecnica, Masson, Mailand 1993.

Moore 1986 Moore, Fuller: Concepts and Practice of Architectural Daylighting, Van Nostrand Reinhold, New York 1986.

Muneer 1997 Muneer, Tariq: Solar Radiation and Daylight Models for the Energy Efficient Design of Buildings, Heinemann, Oxford 1997.

Museums Association 1987 The Museums Association (Eds.): Lighting. A Conference on Lighting in Museums, Galleries and Historic Houses, Bristol 1987.

Nuckolls 1983 Nuckolls, James L.: Interior Lighting for Environmental Designers, John Wiley & Sons, New York 1983.

Phillips 1997 Phillips, Derek: Lighting Historic Buildings, Heinemann Publishers, Oxford 1997.

Pracht 1994 Pracht, Klaus: Licht + Raumgestaltung: Beleuchtung als Element derArchitekturplanung, C.F. Müller, Heidelberg 1994.

Robbins 1986 Robbins, Claude L.: Daylighting. Design and Analysis, Van Nostrand Reinhold, New York 1986.

Sabra 1981 Sabra, A.I.: Theories of Light from Descartes to Newton, Cambridge University Press, Cambridge 1981.

Schiler 1992 Schiler, Mark: Simplified Design of Building Lighting, John Wiley & Sons, New York 1992.

Schmitt 1896 Schmitt, Eduard: Erhellung der Räume mittels Sonnenlicht, in: Durm, Josef (Eds.): Handbuch der Architektur (3. Bd.), Arnold Bergsträsser, Darmstadt 1896.

Schmitz 1981 Schmitz, E.H.: Handbuch der Geschichte der Optik, Bonn 1981.

Schneider/Focus Film 1996 Schneider, Astrid and Focus Film (Eds.): Solararchitektur für Europa, Birkhäuser, Basel, Berlin and Boston 1996.

Schricker 1994 Schricker, Rudolf: Licht-Raum, Raum-Licht. Die Inszenierung der Räume mit Licht. Planungsleitfaden, Deutsche Verlagsanstalt, Stuttgart 1994.

Schröder 1990 Schröder, Gottfried: Technische Optik. Grundlagen und Anwendungen, Vogel, Würzburg 1990.

Sewig 1938 Sewig, R. (Eds.): Handbuch der Lichttechnik (2 Bde.), Verlag Julius Springer, Berlin 1938.

Smith/Bertolone 1986 Smith, Fran Kellogg and Bertolone, Fred J.: Bringing Interiors to Light. The Principles and Practices of Lighting Design, Whitney Library of Design, New York 1986.

Steffy 1990 Steffy, Gary R.: Architectural Lighting Design,
Van Nostrand Reinhold, New York 1990.

Tragenza / Loe 1998 Tragenza, Peter and Loe, David: The Design
of Lighting, Routledge, New York 1998.

Turner 1994 Turner, Janet: Lighting. An Introduction to Light,
Lighting and Light Use, BT. Batsford, London 1994.

Turner 1998 Turner, Janet: Designing with Light. Retail Spaces.
Lighting Solutions for Shops, Malls and Markets, Roto Vision,
Cran-Près-Céligny 1998.

Trilux 1997 Trilux (Eds.): Beleuchtungsplanung. Lichttechnik,
Elektrotechnik, Arnsberg 1997.

Vandeplanque 1995 Vandeplanque, Patrick: L'Eclairage: Notions
de base-projets d'installations, Lavoisier, Paris 1995.

Weigel 1952 Weigel, R.: Grundzüge der Lichttechnik, Girardet,
Essen 1952.

Weis 1985 Weis, Bruno: Not-Beleuchtung, Pflaum, Munich 1985.

Weis 1996 Weis, Bruno: Beleuchtungstechnik. Grundlagen,
Lichtquellen, Leuchten, Pflaum, Munich 1996.

Ziesebiß 1996 Ziesebiß, Carl-Heinz: Beleuchtungstechnik für den
Elektrofachmann, Hüthig, Heidelberg 1996.

Zimmermann 1990 Zimmermann, Ralf (Eds.): Wörterbuch
Lichttechnik, VEB Verlag Technik, Berlin 1990.

Selected Journals

Design & Licht, Siteco Beleuchtungstechnik GmbH, Traunreut.

Erco Lichtbericht, Erco Leuchten GmbH, Lüdenscheid.

Internationale Licht Rundschau, Stichting Prometheus (Eds.),
Amsterdam (NL).

Licht. Technik, Handel, Planung, Design, Pflaum Verlag,
Munich.

Licht & Architektur, Bertelsmann Fachzeitschriften GmbH,
Gütersloh.

Lighting Equipment News, Emap Maclaren Limited,
Croydon (UK).

Index

Bolded page numbers refer to the page in the glossary, where the relevant term is explained. Italicized terms indicate software.

250

Photo Credits

The English translations of German captions are listed in the photo credits under the corresponding illustration number.

CHAPTER 1: IMAGES OF LIGHT

No.	Subject	Place	Country	Architect	Lighting Planner	Copyright
1	Representation of light by means of red arrow				ULRIKE BRANDI LICHT	ULRIKE BRANDI LICHT
2	Representation by means of yellow cones				ULRIKE BRANDI LICHT	ULRIKE BRANDI LICHT
3, 4	Light diagram by Henri Alekan for a scene from Juliette ou la *clé des songes*	Square	France		Henri Alekan	Henri Alekan
	From: Henri Alekan: Des lumières et des ombres. Nouvelle édition.	Caulaincourt				Librairie du Collectionneur,
	Paris: Librairie du Collectionneur 1991. p. 96.					4, rue Cassette, F-75006 Paris
5	EXPO Café	Hanover	Germany	Pax Hadamczik Arndt Brüning	ULRIKE BRANDI LICHT	ULRIKE BRANDI LICHT
6, 7	Lighting plans for the Palazzo Grassi	Venice	Italy	Gae Aulenti, Antonio Foscari	Piero Castiglioni	Piero Castiglioni
	From: *domus* 674, July/August 1986. p. 56.					
8	Simulations of Glass Factory	Dresden	Germany	HENN Architekten Ingenieure	ULRIKE BRANDI LICHT	ULRIKE BRANDI LICHT
9	Cologne Train Station	Cologne	Germany	ECE		ULRIKE BRANDI LICHT
10	Light atmosphere					Silke Lauffs
11	Model of Bosch-Pavilion, EXPO 2000	Hanover	Germany	Milla & Partner	ULRIKE BRANDI LICHT	Milla & Partner
12	Graphical representation of illuminance					ULRIKE BRANDI LICHT
	Illuminance [lx]					
	User level (distance from ground)					
	Mean illuminance E_m					
	Minimal illuminance E_{min}					
	Maximal illuminance E_{max}					
	Uniformity E_{min}/E_m					
	Uniformity E_{min}/E_{max}					
13	Computer simulation					ULRIKE BRANDI LICHT
14	Grid chart					ULRIKE BRANDI LICHT

CHAPTER 2: THE FUNDAMENTALS: LIGHT PLANNING

No.	Subject	Place	Country	Architect	Lighting Planner	Copyright
	Natural Light					
1	The sun in the Galerie de l'Evolution in Paris	Paris	France	Conversion Chemetov et Huidobro	ULRIKE BRANDI LICHT	ULRIKE BRANDI LICHT
	Time of Day/ Month; Highest Position during Day: June, May, April, March, February, January, December, November, October, September, August, July					
2	Deep window reveals					ULRIKE BRANDI LICHT
3	Window bar					ULRIKE BRANDI LICHT
4, 5, 6	Pantheon in Rome	Rome	Italy			ULRIKE BRANDI LICHT
7	Light reflecting on water					ULRIKE BRANDI LICHT
8	Light shelf					ULRIKE BRANDI LICHT
9	Heliostat					ULRIKE BRANDI LICHT
10	House in Barcelona	Barcelona	Spain			Authors' archive
11	Redirecting mirror in the Hong Kong Shanghai Bank	Hong Kong	China	Foster Associates		ULRIKE BRANDI LICHT
12, 13	Natural light system with asymmetric heliostats		Germany		ULRIKE BRANDI LICHT	ULRIKE BRANDI LICHT
14, 15, 16	Light-directing blinds					ULRIKE BRANDI LICHT
17	Natural light system with asymmetric heliostats				ULRIKE BRANDI LICHT	ULRIKE BRANDI LICHT
18	Light-directing blinds					Okalux
19	Light-directing blinds, detail					Okalux
20	Light-directing glass, horizontal; light-directing glass, detail, vertical and horizontal					ULRIKE BRANDI LICHT
21	Light-directing glass at roof level					ULRIKE BRANDI LICHT
22	Mirror profiles in interstice between glass					
	Summer; Transition; Winter					
23	Solar protection and direction of diffuse light by means of prism sheets					ULRIKE BRANDI LICHT
24	Prism sheets as blinds with slats					ULRIKE BRANDI LICHT
25	Laser cut panel with skylight					ULRIKE BRANDI LICHT
	Summer Sun; Winter Sun					
26	Laser cut panel, detail					ULRIKE BRANDI LICHT
27	Holographic-optical element in skylight					ULRIKE BRANDI LICHT
28	Holographic-optical element with photovoltaic modules					ULRIKE BRANDI LICHT
29	Holographic-optical element at the Fortbildungsakademie	Herne	Germany	Jourda et Perraudin	GLB GmbH	ULRIKE BRANDI LICHT
30	Mirror screens					ULRIKE BRANDI LICHT
	Float glass;					
	Float glass;					
	Plastic screen with metal-coated surfaces					
31	Anidolic systems					ULRIKE BRANDI LICHT
32	Periods of daylight in the northern hemisphere					ULRIKE BRANDI LICHT
33	Incline of the earth's axis in its orbit					ULRIKE BRANDI LICHT
	March 21, Spring Equinox; February 19; January 20; December, Winter Solstice; November 22;					
	October 23; September 23, Fall Equinox; August 23; July 23; June 21, Summer Solstice;					
	May 21; April 20					
34	Insolation in Winter and Summer, northern hemisphere (Hamburg)					ULRIKE BRANDI LICHT
	Rays of the Sun					
35	Sun position graph 51.5° northern latitude					ULRIKE BRANDI LICHT
36	Insolation at the Francke'sche Stiftungen	Halle	Germany		ULRIKE BRANDI LICHT	ULRIKE BRANDI LICHT
37	Natural light simulator at ERCO					ERCO
I–VI	S. 34/35 Natural light conditions with different types of windows					Software: Relux
	Refers to each illustration:					Model: ULRIKE BRANDI LICHT
	Result user level:					
	Mean natural light factor D_m;					
	Minimal natural light factor D_{min};					
	Maximal natural light factor D_{max}					
I–VI	S. 36/37 Natural light conditions with different types of room proportions					Software: Relux
	Refers to each illustration:					Model: ULRIKE BRANDI LICHT
	Result user level:					
	Mean natural light factor D_m;					
	Minimal natural light factor D_{min};					
	Maximal natural light factor D_{max}					

						Software: Relux
I–III	S. 40/41 Natural light conditions at various ceiling heights					Model: ULRIKE BRANDI LICHT
	Refers to each illustration:					
	Result user level:					
	Mean natural light factor Dm;					
	Minimal natural light factor Dmin;					
	Maximal natural light factor Dmax					

Artificial Light

No.	Subject	Place	Country	Architect	Lighting Planner	Copyright
1	Aerial photograph	Lüneburg Heath	Germany			ULRIKE BRANDI LICHT
2	Window (photograph of Ernst and Emma Wiemann, Dührkoop 1905, Lille Niebuhr Archive)					ULRIKE BRANDI LICHT
3	Regular reflection					ULRIKE BRANDI LICHT
	Mirror, shiny surface (such as the paint on the body of an automobile)					
4	Aerial photograph	near Munich	Germany			ULRIKE BRANDI LICHT
5	Diffuse reflection					ULRIKE BRANDI LICHT
	Dull surface (such as wall with dispersion paint, exposed concrete)					
6	Aerial photograph	near Munich	Germany			ULRIKE BRANDI LICHT
7	Reflected light on golden wall, Fondation Cartier; (photograph from ERCO Lichtbericht 61, 8/99)	Paris	France	Jean Nouvel		ERCO
8	Reflection on colored pillar, Uhlandstrasse 184	Berlin	Germany	Conversion Feige + Döring	ULRIKE BRANDI LICHT	ULRIKE BRANDI LICHT
9	Reflection on shiny wall					ULRIKE BRANDI LICHT
10	Refraction of light air/water					ULRIKE BRANDI LICHT
11	Refraction of light air/glass/air					ULRIKE BRANDI LICHT
12	Total reflection					ULRIKE BRANDI LICHT
13	Mirage					ULRIKE BRANDI LICHT
14	Total reflection in prism sheet					ULRIKE BRANDI LICHT
15	Drop of rainbow					ULRIKE BRANDI LICHT
16	Refraction in a prism					ULRIKE BRANDI LICHT
17	Rainbow					ULRIKE BRANDI LICHT
18	Refraction of light at the crystal of a chandelier			Christine Brandi		Christine Brandi
19	Convex glass walls as projection surfaces	London	England	Ian Ritchie Architects		Ian Ritchie Architects
20	Light on various types of material	London	England	Ian Ritchie Architects		Ian Ritchie Architects
21	Medical technology factory B. Braun, rib mesh above staircase	Melsungen	Germany	Stirling, Wilford and Associates	ULRIKE BRANDI LICHT	ULRIKE BRANDI LICHT
22	Installation Lichtfest	Ingolstadt	Germany	Ian Ritchie		von Bassewitz
23	Ceiling lamps					ULRIKE BRANDI LICHT
24	Wall floods					ULRIKE BRANDI LICHT
25	Downlights					ULRIKE BRANDI LICHT
26	Downlight: pendant					ULRIKE BRANDI LICHT
27	Chandelier in the Bundesmobiliendepot	Vienna	Austria			ULRIKE BRANDI LICHT
28	Pendant lamps, rotationally symmetrical					ULRIKE BRANDI LICHT
29	Linear fluorescent lamp					ULRIKE BRANDI LICHT
30	Linear fluorescent lamps					ULRIKE BRANDI LICHT
31	Linear fluorescent lamp, pendant, radiating directly and direct-indirectly					ULRIKE BRANDI LICHT
32	Lamp with secondary reflector					ULRIKE BRANDI LICHT
33	Wall lamps, radiating diffusely; built-in ceiling and wall floodlights					ULRIKE BRANDI LICHT
34	Wall lamps, shaded, radiating indirectly; surface-mounted ceiling floodlight					ULRIKE BRANDI LICHT
35	Cafeteria at the publishing house Der Spiegel	Hamburg	Germany	Verner Panton	Verner Panton	Authors' archive
36	Built-in floor lamps, radiating asymmetrically, sided light on ground					ULRIKE BRANDI LICHT
37	End-emitting fiber glass as built-in floor lamps					ULRIKE BRANDI LICHT
38	Sided light					Bega
39	Table lamps, rigid and swiveling					ULRIKE BRANDI LICHT
40	Floor standard lamps, rigid and swiveling					ULRIKE BRANDI LICHT
41	Floor standard lamps, radiating indirectly as well as direct-indirectly					ULRIKE BRANDI LICHT
42	Outdoor lamps: bollard; top-mounted pole lamp; side-mounted poll lamp					ULRIKE BRANDI LICHT
43	Induction lamp					
44	LED					Philips
45	Metal halide lamp					Philips
46	High-pressure sodium lamp					Philips
47	Incandescent lamp					Osram
48	Mercury vapor lamp					Philips
49	Low-voltage halogen lamp					Philips
50	Fluorescent lamp					Philips
51	Compact fluorescent lamp					Philips
52	PAR reflector lamp					Philips
53	High-voltage halogen incandescent lamp					Osram
54	Metal halide lamp					Philips

CHAPTER 3: PROCESSES AND PROCEDURES: DESIGN, IMPLEMENTATION, SUPERVISION

No.	Subject	Place	Country	Architect	Lighting Planner	Copyright
1	Lighting plan for outdoor area	Miltenberg	Germany	Dr. Hartmut Holl	ULRIKE BRANDI LICHT	ULRIKE BRANDI LICHT
2	Francke'sche Stiftungen, interior view of the song and prayer hall	Halle	Germany		ULRIKE BRANDI LICHT	ULRIKE BRANDI LICHT
3, 4	Francke'sche Stiftungen, lighting plans	Halle	Germany		ULRIKE BRANDI LICHT	ULRIKE BRANDI LICHT
	A = Entrance Area, B = Reading Room, C = Stacks;					
	1 Illumination Entrance Area and Balcony, direct; 2 Illumination Reading Room, direct and indirect;					
	3 Illumination Stacks, direct and indirect; 4 Sun Protection, suspended; 5 Sun Protection, inserted					
5, 6	Gynecological and children's clinic, university hospital of the TU Dresden, model, top view and frontal view	Dresden	Germany	Heinle, Wischer und Partner	ULRIKE BRANDI LICHT	Heinle, Wischer und Partner
7	Materials, surface properties	Dresden	Germany	Heinle, Wischer und Partner	ULRIKE BRANDI LICHT	Heinle, Wischer und Partner
	Captions concrete surface:					
	Concrete surfaces;					
	Walls with coated concrete surface (e.g. plaster, tiles ...);					
	Ceilings with exposed concrete surfaces;					
	Walls with coated concrete surface (e.g. plaster, tiles ...);					
8	Sketches of ceiling lamps, axial measurement	Dresden	Germany	Heinle, Wischer und Partner	ULRIKE BRANDI LICHT	ULRIKE BRANDI LICHT
9	Section of glass hall	Dresden	Germany	Heinle, Wischer und Partner	ULRIKE BRANDI LICHT	ULRIKE BRANDI LICHT
	09 - Ceiling Lamp Built-in (L = 120 cm) Linear, T16 28W; 08 - Ceiling Lamp Built-in (L = 120 cm)					
	Linear, T16 54W; 07 - Ceiling Lamp Built-in (d = 25 cm) 2 TC-D 26W asym.;					
	04 - Ceiling Lamp Built-in (d= 22 cm) 1 TC-D 26W sym.					
10	Excerpts from HU-Bau with legend	Dresden	Germany	Heinle, Wischer und Partner	ULRIKE BRANDI LICHT	ULRIKE BRANDI LICHT
11	Excerpt from lamp catalogue				ULRIKE BRANDI LICHT	Catalogues of manufacturers
12	Excerpt from lamp catalogue	Dresden	Germany	von Gerkan Marg und Partner	ULRIKE BRANDI LICHT	Hapag Lloyd
13	Historical photograph of Hapag Lloyd, central hall	Hamburg	Germany	von Gerkan Marg und Partner	ULRIKE BRANDI LICHT	Hapag Lloyd
14	Table of natural light simulation				ULRIKE BRANDI LICHT	ULRIKE BRANDI LICHT
	Natural Light (left); Natural Light Simulation, Superlite File (right)					

No.	Subject	Place	Country	Architect	Lighting Planner	Copyright
15	Grundriß Hapag Lloyd	Hamburg	Germany	von Gerkan Marg und Partner	ULRIKE BRANDI LICHT	ULRIKE BRANDI LICHT
16	Section of Hapag Lloyd through entrance as well as hall and conference room	Hamburg	Germany	von Gerkan Marg und Partner	ULRIKE BRANDI LICHT	ULRIKE BRANDI LICHT
17	Lamp catalogue for Hapag Lloyd	Hamburg	Germany	von Gerkan Marg und Partner	ULRIKE BRANDI LICHT	ULRIKE BRANDI LICHT
18	Space between ceiling and roof above hall, Hapag Lloyd	Hamburg	Germany	von Gerkan Marg und Partner	ULRIKE BRANDI LICHT	ULRIKE BRANDI LICHT
19	Hall before reconstruction, Hapag Lloyd	Hamburg	Germany	von Gerkan Marg und Partner	ULRIKE BRANDI LICHT	ULRIKE BRANDI LICHT
20	Detail of hall ceiling, Hapag Lloyd	Hamburg	Germany	von Gerkan Marg und Partner	ULRIKE BRANDI LICHT	ULRIKE BRANDI LICHT
21	Ceiling above hall, Hapag Lloyd	Hamburg	Germany	von Gerkan Marg und Partner	ULRIKE BRANDI LICHT	ULRIKE BRANDI LICHT
22	Hall during reconstruction, Hapag Lloyd	Hamburg	Germany	von Gerkan Marg und Partner	ULRIKE BRANDI LICHT	ULRIKE BRANDI LICHT
23	Hall during reconstruction, Hapag Lloyd	Hamburg	Germany	von Gerkan Marg und Partner	ULRIKE BRANDI LICHT	ULRIKE BRANDI LICHT
24	Hall following reconstruction, Hapag Lloyd	Hamburg	Germany	von Gerkan Marg und Partner	ULRIKE BRANDI LICHT	ULRIKE BRANDI LICHT
25	Detail of hall ceiling, Hapag Lloyd	Hamburg	Germany	von Gerkan Marg und Partner	ULRIKE BRANDI LICHT	ULRIKE BRANDI LICHT
26	Detail of hall ceiling, Hapag Lloyd	Hamburg	Germany	von Gerkan Marg und Partner	ULRIKE BRANDI LICHT	ULRIKE BRANDI LICHT
27	Detail of hall ceiling, Hapag Lloyd	Hamburg	Germany	von Gerkan Marg und Partner	ULRIKE BRANDI LICHT	ULRIKE BRANDI LICHT
28	Hollow moulding above conference room prior to reconstruction, Hapag Lloyd	Hamburg	Germany	von Gerkan Marg und Partner	ULRIKE BRANDI LICHT	ULRIKE BRANDI LICHT
29	Space between ceiling and roof above conference room prior to reconstruction, Hapag Lloyd	Hamburg	Germany	von Gerkan Marg und Partner	ULRIKE BRANDI LICHT	ULRIKE BRANDI LICHT
30	New roof above conference room, Hapag Lloyd	Hamburg	Germany	von Gerkan Marg und Partner	ULRIKE BRANDI LICHT	ULRIKE BRANDI LICHT
31	New roof above conference room, Hapag Lloyd	Hamburg	Germany	von Gerkan Marg und Partner	ULRIKE BRANDI LICHT	ULRIKE BRANDI LICHT
32	Detail of lamp fixtures, Hapag Lloyd	Hamburg	Germany	von Gerkan Marg und Partner	ULRIKE BRANDI LICHT	ULRIKE BRANDI LICHT
33	Core drilling in conference room, Hapag Lloyd	Hamburg	Germany	von Gerkan Marg und Partner	ULRIKE BRANDI LICHT	ULRIKE BRANDI LICHT
34	Built-in floor lamps, Hapag Lloyd	Hamburg	Germany	von Gerkan Marg und Partner	ULRIKE BRANDI LICHT	ULRIKE BRANDI LICHT
35	Built-in floor lamps, Hapag Lloyd	Hamburg	Germany	von Gerkan Marg und Partner	ULRIKE BRANDI LICHT	ULRIKE BRANDI LICHT
36	Conference room during reconstruction, Hapag Lloyd	Hamburg	Germany	von Gerkan Marg und Partner	ULRIKE BRANDI LICHT	ULRIKE BRANDI LICHT
37	Conference room, Hapag Lloyd	Hamburg	Germany	von Gerkan Marg und Partner	ULRIKE BRANDI LICHT	ULRIKE BRANDI LICHT
38	Conference room, Hapag Lloyd	Hamburg	Germany	von Gerkan Marg und Partner	ULRIKE BRANDI LICHT	ULRIKE BRANDI LICHT
39	Conference room, Hapag Lloyd	Hamburg	Germany	von Gerkan Marg und Partner	ULRIKE BRANDI LICHT	ULRIKE BRANDI LICHT
40	Conference room, Hapag Lloyd	Hamburg	Germany	von Gerkan Marg und Partner	ULRIKE BRANDI LICHT	ULRIKE BRANDI LICHT
41	Conference room, Hapag Lloyd	Hamburg	Germany	von Gerkan Marg und Partner	ULRIKE BRANDI LICHT	ULRIKE BRANDI LICHT
42	Conference room, Hapag Lloyd	Hamburg	Germany	von Gerkan Marg und Partner	ULRIKE BRANDI LICHT	ULRIKE BRANDI LICHT
43	Entrance area, Hapag Lloyd	Hamburg	Germany	von Gerkan Marg und Partner	ULRIKE BRANDI LICHT	ULRIKE BRANDI LICHT
44	Bar, Hapag Lloyd	Hamburg	Germany	von Gerkan Marg und Partner	ULRIKE BRANDI LICHT	ULRIKE BRANDI LICHT
45	Lighting test, Friedrichstraße train station	Berlin	Germany	Weinkamm und Partner	ULRIKE BRANDI LICHT	ULRIKE BRANDI LICHT
46	Mock-up room, ERCO	Lüdenscheid	Germany			Erco

CHAPTER 4: EXAMPLES: DESIGNING WITH LIGHT

No.	Subject	Place	Country	Architect	Lighting Planner	Copyright
1	Tokyo International Forum, exterior view	Tokyo	Japan	Rafael Vinoly	Danielle & Claude Engele and LPA	ERCO
2	Tokyo International Forum, interior courtyard	Tokyo	Japan	Rafael Vinoly	Danielle & Claude Engele and LPA	LPA
3	Hotel Poluinya	Hokkaido	Japan	Toyo Ito	LPA	LPA
4	Façade of the Louvre, section	Paris	France		Electricité de France	ULRIKE BRANDI LICHT
5	Louvre, Façade Sully	Paris	France		Electricité de France	Agabekov S.A.
6	Deutsches Schauspielhaus	Hamburg	Germany	Renovierung Eingang R. Klamp	ULRIKE BRANDI LICHT	ULRIKE BRANDI LICHT
7	Uhlandstraße 184, entrance	Berlin	Germany	Umbau Feige + Döring	ULRIKE BRANDI LICHT	ULRIKE BRANDI LICHT
8	Uhlandstraße 184, passage	Berlin	Germany	Umbau Feige + Döring	ULRIKE BRANDI LICHT	ULRIKE BRANDI LICHT
9	RWE high-rise, bottom view of ceiling	Essen	Germany	Ingenhoven Overdiek + Partner	HL-Technik AG	H. Knauf
10	RWE-Hochhaus, Eingangshalle	Essen	Germany	Ingenhoven Overdiek + Partner	HL-Technik AG	H. Knauf
11	Museum of Contemporary Art	Strasbourg	France	Adrien Fainsilber		ERCO
12	Headquarters of adidas, exterior view	Herzogenaurach	Germany	Babler + Lode		Jan Kraege
13	Headquarters of adidas	Herzogenaurach	Germany	Babler + Lode	ULRIKE BRANDI LICHT	Jan Kraege
14	Medical technology factory B. Braun, glass connecting passage	Melsungen	Germany	Stirling, Wilford and Associates	ULRIKE BRANDI LICHT	ULRIKE BRANDI LICHT
15	Medical technology factory B. Braun, stairwell with vertical lamp	Melsungen	Germany	Stirling, Wilford and Associates	ULRIKE BRANDI LICHT	ULRIKE BRANDI LICHT
16	Medical technology factory B. Braun, connecting passage	Melsungen	Germany	Stirling, Wilford and Associates	ULRIKE BRANDI LICHT	ULRIKE BRANDI LICHT
17	Forum Elbflorenz Dresden, hallway ceiling with ventilation ducts	Dresden	Germany	Nietz Prasch Sigl	ULRIKE BRANDI LICHT	ULRIKE BRANDI LICHT
18	Forum Elbflorenz Dresden, hallway ceiling with ventilation ducts	Dresden	Germany	Nietz Prasch Sigl	ULRIKE BRANDI LICHT	ULRIKE BRANDI LICHT
19	Forum Elbflorenz Dresden, elevator foyer, half-finished	Dresden	Germany	Nietz Prasch Sigl	ULRIKE BRANDI LICHT	ULRIKE BRANDI LICHT
20	Forum Elbflorenz Dresden, finished hallway	Dresden	Germany	Nietz Prasch Sigl	ULRIKE BRANDI LICHT	ULRIKE BRANDI LICHT
21	Forum Elbflorenz Dresden, elevator foyer, finished	Dresden	Germany	Nietz Prasch Sigl	ULRIKE BRANDI LICHT	ULRIKE BRANDI LICHT
22	Medical technology factory B. Braun, elevator foyer	Melsungen	Germany	Stirling, Wilford and Associates	ULRIKE BRANDI LICHT	ULRIKE BRANDI LICHT
23	Medical technology factory B. Braun, stairwell	Melsungen	Germany	Stirling, Wilford and Associates	ULRIKE BRANDI LICHT	ULRIKE BRANDI LICHT
24	Norddeutsche Landesbank, stairwell	Hamburg	Germany	von Gerkan Marg und Partner	ULRIKE BRANDI LICHT	Klaus Frahm
25	Norddeutsche Landesbank, staircase	Hamburg	Germany	von Gerkan Marg und Partner	ULRIKE BRANDI LICHT	Klaus Frahm
26	Norddeutsche Landesbank, sections	Hamburg	Germany	von Gerkan Marg und Partner	ULRIKE BRANDI LICHT	ULRIKE BRANDI LICHT
27	Norddeutsche Landesbank, floor plan	Hamburg	Germany	von Gerkan Marg und Partner	ULRIKE BRANDI LICHT	ULRIKE BRANDI LICHT
28	Office building of the Großhandels- und Lagergesellschaft	Bremen	Germany	Kleffel, Köhnhold, Gundermann	ULRIKE BRANDI LICHT	Oliver Heissner
29	Office building Heidenkampsweg, staircase	Hamburg	Germany	Böge, Lindner-Böge	ULRIKE BRANDI LICHT	ULRIKE BRANDI LICHT
30	Round staircase at the Alexanderplatz train station	Berlin	Germany	Rebecca Chestnutt + Robert Niess	ULRIKE BRANDI LICHT	ULRIKE BRANDI LICHT
31	Syltquelle, staircase	Rantum	Germany	Alsop und Störmer	ULRIKE BRANDI LICHT	Oliver Heissner
32	Norddeutsche Landesbank, staircase of the client hall	Hamburg	Germany	von Gerkan Marg und Partner	ULRIKE BRANDI LICHT	Klaus Frahm
33	Forum Elbflorenz Dresden, elevator car	Dresden	Germany	Nietz Prasch Sigl	ULRIKE BRANDI LICHT	ULRIKE BRANDI LICHT
34	EXPO Café, staircase	Hannover	Germany	Pax Hadamczick Arndt Brüning	ULRIKE BRANDI LICHT	ULRIKE BRANDI LICHT
35	Office building of the Götz GmbH, office	Würzburg	Germany	Webler + Geissler, Stuttgart	Rudi Wolff	ERCO
36	Office building of the Götz GmbH, façade	Würzburg	Germany	Webler + Geissler, Stuttgart	Rudi Wolff	ERCO
37	Office building of the Götz GmbH, ceiling element	Würzburg	Germany	Webler + Geissler, Stuttgart	Rudi Wolff	ERCO
38	Office building of the Götz GmbH, ceiling element	Würzburg	Germany	Webler + Geissler, Stuttgart	Rudi Wolff	ERCO
39	Lloyds, façade	London	United Kingdom	Richard Rogers Partnership	Christian Bartenbach	Felix Krämer
40	Lloyds, hall	London	United Kingdom	Richard Rogers Partnership	Christian Bartenbach	Felix Krämer
41	Lloyds, hall, ground floor	London	United Kingdom	Richard Rogers Partnership	Christian Bartenbach	Felix Krämer
42	Lloyds, office area	London	United Kingdom	Richard Rogers Partnership	Christian Bartenbach	Felix Krämer
43	Office building of Pihl & Sons, foyer	Lyngby	Denmark	KHR Architects	KHR Architects	Louis Poulsen
44	Office building of Pihl & Sons, office	Lyngby	Denmark	KHR Architects	KHR Architects	Louis Poulsen
45	Office building of Pihl & Sons, skylights	Lyngby	Denmark	KHR Architects	KHR Architects	Louis Poulsen
46	RWE high-rise, complete view	Essen	Germany	Ingenhoven Overdiek + Partner	HL-Technik AG	H. Knauf
47	RWE high-rise, office	Essen	Germany	Ingenhoven Overdiek + Partner	HL-Technik AG	H. Knauf

No.	Description	City	Country			
48	RWE high-rise, bottom view of ceiling	Essen	Germany	Ingenhoven Overdiek + Partner	HL-Technik AG	H. Knauf
49	RWE high-rise, ceiling drawing	Essen	Germany	Ingenhoven Overdiek + Partner	HL-Technik AG	Ingenhoven Overdiek + Partner
50	Tokyo International Forum, hall	Tokyo	Japan	Rafael Vinoly	Danielle & Claude Engle and LPA	ERCO
51	Tokyo International Forum, bottom view of ceiling and galleries	Tokyo	Japan	Rafael Vinoly	Danielle & Claude Engle and LPA	ERCO
52	Tokyo International Forum, hall, elevator foyers	Tokyo	Japan	Rafael Vinoly	Danielle & Claude Engle and LPA	ERCO
53	Tokyo International Forum, events hall	Tokyo	Japan	Rafael Vinoly	Danielle & Claude Engle und LPA	ERCO
54	Tokyo International Forum, large events hall	Tokyo	Japan	Rafael Vinoly	Danielle & Claude Engle und LPA	ERCO
55	Lecture hall building of the Technical University Chemnitz, lecture hall	Chemnitz	Germany	von Gerkan Marg und Partner	ULRIKE BRANDI LICHT	ULRIKE BRANDI LICHT
56	Lecture hall building of the Technical University Chemnitz, lecture hall	Chemnitz	Germany	von Gerkan Marg und Partner	ULRIKE BRANDI LICHT	ULRIKE BRANDI LICHT
57	Lecture hall building of the Technical University Chemnitz, foyer	Chemnitz	Germany	von Gerkan Marg und Partner	ULRIKE BRANDI LICHT	ULRIKE BRANDI LICHT
58	Lecture hall building of the Technical University Chemnitz	Chemnitz	Germany	von Gerkan Marg und Partner	ULRIKE BRANDI LICHT	ULRIKE BRANDI LICHT
59	St. Katharinen church, lighting element	Stendal	Germany	Jochen Brandi + Partner	ULRIKE BRANDI LICHT	Christian Richters
60	St. Katharinen church, model of the concert hall	Stendal	Germany	Jochen Brandi + Partner	ULRIKE BRANDI LICHT	Brandi + Partner
61	St. Katharinen church, lighting element	Stendal	Deutschland	Jochen Brandi + Partner	ULRIKE BRANDI LICHT	ULRIKE BRANDI LICHT

WIRE CABLE SUSPENSION;

BARE LAMP;

POINT OF CONTACT;

PERFORATED PLATE D = 1.5mm, ANODIZED ALUMINUM;

LIGHTING ELEMENTS (16 ELEMENTS);

FROSTED GLASS COVER

No.	Description	City	Country			
62	St. Katharinen church, floor plan	Stendal	Germany	Jochen Brandi + Partner	ULRIKE BRANDI LICHT	ULRIKE BRANDI LICHT
63	Hong Kong Shanghai Bank, conference room	Hongkong	China	Foster Associates	Danielle & Claude Engle	ERCO
64	Hong Kong Shanghai Bank, chandelier, test	Hongkong	China	Foster Associates	Danielle & Claude Engle	ERCO
65	Panasonic Data & Communications Center, section of the atrium	Tokyo	Japan	Nikken Sekkei	LPA	LPA
66	Panasonic Data & Communications Center, atrium	Tokyo	Japan	Nikken Sekkei	LPA	LPA
67	Panasonic Data & Communications Center, alignment plan	Tokyo	Japan	Nikken Sekkei	LPA	LPA
68	Restaurant Marema	Tokyo	Japan		LPA	LPA
69	Restaurant Marema	Tokyo	Japan		LPA	LPA
70	Restaurant Marema	Tokyo	Japan		LPA	LPA
71	Restaurant Nil	Hamburg	Germany		ULRIKE BRANDI LICHT + Christine Brandi	ULRIKE BRANDI LICHT
72	Skippers Society, floor plan	Lübeck	Germany		Teilbereich ULRIKE BRANDI LICHT	ULRIKE BRANDI LICHT
73	Skippers Society	Lübeck	Germany		Teilbereich ULRIKE BRANDI LICHT	ULRIKE BRANDI LICHT
74	Office building of the Großhandels- und Lagergesellschaft, cafeteria	Bremen	Germany	Kleffel, Köhnhold, Gundermann	ULRIKE BRANDI LICHT	Oliver Heissner
75	Office building of the Großhandels- und Lagergesellschaft, cafeteria	Bremen	Germany	Kleffel, Köhnhold, Gundermann	ULRIKE BRANDI LICHT	ULRIKE BRANDI LICHT

CABLE;

GLASS CYLINDER, PRINTED ON LOWER SIDE OR FITTED WITH PERFORATED

PLATE, 70% TRANSPARENCY;

SOCKET;

FIXTURE WITH ATTACHMENT OF

TENSIONING ROPE;

TENSIONING ROPE;

DETAIL;

CONCRETE CEILING, PLASTER;

LAMP;

CONCRETE CEILING, PLASTER;

LAMP;

No.	Description	City	Country			
76	Occupational Training Center, cafeteria	Staßfurt	Germany	Pook und Leiska	ULRIKE BRANDI LICHT	ULRIKE BRANDI LICHT
77	Occupational Training Center, cafeteria	Staßfurt	Germany	Pook und Leiska	ULRIKE BRANDI LICHT	ULRIKE BRANDI LICHT
78	EXPO Café	Hanover	Germany	Pax Hadamczik Arndt Brüning	ULRIKE BRANDI LICHT	ULRIKE BRANDI LICHT
79	Shopping arcade	Paris	France			ULRIKE BRANDI LICHT
80	Nordseepassage, main shopping arcade	Wilhelmshaven	Germany	von Gerkan Marg und Partner	ULRIKE BRANDI LICHT	ULRIKE BRANDI LICHT
81	Nordseepassage, special lamp	Wilhelmshaven	Germany	von Gerkan Marg und Partner	ULRIKE BRANDI LICHT	ULRIKE BRANDI LICHT

REFLECTOR 1100G ALAMOD

MARTINELLI

ZH1 70W ATTACHED TO POLE BY MEANS OF PIPE CLAMPS;

LAMP POLE WEEF

No.	Description	City	Country			
82	Nordseepassage, transverse arcade	Wilhelmshaven	Germany	von Gerkan Marg und Partner	ULRIKE BRANDI LICHT	ULRIKE BRANDI LICHT
83	Nordseepassage, floor plan, entrance	Wilhelmshaven	Germany	von Gerkan Marg und Partner	ULRIKE BRANDI LICHT	ULRIKE BRANDI LICHT

ACTIVITY AREA

No.	Description	City	Country			
84	Biblioteca de Catalunya	Barcelona	Spain	Joan Rodon		ERCO
85	Biblioteca de Catalunya, bookshelves	Barcelona	Spain	Joan Rodon		ERCO
86	Bibliothek am Luisenbad, exterior view	Berlin	Germany	Rebecca Chestnutt + Robert Niess	Rebecca Chestnutt + Robert Niess	Reinhard Görner
87	Bibliothek am Luisenbad, "table" in the reading room	Berlin	Germany	Rebecca Chestnutt + Robert Niess	Rebecca Chestnutt + Robert Niess	Reinhard Görner
88	Bibliothek am Luisenbad, detail of ceiling lamp	Berlin	Germany	Rebecca Chestnutt + Robert Niess	Rebecca Chestnutt + Robert Niess	ULRIKE BRANDI LICHT
89	Mira Mesa Library, interior	San Diego	USA	Carrier Johnson		Louis Poulsen
90	Mira Mesa Library, exterior	San Diego	USA	Carrier Johnson		Louis Poulsen
91	Galerie d'Evolution, view into the large hall	Paris	France	Conversion Chemetov et Huidobro	ULRIKE BRANDI LICHT	ERCO
92	Galerie d'Evolution, front view and section	Paris	France	Conversion Chemetov et Huidobro	ULRIKE BRANDI LICHT	ULRIKE BRANDI LICHT
93	Galerie d'Evolution, bottom view of ceiling and section	Paris	France	Conversion Chemetov et Huidobro	ULRIKE BRANDI LICHT	ULRIKE BRANDI LICHT
94	Galerie d'Evolution, colored sky	Paris	France	Conversion Chemetov et Huidobro	ULRIKE BRANDI LICHT	ULRIKE BRANDI LICHT
95	Galerie d'Evolution, colored sky	Paris	France	Conversion Chemetov et Huidobro	ULRIKE BRANDI LICHT	ULRIKE BRANDI LICHT
96	Galerie d'Evolution, colored sky	Paris	France	Conversion Chemetov et Huidobro	ULRIKE BRANDI LICHT	ULRIKE BRANDI LICHT
97	Galerie d'Evolution, colored sky	Paris	France	Conversion Chemetov et Huidobro	ULRIKE BRANDI LICHT	ULRIKE BRANDI LICHT
98	Galerie d'Evolution, animals with shadows	Paris	France	Conversion Chemetov et Huidobro	ULRIKE BRANDI LICHT	ERCO
99	Galerie d'Evolution, drawings	Paris	France	Conversion Chemetov et Huidobro	ULRIKE BRANDI LICHT	ULRIKE BRANDI LICHT
100	Galerie d'Evolution, view into the gallery	Paris	France	Conversion Chemetov et Huidobro	ULRIKE BRANDI LICHT	ULRIKE BRANDI LICHT
101	Galerie d'Evolution, animals	Paris	France	Conversion Chemetov et Huidobro	ULRIKE BRANDI LICHT	ERCO
102	Galerie d'Evolution, hall and basement level	Paris	France	Conversion Chemetov et Huidobro	ULRIKE BRANDI LICHT	ULRIKE BRANDI LICHT
103	Galerie d'Evolution, animal skeleton	Paris	France	Conversion Chemetov et Huidobro	ULRIKE BRANDI LICHT	ERCO
104	Galerie d'Evolution, animals in light cone	Paris	France	Conversion Chemetov et Huidobro	ULRIKE BRANDI LICHT	ULRIKE BRANDI LICHT
105	Galerie d'Evolution, fish	Paris	France	Conversion Chemetov et Huidobro	ULRIKE BRANDI LICHT	ULRIKE BRANDI LICHT
106	American Museum of Natural History, exhibition area (blue ceiling)	New York	USA	Polshek & Partners	Fisher Marantz Stone	Fisher Marantz Stone
107	American Museum of Natural History, front view	New York	USA	Polshek & Partners	Fisher Marantz Stone	Fisher Marantz Stone
108	American Museum of Natural History, exhibition area	New York	USA	Polshek & Partners	Fisher Marantz Stone	Fisher Marantz Stone

109	American Museum of Natural History, exhibition area	New York	USA	Polshek & Partners	Fisher Marantz Stone	Fisher Marantz Stone
110	American Museum of Natural History, sphere	New York	USA	Polshek & Partners	Fisher Marantz Stone	Fisher Marantz Stone
111	American Museum of Natural History, ramp	New York	USA	Polshek & Partners	Fisher Marantz Stone	Fisher Marantz Stone
112	American Museum of Natural History, spheres	New York	USA	Polshek & Partners	Fisher Marantz Stone	Fisher Marantz Stone
113	American Museum of Natural History, planets	New York	USA	Polshek & Partners	Fisher Marantz Stone	Fisher Marantz Stone
114	Museum Inam, front view	Toyama	Japan	Peter Salter	ULRIKE BRANDI LICHT	ULRIKE BRANDI LICHT
115	Museum Inam, lighting plan	Toyama	Japan	Peter Salter	ULRIKE BRANDI LICHT	ULRIKE BRANDI LICHT
116	Museum Inam, view into the exhibit	Toyama	Japan	Peter Salter	ULRIKE BRANDI LICHT	ULRIKE BRANDI LICHT
117	Museum Inam, detail	Toyama	Japan	Peter Salter	ULRIKE BRANDI LICHT	ULRIKE BRANDI LICHT
118	Museum Inam, view into the exhibit	Toyama	Japan	Peter Salter	ULRIKE BRANDI LICHT	ULRIKE BRANDI LICHT
119	Museum Inam, skylights	Toyama	Japan	Peter Salter	ULRIKE BRANDI LICHT	ULRIKE BRANDI LICHT
120	Cultural Center Jean-Marie Tjibaou, exhibition room	Nouméa	New Zealand	Renzo Piano	Renzo Piano	architekturphoto, Hans Schlupp
121	Cultural Center Jean-Marie Tjibaou, front view	Nouméa	New Zealand	Renzo Piano	Renzo Piano	architekturphoto, Hans Schlupp
122	Fondation Beyeler, roof element	Basel	Switzerland	Renzo Piano	Neuco AG	ERCO
123	Fondation Beyeler, roof element and exhibit	Basel	Switzerland	Renzo Piano	Neuco AG	ERCO
124	Fondation Beyeler, exhibit	Basel	Switzerland	Renzo Piano	Neuco AG	ERCO
125	Fondation Beyeler, exhibit	Basel	Switzerland	Renzo Piano	Neuco AG	ERCO
126	Illuminated intersection	Lisbjerg	Denmark	H. Thule Hansen	H. Thule Hansen	ILR
127	Campidogli	Rome	Italy			Agabekov S.A.
128	Schloß Schönbrunn, fountain	Vienna	Austria		ULRIKE BRANDI LICHT	ULRIKE BRANDI LICHT
129	Schloß Schönbrunn, historical layout plan	Vienna	Austria			Authors' archive
130	Schloß Schönbrunn, Gloriette	Vienna	Austria		ULRIKE BRANDI LICHT	ULRIKE BRANDI LICHT
131	VW-Autostadt, "black plan"	Wolfsburg	Germany		ULRIKE BRANDI LICHT	ULRIKE BRANDI LICHT
132	VW-Autostadt, path along the banks with bridge	Wolfsburg	Germany		ULRIKE BRANDI LICHT	ULRIKE BRANDI LICHT
133	VW-Autostadt, hotel forecourt	Wolfsburg	Germany		ULRIKE BRANDI LICHT	ULRIKE BRANDI LICHT
134	VW-Autostadt, bridge connecting park with southern promenade	Wolfsburg	Germany		ULRIKE BRANDI LICHT	ULRIKE BRANDI LICHT
135	VW-Autostadt, path along the banks at the museum	Wolfsburg	Germany		ULRIKE BRANDI LICHT	ULRIKE BRANDI LICHT
136	EXPO 2000, urban master plan	Hanover	Germany	A. Speer + Partner	ULRIKE BRANDI LICHT	ULRIKE BRANDI LICHT
137	EXPO 2000, master plan for lighting	Hanover	Germany		ULRIKE BRANDI LICHT	ULRIKE BRANDI LICHT
138 -142	EXPO 2000, bridges with rows of lamps	Hanover	Germany	von Gerkan Marg und Partner	ULRIKE BRANDI LICHT	ULRIKE BRANDI LICHT
143	EXPO 2000, lamps on parking lot	Hanover	Germany		ULRIKE BRANDI LICHT	ULRIKE BRANDI LICHT
144	EXPO 2000, intersections	Hanover	Germany		ULRIKE BRANDI LICHT	ULRIKE BRANDI LICHT
145	EXPO 2000, lighting principles	Hanover	Germany		ULRIKE BRANDI LICHT	ULRIKE BRANDI LICHT
146	EXPO 2000, lighting principles	Hanover	Germany		ULRIKE BRANDI LICHT	ULRIKE BRANDI LICHT
147	EXPO 2000, EXPO 2000, lighting principles, lawn cones in the earth garden	Hanover	Germany		ULRIKE BRANDI LICHT	ULRIKE BRANDI LICHT
148	EXPO 2000, lawn cones by daylight	Hanover	Germany	Kienast Vogt + Partner	ULRIKE BRANDI LICHT	ULRIKE BRANDI LICHT
149	EXPO 2000, lawn cones illuminated	Hanover	Germany	Kienast Vogt + Partner	ULRIKE BRANDI LICHT	ULRIKE BRANDI LICHT
150	EXPO 2000, lighting principle	Hanover	Germany	Kienast Vogt + Partner	ULRIKE BRANDI LICHT	ULRIKE BRANDI LICHT
151	EXPO 2000, EXPO roof with EXPO lake	Hanover	Germany	Thomas Herzog + Partner	ULRIKE BRANDI LICHT	ULRIKE BRANDI LICHT
152	EXPO 2000, EXPO roof, support	Hanover	Germany	Thomas Herzog + Partner	ULRIKE BRANDI LICHT	ULRIKE BRANDI LICHT
153	EXPO 2000, EXPO roof, support illumination	Hanover	Germany	Thomas Herzog + Partner	ULRIKE BRANDI LICHT	ULRIKE BRANDI LICHT
154	EXPO 2000, park wave	Hanover	Germany	Kienast Vogt + Partner	ULRIKE BRANDI LICHT	ULRIKE BRANDI LICHT
155	EXPO 2000, sided light	Hanover	Germany	Kienast Vogt + Partner	ULRIKE BRANDI LICHT	ULRIKE BRANDI LICHT
156	EXPO 2000, built-in ground lights at the Avenue of the United Trees	Hanover	Germany	Kienast Vogt Partner	ULRIKE BRANDI LICHT	ULRIKE BRANDI LICHT
157	EXPO 2000, light atmosphere at plaza	Hanover	Germany	WES + Partner	ULRIKE BRANDI LICHT	ULRIKE BRANDI LICHT
158	EXPO 2000, light atmosphere at seating stairs	Hanover	Germany	WES + Partner	ULRIKE BRANDI LICHT	ULRIKE BRANDI LICHT
159	EXPO 2000, seating stairs at plaza	Hanover	Germany	WES + Partner	ULRIKE BRANDI LICHT	ULRIKE BRANDI LICHT
160	Erasmus bridge	Rotterdam	Holland	Van Berkel & Bos	LDP	LDP
161	EXPO 2000, Skywalk, exterior view	Hanover	Germany	Schulitz + Partner	ULRIKE BRANDI LICHT	ULRIKE BRANDI LICHT
162	EXPO 2000, Skywalk, bottom view	Hanover	Germany	Schulitz + Partner	ULRIKE BRANDI LICHT	ULRIKE BRANDI LICHT
163	EXPO 2000, Skywalk, interior	Hanover	Germany	Schulitz + Partner	ULRIKE BRANDI LICHT	ULRIKE BRANDI LICHT
164	Miho Museum, entrance tunnel	Kyoto	Japan	Pei & Partner		ERCO
165	Miho Museum, tunnel at night	Kyoto	Japan	Pei & Partner		ERCO
166	Miho Museum, tunnel at night	Kyoto	Japan	Pei & Partner		ERCO
167	Miho Museum, ground illumination	Kyoto	Japan	Pei & Partner		ERCO
168	Alexanderplatz train station, cross section	Berlin	Germany	Rebecca Chestnutt + Robert Niess		Authors' archive
169	Alexanderplatz train station, longitudinal section	Berlin	Germany	Rebecca Chestnutt + Robert Niess		Authors' archive
170	Alexanderplatz train station, lighting test	Berlin	Germany	Rebecca Chestnutt + Robert Niess	ULRIKE BRANDI LICHT	ULRIKE BRANDI LICHT
171	Alexanderplatz train station, platform hall	Berlin	Germany	Rebecca Chestnutt + Robert Niess	ULRIKE BRANDI LICHT	ULRIKE BRANDI LICHT
172	Alexanderplatz train station, staircase, detail	Berlin	Germany	Rebecca Chestnutt + Robert Niess	ULRIKE BRANDI LICHT	ULRIKE BRANDI LICHT
173	Alexanderplatz train station, round staircase	Berlin	Germany	Rebecca Chestnutt + Robert Niess	ULRIKE BRANDI LICHT	ULRIKE BRANDI LICHT
174	Alexanderplatz train station, mall	Berlin	Germany	Rebecca Chestnutt + Robert Niess	ULRIKE BRANDI LICHT	ULRIKE BRANDI LICHT
175	Gardermoen Airport train station, lamps	Oslo	Norway	Aviaplan	LDP	ULRIKE BRANDI LICHT
176	Gardermoen Airport train station, entrance area	Oslo	Norway	Aviaplan	LDP	ULRIKE BRANDI LICHT
177	Brisbane Airport	Brisbane	Australia		LDP	LDP
178	Hamburg Airport, hall of Terminal 4	Hamburg	Germany	von Gerkan Marg und Partner with Karsten Bauer	Peter Andres	ULRIKE BRANDI LICHT
179	Hamburg Airport, check-in counter	Hamburg	Germany	von Gerkan Marg und Partner with Karsten Bauer	Peter Andres	ULRIKE BRANDI LICHT
180	Hamburg Airport, supports	Hamburg	Germany	von Gerkan Marg und Partner with Karsten Bauer	Peter Andres	ULRIKE BRANDI LICHT
181	Hamburg Airport, pier	Hamburg	Germany	von Gerkan Marg und Partner with Karsten Bauer	Peter Andres	ULRIKE BRANDI LICHT
182	Chek Lap Kok Airport, aerial photograph	Hongkong	China	Foster and Partners	Fisher Marantz Stone	Fisher Marantz Stone
183	Chek Lap Kok Airport, view into hall	Hongkong	China	Foster and Partners	Fisher Marantz Stone	Fisher Marantz Stone
184	Chek Lap Kok Airport, hall	Hongkong	China	Foster and Partners	Fisher Marantz Stone	Fisher Marantz Stone
185	Chek Lap Kok Airport, entrance area	Hongkong	China	Foster and Partners	Fisher Marantz Stone	Fisher Marantz Stone
186	Chek Lap Kok Airport, section	Hongkong	China	Foster and Partners	Fisher Marantz Stone	Fisher Marantz Stone
187	Chek Lap Kok Airport, detail of ceiling	Hongkong	China	Foster and Partners	Fisher Marantz Stone	Fisher Marantz Stone
188	Chek Lap Kok Airport, reflector element	Hongkong	China	Foster and Partners	Fisher Marantz Stone	Fisher Marantz Stone
189	Gardermoen Airport, ceiling, outside	Oslo	Norway	Aviaplan	LDP	ULRIKE BRANDI LICHT
190	Gardermoen Airport, hall	Oslo	Norway	Aviaplan	LDP	ULRIKE BRANDI LICHT
191	Gardermoen Airport, arrivals area	Oslo	Norway	Aviaplan	LDP	ULRIKE BRANDI LICHT
192	Gardermoen Airport, hall	Oslo	Norway	Aviaplan	LDP	ULRIKE BRANDI LICHT
193	Gardermoen Airport, offices	Oslo	Norway	Aviaplan	LDP	ULRIKE BRANDI LICHT

Authors:

Ulrike Brandi, Christoph Geissmar-Brandi, Hamburg

Numerous Photographs, Photo Editing, Photo Documentary, and Bibliography:

Felix Krämer, Hamburg

Graphics (CAD) and Drawings:

Annika Prätzlich, Hamburg

Technical Editing:

Harald Hofmann, Lüdenscheid

Research and Drawings:

Mariana Theiling, Hamburg

Oliver Ost, Hamburg

Network and CAD Operations:

Christof Fielstette, Hamburg

Cooperation:

Kaoru Mende, Reiko Kasai, LPA, Tokyo/Singapore

Charles Stone, Fisher Marantz Stone & Partner, New York

Child care:

Linda Scott, Emily Seed, Oksana Schewtschenko, Katarzyna Dziekan, Tatjana Sytnik,
Marta Wesolowska

Dorothee Brandi-Effenberg, Hamburg

Gisela and Alfred Geissmar, Braunschweig

The teachers of the Protestant Kindergarten in Bad Bevensen

Translation:

Hans-Jakob Wilhelm, Damus Communications, Outremont/New York

Contact information for Ulrike Brandi and Christoph Geissmar-Brandi:

E-mail: info@ulrike-brandi.de

www.ulrike-brandi.de

www.tanteidan.org

Layout and Cover:

Muriel Comby, Basel

Deutsche Bibliothek Cataloging-in-Publication Data

Brandi, Ulrike:

Lightbook: the practice of lighting design/Ulrike Brandi ; Christoph Geissmar-Brandi. [Transl. German/Engl.: Hans-Jakob Wilhelm]. – Basel ; Boston ; Berlin : Birkhäuser 2001

Dt. Ausg. u.d.T.: Brandi, Ulrike: Lichtbuch

ISBN 3-7643-6303-7

This book is also available in a German language edition (ISBN 3-7643-6302-9).

© 2001 Birkhäuser – Publishers for Architecture, P.O.Box 133, CH-4010 Basel, Switzerland

A member of the BertelsmannSpringer Publishing Group.

Printed on acid-free paper produced from chlorine-free pulp. TCF ∞

Printed in Germany

ISBN 3-7643-6303-7

9 8 7 6 5 4 3 2 1